Intimacy and Friendship on Facebook

Intimacy and Friendship on Facebook

Alex Lambert

First published 2013 by
PALGRAVE MACMILLAN

Palgrave Macmillan in the UK is an imprint of Macmillan Publishers Limited, registered in England, company number 785998, of Houndmills, Basingstoke, Hampshire RG21 6XS.

Palgrave Macmillan in the US is a division of St Martin's Press LLC, 175 Fifth Avenue, New York, NY 10010.

Palgrave Macmillan is the global academic imprint of the above companies and has companies and representatives throughout the world.

Palgrave® and Macmillan® are registered trademarks in the United States, the United Kingdom, Europe and other countries

ISBN: 978–1–137–28713–7 hardback
ISBN: 978–1–137–32284–5 paperback

This book is printed on paper suitable for recycling and made from fully managed and sustained forest sources. Logging, pulping and manufacturing processes are expected to conform to the environmental regulations of the country of origin.

A catalogue record for this book is available from the British Library.

A catalog record for this book is available from the Library of Congress.

10   9   8   7   6   5   4   3   2   1
22 21 20 19 18 17 16 15 14 13

Printed and bound in Great Britain by
CPI Antony Rowe, Chippenham and Eastbourne

Contents

Acknowledgements

I would not have been able to complete this book without the efforts of Scott McQuire and Audrey Yue. More than anyone, Scott's incredible knowledge, patience, and generous assistance has shaped my personal intellectual journey. Moreover, Scott has supplied the incisive critique without which I would have found myself content with wanting methods, under-considered ideas, and half-complete theories. Where Scott influenced content, Audrey's advice influenced shape. She helped sculpt and trim when I was glutted with data. Audrey's kind enthusiasm, combined with her subtle ability to motivate others, helped turn endless memos into structured chapters. Scott and Audrey, thank you.

I would also like to thank Sue and Tim, for supporting me when times were tough and compelling me forward when I doubted myself. And where would I be without having to defend the ways of the social sciences to an economist and a psychiatrist? Ultimately it is to them that I owe my love of ideas and the study of social life.

To my participants, and the various people I have met both offline and in the open and cloistered rooms of Facebook, thank you for steering me toward the things which matter.

Finally, I would like to thank Renée, whose love lies behind every word.

Introduction

For many people life goes on within a complex media ecology. Within this ecology *social media* have become a dominant genus and Facebook the dominant species. Facebook's massive population, third to India and China, makes it a significant global phenomenon with deep-reaching social and cultural effects. Consequently, Facebook has fallen under the microscope of social scientists from numerous disciplines and generated a rich body of political, economic, legal, psychological, sociological, anthropological and technological insights. These construct Facebook in different ways, and this suggests that Facebook is not one 'thing'. Rather, it is an assemblage of protocols, software, interfaces, media, content, contracts, marketing, public relations, surveillance systems, bureaucracies, shareholders, users and global and local cultures – the list goes on. I am concerned with one 'field' within this arabesque: Facebook's influence on everyday social relationships and identities. Facebook is having a significant effect on these phenomena which, I argue, can be theorised in terms of *intimacy*.

I began this project as a grounded ethnographic study of the influence of Facebook on everyday life. Soon, intimacy emerged as the central concept which explained the participants in my study. Facebook offers amazing opportunities to enrich interpersonal life and generate intimacy. However, Facebook also makes intimacy problematic, and this determines much about how my participants use it. These benefits and problems spring from Facebook's peculiar publicity. When people become Facebook 'friends' they grant a kind of public access to each other's personal profiles (called 'timelines'). That is, when people create personal Facebook networks, they construct publics out of social connections. Much has been said regarding this process, though much has been missed with regard to how it influences intimacy. Publicity provides the opportunity to sustain interpersonal connections in a rewarding fashion, in particular through a kind of gregarious group intimacy. Publicity allows zones of gregarious intimacy to expand unpredictably in playful and affectionate ways.

However, publicity also makes it difficult to control intimate information. Disclosures circulate beyond their intended audiences, disclosures that are free to act on the minds of unknown others. Indeed, some of these unknowns will have been 'friended' (*verb*) because of a nascent politics of intimacy associated with the popularisation of Facebook. When intimate information is circulating in this way, participants experience this as a kind of loss of self. The intimate self is 'doubled', and the unreachable, undetectable agency of this double causes insecurity. Who knows what the intimate self is saying, doing, becoming? At the same time, my participants experience various problems to do with Facebook's mediated nature. In order for a person to participate in its intimate spaces, Facebook demands that the self be constantly updated. A surplus of information builds up which exceeds the attentive capabilities of every user. Consequently, the attention of others and the resulting possibility of interpersonal acknowledgment becomes scarcer. This further animates the desire for dependable, regular acknowledgment and interaction. Furthermore, the mediated gaze of one's Facebook friends, invisible but potentially 'there', encourages the production of intimacies. But while this impels the production of subjectivity it can also lead to the user feeling objectified. This is further enhanced by the sense of alienated connection which can sometimes occur when witnessing the intimacies of Facebook 'friends' who, nonetheless, are not friends at all. All this – the compulsion to update, self-objectification, alienation through connection – is felt as intensely frustrating, and this hides a more subtle form of insecurity.

I understand these problems as disruptions in the nature of subjectivity, objectivity, space and time. Here, I find Martin Buber's distinction between 'I–thou' and 'I–it' relationships highly useful. The former describes a transcendent sense of connectedness, while the latter describes the recognition of worldly objects, which occurs when standing apart from them. The former describes relation, while the latter describes separation. In regard to human relations, the 'I–thou' is achieved when two people are within a dialogical space – a co-present space in which each perceives the other's intentional conscious presence directed at himself or herself. Intimate spaces have this nature because intimacy involves seeing and treating another as a subject rather than as an object. Facebook is very different from the kind of co-present social spaces which concerned Buber nearly a century ago. Facebook offers the opportunity for a different kind of dialogical space, for a different kind of intimacy. Yet this spatiality is precarious. It can sometimes become inverted such that participants see others and themselves as objects rather than subjects. Interpersonal intimacy is deferred. In order to understand this, intimacy must become a broad, flexible concept, capable of understanding 'I–it' relations. We must understand the transmutation of intimacies from affectionate self-disclosures into different objects, such as media, texts, images and interfaces.

Both the problems and solutions I discuss are elements of a socio-cultural state of affairs, which I term 'intensive intimacy'. Problems are experienced in an intense fashion. They involve intense emotions such as frustration, nausea and insecurity. Concurrently, the solutions to these problems involve intensive social labour. That is, the intensive surveillance and organisation – the *bureaucratisation* – of social ties and the intensive management of personal information. Interestingly, this intensive quality has become a normalised part of everyday life. It is often *not* a subject of self-reflective thought. This is partly because intensive intimacy is not new and did not begin with Facebook. Rather, it is the result of changes in the nature of complex social relations and forms of technological mediation which arguably have been occurring since the onset of Industrial Modernity. Mobility and photography, for instance, are both tied up with intensive intimacy, and neither began with Facebook. However, Facebook fixes the different characters met throughout a mobile lifespan in an online public space and, hence, demands that they be considered, organised, accepted, rejected, blocked, tagged, edited and so forth. It allows photographic self-portraits to reawaken intimacies, but turns photographs into complex objects which must be continually negotiated. Hence, Facebook further amplifies these deeply structured processes which I associate with intensive intimacy.

Yes, Facebook creates social and self-expressive opportunities which previously did not exist. However, I argue against the idea that Facebook marks a radical paradigm shift in the way we construct our identities and interpersonal relationships. Certain commentators describe such a shift in relation to privacy and intimacy. It is said that users are no longer concerned with their own privacy, that we live in a new age defined by complicit sharing without negative consequences. This position, held by people in power such as Facebook's CEO, Mark Zuckerberg, attempts to legitimate many of the functional innovations that have subverted user privacy. Another position holds that people purposefully expose their private, intimate lives to public audiences. Here, intimacy is no longer framed in terms of interpersonal relationships. Intimacy has supposedly transformed from a 'relational' to an 'instrumental' aspect of human association, into a performative tool for garnering attention and esteem and, hence, narcissistic gratification. Facebook and like social network services (SNSs) are thus thought to be emblematic of a broader shift toward a 'culture of narcissism' in which meaningful relationships cease to significantly motivate people. In this sense people become objects, 'its' rather than 'thous'.

Two paradigms are clear: On the one hand, private, dyadic intimacy which is characteristically 'other-concerned'; on the other, public, narcissistic intimacy which is essentially 'self-concerned'. The 'I–thou' and the 'I–it'. However, intensive intimacy reveals, I argue, the struggle between these two paradigms rather than the dominance of one over the other. Yes, people desire a form of public intimacy. However, this remains *interpersonal*. Moreover, people still desire privacy, yet they must grapple with a variety of socio-technical contingencies which make privacy, intimacy, friendship and identity problematic. In a way, intensive intimacy is a framework which helps the understanding of these contingencies, whereupon 'thou' and 'it' conflict, diverge, overlap and enfold one another.

In Chapters 1 and 2 I explore existing literature relevant to the task at hand. Chapter 1 looks at literature which deals with aspects of interpersonal intimacy on SNSs, specifically relationships and self-disclosures. Given that these play out publicly, I turn to cultural criticisms of public intimacy, probing their values and limitations.

SNS research has heavily focused on privacy, the performance of identity, and social capital. Certainly these are very useful concepts, although the relationship between them is often underexplored. I synthesise these frameworks so as to understand intimacy on Facebook. In Chapter 2 I cover privacy, performance and social capital literature, and argue that a more fine-grained, qualitative understanding of each is required. In this vein, I ask: How can we understand intimacy problems in terms of privacy problems? To answer this, privacy cannot be thought of generically. Specific risks and contexts, as well as appropriate theories, must be identified. I also ask: How is intimacy performed on Facebook? In response, I go beyond Goffmanian theories of performance. Facebook asks us to probe the mediated, textual nature of performances. Finally, social capital involves relying on others for intimacy, but how does Facebook influence this? There is more to social capital than its effects, though SNS literature has heavily focused on one such effect:

elevated self-esteem. Social capital also involves exchanging social resources. How can these resources be conceptualised in terms of intimacy? How does this moment of exchange play out on Facebook?

In Chapter 3 I detail my methodology. Research into SNSs is dominated by deductive methodologies. Although some ethnography has been produced, there remains a need for fine-grained, qualitative research. Also, deductive approaches have produced a range of useful but disparate concepts. There remains a need for conceptual *relations*, for theory. I utilise ethnographic techniques to gather data and employ grounded theory techniques to develop a conceptual, rather than descriptive, understanding of this data. My hope is to produce a theoretical account and a collection of new concepts which others will find interesting and useful in their own studies.

In Chapter 4 I discuss my participants' core motivation for using Facebook: the 'performance of connection'. This constitutes what researchers employing the grounded theory method call a 'basic social process'. This process occurs in all aspects of social life, although it takes on novel properties and dimensions on Facebook. On the one hand, it describes the desire for sociality in and for itself and, on the other, the performance of this sociality toward a broad public such that a social connection is recognised. In seeking this recognition, participants take their relationships as subjects of self-conscious thought and labour and in this way sustain the interpersonal intimacy therein. The ultimate performance of connection achieves a playful, gregarious interaction. The performance of connection works through claims on social capital, which generates social spaces. These spaces have a private, intimate nature which aids in self-conscious identification and heightens the pleasure of belonging.

In Chapter 5 I describe how the performance of connection takes on unique properties in relation to distant ties. Facebook allows distant and estranged ties to be reclaimed and sustained through online interactions. Participants utilise Facebook to overcome the loss of distant ties, and this infuses their online encounters with these ties with a specific kind of intimacy. However, not every distant tie is reclaimed and sustained. Many remain weak ties, floating in the grey area of one's Facebook network. On the one hand, this potentiates unexpected, surprising moments of sociality. On the other, it sometimes engenders conflict between those who have radically changed their opinions, desires, and feelings toward one another.

In Chapter 6 I describe the social surveillance practices my participants engage in. People use Facebook to gather information on their connections. Often this information informs future interactions. However, Facebook offers the opportunity to connect with people without performing these connections. Between these two poles exist a gamut of 'surveillance contexts' which depend on who is being watched, why they are being watched, and the socio-technical context which frames the moment of watching. Surveillance can often be habitual; however, it becomes self-conscious when participants engage in what they term 'spying', the furtive observation of information which would be impossible or inappropriate to gather in other forums. Spying points to an interesting point of tension in the evolving fabric of intensive intimacy. Participants recognise that it is increasingly normative, yet they also experience a kind of moral self-consciousness when spying on others. I conceptualise the various aspects of this moral dilemma in terms of voyeurism. This voyeurism is unique and is indicative of a process I term 'prosthetic intimacy', the constitution of self through the technologically mediated integration of someone else's intimacies. In this chapter I also explore the way in which Facebook allows information to move into the realm of 'first-hand judgement' and, hence, gives it an objective quality.

Chapter 7 delves into the problems my participants experience with regard to fulfilling their main goal, the performance of connection. Participants accumulate a heterogeneous amalgam of social ties on Facebook with differing gradations of intimacy. While theorists have looked at how this creates problems by compromising one's ability to keep social contexts separate from one another, I explore how it creates problems for intimacy by undermining regular performances of connection, by subverting dialogical spaces.

In Chapter 8 I conceptualise, in terms of the 'negotiation of intimacy', the novel solutions my participants invent for these problems. On the one hand, this involves the control of information flows and the organisation of social connections. This reins in, shelters, protects and silences intimacy. On the other hand, this involves mobilising specific kinds of intimacy so as to generate specific kinds of social interactions. The mobilisation of intimacy is particularly interesting, as it involves making claims on various 'kinds' of social capital. The accumulation of these 'capitals' over time can lead to regular performances of connection. The most important of these is 'intimacy capital', the careful investment of which will lead to rewarding performances of connection. However, if intimacy capital is not properly invested, and intimacy is badly negotiated, people can alienate audiences and, hence, stifle the performance of connection. Here, I observe nascent norms with regard to what is acceptable public information and what is considered *too intimate*: disclosures which nauseate, alienate, 'miss the mark' and bore. Overall, participants come to actualise a rewarding form of public intimacy which is thoroughly interpersonal: gregarious playfulness. This playfulness is both a desired outcome in and of itself and is the result of a series of reflexive experiences with the pitfalls of public intimacy.

In the conclusion I reflect on how inquiries into 'intensive intimacy', on Facebook and in other domains, may continue. The research presented in this book is by no means conclusive but, rather, is an inductive journey which must be taken up in different fields and applied to varying cultural groups. As our lives are becoming further entangled with social media such as Facebook, it is important to recognise how intensive processes are both enhancing our interpersonal experiences and jeopardising them. Will we be able to keep up with the pace of change? Will we be able to develop the emotional and social competencies needed? What factors determine such competencies? How are they learnt? How are they managed from within and without? How are they made objects of value, not only for ourselves, but for the businesses which subtly design the digital architectures of our social lives? Hopefully, these questions stimulate further scholarship in a burgeoning and baffling world.

1
Discovering Intimacy on Facebook

Positioning Facebook

Fundamentally, SNSs are online worlds which facilitate the creation of personal profiles capable of connecting people with other users (Lenhart & Madden 2007a; boyd & Ellison 2008). Profiles often afford forms of social interaction and the expression of personal information such as tastes, interests, political views, sexual orientation, and so forth (Stutzman 2006). They also afford the articulation of one's connections, commonly displayed as a 'friends list' (Donath & boyd 2004).

Profiles and connections can range from being 'semi-public within a bounded system' (boyd & Ellison 2008: 211), to being public to the entire Internet. SNSs are distinguished partly by these degrees of publicity. For instance, ASmallWorld is a relatively closed service in which people must be invited by users to join and access member profiles. On the other hand, Twitter is open to the Internet proper, and does not prejudice membership. Somewhere in between, Facebook affords varying degrees of self-tailored publicity. People can choose to set their profiles to 'public', thus open to anyone, or restrict them to 'friends only'. They can also customise individual posts such that only specific friends may see them.

According to boyd and Ellison (2008), SNS users connect with people they share a prior relationship with. Various studies confirm this (Lampe, Ellison, & Steinfield 2006; Ellison, Steinfield, & Lampe 2007; Zhao, Grasmuch, & Martin 2008). Where SNS networks are found to contain weak ties and strangers, these are explained as 'friends-of-friends' who are contacted through mutual friends to reap social capital benefits (Ellison, Steinfield, & Lampe 2011).

People use Facebook and like SNSs to socialise with their connections (Pempek, Yermolayeva and Calvert 2009), gather information on these people (Joinson 2008, Rau, Gao and Ding 2008, Burke, Marlow and Lento 2010), increase their self-esteem and popularity (Zhao, Grasmuch, & Martin 2008; Zywica & Danowski 2008; Barker 2009; Ross et al. 2009), express their identities through novel forms of content and association (Zhao, Grasmuch, and Martin 2008, Liu 2008, Pempek, Yermolayeva, and Calvert 2009, Donath and boyd 2004), and entertain themselves through interactive applications such as social games (Rao 2008).

Scholars find that certain SNSs, Facebook in particular, are deeply embedded in everyday life, weaving through online and offline experience (Ellison, Steinfield, and Lampe 2011, Debatin, et al. 2009, Tufekci 2008, Dwyer, Hiltz, and Passerini 2007). Facebook has been referred to as a 'pervasive technology', 'deeply ingrained in [peoples'] daily routines' (Debatin et al. 2009: 96). I am particularly concerned with how this rich entanglement influences intimacy.

In this chapter I review literature which either explicitly or implicitly investigates intimacy on Facebook and like SNSs. Modern conceptions of intimacy are firmly routed in relationships which share genuine love, liking, care and commitment (Inness 1992; Prager 1995; Jamieson 1998). As thinkers such as Giddens (1991, 1992) and Illouz (2007) note, the upkeep of healthy intimate relationships has become a central value in the West, vitally entangled with the ideal of personal happiness. These writers, combined with a host of social psychologists (Reis & Shaver 1988; Prager 1995; Parks & Floyd 1996; Laurenceau, Pietromonaco, & Barret 1998), emphasise the importance of self-disclosure in the construction of intimate relationships. Interestingly, 'self-disclosures' and 'relationships' (friendships in particular) constitute key areas of interest for SNS scholars. These are conventionally valued as private phenomena. Intimacy is fostered over time through private interactions in which both parties disclose and validate each other's emotional inner selves (Reis & Shaver 1988). Hence, a chief question is: what happens to these factors when they play out publicly on SNSs? In what follows, I interrogate how SNS scholarship has dealt with friendships, romantic relationships and self-disclosures; then I turn to a broader cultural critique of public intimacy.

Friends and lovers

People utilise SNSs to connect with strong and weak ties. Various studies find the latter number far exceeds the former. For example, Ellison and colleagues (2011) find that American university students possess a mean of 300 Facebook 'friends', but only 25 per cent are considered 'actual friends'. Similarly, West and colleagues find users from the United Kingdom possess a mean of 200 Facebook 'friends', a mean of 82 'real friends', and a mean of 19 'close friends'. It seems Facebook users express complex gradations of friendship. Moreover, terms such as 'actual' and 'real' bring into question the relationship between friendship and authenticity (boyd 2006). It is important to probe the different benefits these different social ties provide. What benefits accrue from articulating one's strong, intimate friendships online? Ellison and colleagues (2007) understand this phenomenon in terms of social capital. That is, people's broader collection of weak ties offer opportunities to claim on bridging social capital, such as new information and the feeling of being in a broader community. On the other hand, people's relatively stable set of strong ties provides the opportunity for bonding social capital, for emotional support and solidarity. Scholarship elucidates how communication with these strong ties on Facebook has become an everyday aspect of social life (Goggin 2010; Robards 2012) which involves sharing emotional disclosures publicly (Mallan 2009; Sas et al. 2009). This suggests that Facebook has become an important tool for the reproduction of interpersonal bonds and, hence, interpersonal intimacy. However, just what this process involves remains fuzzy. One of the central aims of this book is to offer a more fine-grained, qualitative understanding of how this occurs, and what benefits Facebook offers in this regard.

Much of the research into SNSs and friendship has focused on adolescent groups. Within this field, the relationship between friendship and selfhood is highly significant. For instance, boyd's (2008a) influential ethnography into adolescents on MySpace views SNSs as autonomous spaces where youths can experiment with identity and friendship. SNSs offer a chance to develop experiences of intimacy, public 'face' and authenticity beyond the bounds of parental authority. Like boyd, Livingstone (2008) locates SNS friendships within developmental processes. Livingstone conducts a series of in-depth interviews with adolescent MySpace and Facebook users from the United Kingdom. Younger users cultivate a form of self-presentation on MySpace which Livingstone terms 'identity as display'. This involves a heavy focus on performing visual self-aspects. However, older youths abandon MySpace for Facebook, where they practice 'identity as connection', the performance of self through the signification of friendships. Robards (2012) notices a similar phenomenon while investigating the migration of Australian youths from MySpace to Facebook. Robards's participants reflect on the autobiographical, introspective nature of MySpace, which is considered 'juvenile', and they privilege the social interaction-focused Facebook, which is 'grown up'. The transition from one to the other is considered a ritualised passage into adulthood.

These ideas echo a central motif in the study of intimacy, namely that selfhood is achieved through voluntary, intimate relationships (Bellah et al. 1985; Giddens 1991). A more direct exposition of this will follow shortly.

The allure of SNSs extends beyond socialising with close friends. As mentioned above, people articulate both strong and weak ties online. What value lies in 'friending' people one does not share a close interpersonal relationship with? Based on an ethnography of teenage Friendster users, boyd (2006) suggests a series of reasons for sending and accepting friend requests. Users genuinely want to connect with actual friends, as well as with acquaintances, family, and colleagues. They also connect with others so as to see their profiles and gather social information. They connect to affiliate with popular peers and in turn look popular and 'cool'. They cultivate a list of friends as a performance of identity. Sometimes they are forced to connect due to social pressures and to avoid the awkwardness of saying 'no'. Hence, users do not follow one distinct strategy, and neither are they completely empowered. Rather, they are embedded within a fabric of different social pressures and motivations.

Research into Facebook also reflects these themes. Pempek and colleagues (2009) find American university students mainly use Facebook to 'keep up' with friends. Implicitly, this involves surveying friends, keeping informed as to what they are posting and who they are interacting with. Similarly, Joinson (2008) finds that people use Facebook to both watch and socialise with friends. He emphasises the powerful allure of social surveillance as a means of acquiring information on different ties. Tufekci (2008b) expands on this, finding that SNSs increased the ability to 'keep in touch' with a wide variety of connections. Facebook's own in-house research reveals that users passively survey about 2.5 times more people than they regularly interact with online (Marlow 2009). Collectively, these results suggest that users are motivated to friend weak ties so as to covertly monitor them. Authors suggest that much of this behaviour is driven by social curiosity, especially in regard to discovering how estranged contacts have changed over time (Joinson 2008; Tufekci 2008b; Pempek, Yermolayeva, & Calvert 2009).

Indeed, Facebook is highly valued for its affordance for reclaiming distant and estranged ties. For example, Ellison et al. (Ellison, Steinfield,

& Lampe 2007), and Manago et al. (2012) find that university students value the ability to reconnect with high school friends. Joinson's (2008) research finds that users are motivated to use Facebook so as to keep in touch with distant friends, and reacquire lost contacts. Madden and Smith (2010) report on a wide-ranging survey into the Internet use of American adults. They find that SNS users are four times more likely than non-users to be contacted by people from their past. It seems that Facebook is emblematic of a highly mobile society, a tool for sustaining bonds over distances of time and space. Hence, Facebook networks are not communities in the traditional sense, defined by 'kinship and acquaintanceship' and a 'common isolation' (Pahl 2005: 622). They transcend locals, and are composed of people from different walks of life. Hence, they can be called 'personal communities' (Wilkinson 2010). They are organised around specific individuals, and in this sense are a matter of perspective. As Pahl writes, personal communities are 'frameworks of belonging' which are provided, not by locals, but by 'the individual's biography' (2005: 636).

Scholars also find that relatively young SNS users friend others so as to accrue popularity, or at least the perception of popularity. For example, boyd (2006) discusses how Friendster users will friend popular kids so as to acquire similar social status. Based on in-depth interviews with Australian MySpace users, Mallan finds that the 'Top Friends' list not only performs a kind of identity through connection, but is taken as a 'quantifiable measure of one's popularity' (2009: 59). Tongand colleagues (2008) seek to confirm whether having a large quantity of friends is perceived by users to indicate popularity. They ask a large sample of American university students to judge mock-up Facebook profiles with differing friend counts; one finding was that profiles with around 300 friends were perceived to be most attractive. However, those who increasingly exceeded this amount decreased in perceived popularity. Following Donath and boyd (2004), they suggest that too many friends can lead to the perception of being a social networking 'whore', 'friending out of desperation rather than popularity' (Tong et al. 2008: 542).

Other scholars have linked the ability to select and grow a personal audience to both popularity and self-esteem. Zywica and Danowski (2008) ask students to address self-esteem measures and answer open-ended questions regarding their popularity online and offline. Extroverted participants with high self-esteem utilise Facebook to further enhance their self-esteem by increasing their sociability. Introverted students with low self-esteem also profit from Facebook by posting images and descriptions which make them look 'cool', and by accumulating friends. These users increase their self-esteem by elevating their self-perception as popular and attractive.

Barker (2009) also explores the relationship between SNS use and self-esteem. Her arguments are based on a large-sample survey of late adolescents, most of whom use Facebook and MySpace. Barker measures for 'collective-self esteem', 'the aspect of identity that has to do with the value placed on group membership' (2009: 210). Hence, as apposed to a measure of self-esteem in general, Barker specifically examines the relationship between self-esteem and the ability to identify with a social group and experience a sense of belonging. Barker finds that people compensate for low collective self-esteem by developing more fulfilling online bonds. Both Barker and Zywica and Danowski confirm the 'social compensation thesis' that Internet environments allow people to overcome negative social identities by re-creating themselves online. This process, however, inevitably involves the searching out of new, weak connections which must be strengthened. Here, Facebook is implicitly cast as a kind of 'psychotherapeutic milieu' (Turkle 1994), in which friending is part of a healing, or self-improvement process.

Another position argues that Facebook users accumulate large networks to act as audiences which provide narcissistic self-gratification (Rosen 2007; Ibrahim 2010; Mehdizadeh 2010; Ong et al. 2011). This key point of critique is highly relevant for this study, as modern conceptions of narcissism and public intimacy are crucially related (Sennett 1977; Lasch 1979). I return to examine this position in detail shortly.

These issues demand that we consider how the concept of intimacy elucidates the relationship between different ties. Throughout this book I respond to this problem by going beyond a mere 'weak/strong' or 'bridging/bonding' dichotomy. Instead I interrogate how intimacy plays out in specific social contexts across a range of different ties.

Relationships are not without their problems on Facebook. Tokunaga (2011) investigates the degree to which relationships are put under strain due to the way Facebook facilitates negative interpersonal events. He asks American university students to recall an SNS-related scenario which caused 'relational distrust, worry, dislike, problems, and/ or damage' (2011: 426). Responses describe denied or ignored friend requests, removed tags, and deleted posts from friends' walls. A denied friend request is a direct affront. Removed tags or posts are similarly hurtful, as they suggest a friend does not want to be socially associated with the one who is denied. Interestingly, Tokunaga finds that much of the activity which causes strain is due to the desire to negotiate social contexts in a complex public space, rather than to intentionally cause harm. In order to protect face within one social sphere, one may need to prevent that sphere from witnessing relationships with peers from other spheres (Binder, Howes, & Smart 2012). The necessity for this form of impression management, argues Tokunaga, sometimes contradicts the expectations on 'politeness and decorum' which friends foster in offline spaces. Various literature, covered in the next chapter, explores how conflicting social contexts jeopardise people's social privacy. This intensifies the politics of friendship on Facebook. It is apparent that friendships can no longer be left to 'go on' according to their own rhythms. Friends are ranked and shuffled, their comments and images tagged, untagged, copied, and removed. Friendships are *bureaucratised*, while the labour of intimacy is *intensified*.

Facebook also complicates romantic relationships. Muise and colleagues (2009) find that undergraduates who are naturally prone to jealousy will monitor their partners covertly on Facebook. When they witness their partners socialising with other friends they are more likely to take what they see out of context, as indicative of suspiciously unfaithful behaviour. This causes a vicious circle of more surveillance activity and, hence, more jealousy. While researching romantic partners from the United Kingdom, Marshall and colleagues (2012) connect Facebook-related jealousy with relationship quality, self-esteem, neuroticism, and attachment style. Of particular salience is 'attachment style', which describes the mode in which a person engages in intimate relationships based on early developmental relationships with his or her parents. The authors find that those with an 'anxious' attachment style (characterised by low trust, low self-esteem and high insecurity – caused by an inconsistently available parent) utilise Facebook to survey their partners and confirm subjective suspicions, causing jealousy and relationship conflict.

Utz and Beukeboom (2011) build on the above empirical work. They recruit a large sample of mostly female Dutch university students and have them complete a survey on the characteristics of their romantic relationships, their propensity toward jealousy, their use of SNSs for relationship maintenance and their surveillance behaviour. Again, they find that those with low self-esteem experience higher degrees of jealousy. Conversely, they also find that those who are in trusting, secure relationships experience an augmentation of relationship quality on Facebook due to monitoring their partners' online activities. The observation of finding a publicly posted comment which lovingly references oneself, for example, is experienced as a positive event.

Importantly, this data does not suggest that Facebook creates bad rela-tionships. Rather, Facebook *intensifies* dispositions which already exist. A common theme in the above literature, I argue, is that Facebook inten-sifies intimacy in one way or another. For example: through projects of constructing the self through intimacy; through maintaining many contacts: through forging and building new relationships; through protecting oneself against weak ties; through the politics of friendship; or through the intensified intimate (and potentially jealous) gaze.

Intimate disclosures

Contemporary social psychology emphasises the importance of self-disclosure in the establishment of intimate relationships (Prager 1995; Laurenceau, Pietromonaco, & Barret 1998). Intimacy is constructed when one reveals one's inner self and perceives the validation and support of another (Reis & Shaver 1988). Likewise, sociologists such as Anthony Giddens (1991) view self-disclosure as an essential ingre-dient in the kinds of relationships which can endure the risky milieus of modern life. Jamieson (1998) refers to today's personal relationships as constructed around a regime of 'intimate disclosure'. Rather than viewing this as an essential aspect of intimacy, Jamieson locates this regime within historical processes which involve the dissemination of therapeutic discourses, the privileging of egalitarian relationships, and the individualisation of self-concepts.

These ideas help frame SNS scholarship, which heavily focuses on self-disclosures. Drawing on a survey of Canadian users, Christofides and colleagues (2009) discover that people are more likely to disclose personal information on Facebook than in general. They hypoth-esise that norms of self-disclosure are more permissive on Facebook. Certainly, researchers have noticed the preponderance of self-disclosures one encounters when navigating Facebook. Some of these constitute people's day-to-day trivialities and ephemeral thoughts (Robards 2012). Some of these are of a more emotional and intimate nature. For example, based on a year-long observation of Facebook profiles, Enli and Thumin (2012) distinguish among three primary ways in which users 'practice' status updating: 'reluctance practice', whereby people post infrequently and refrain from disclosing intimate information; 'promoting practice', whereby people only post when they can paint themselves in a posi-tive light; and 'sharing practice', whereby they liberally disclose aspects of themselves, including intimate information. Describing the last of these, they write: 'People might use their status updates to inform about their private life, including personal weaknesses and mistakes, and thus invite their online friends to engage in a more private and personal conversation' (2012: 96).

There is a general sense that one cannot help but encounter emotional self-disclosures when logging on, especially given that Facebook's central zone is the News Feed, an aggregate reportage of one's friends' posts. Hence, Facebook is referred to as a space of 'ambient intimacy' (Thompson 2008) which facilitates 'emotional contagion' (Kramer 2012).

Facebook is a highly convergent technology. Self-disclosures can be articulated via different media, through different interface functions, and in different communication spaces (Valesco-Martin 2011). Consider autobiographical self-descriptions, status updates, group messages, comments, geo-tags, links to content elsewhere on the web, 'liked' pages and groups, videos, and photographs. Different communication tools are used to construct different forms of intimacy on Facebook. Take photographs. Facebook holds more photographs than any other website (Schonfeld 2009). It is an abyssal user-generated photo archive of everyday life and signals the social dominance of photographic self-expression. Photographs are valued for how they can picture the self in social situations, thus implicitly disclosing one's interpersonal relationships (Livingstone 2008; Zhao, Grasmuch, & Martin 2008; Mallan 2009; Mendelson & Papacharissi 2011). Berger (1982) describes what he terms 'private photographs': images which emotionally resonate with a specific social group. Unlike historical images or advertisements, private photographs circumscribe a specific meaning for those who are interpersonally invested in them. These people can construct an affect-laden narrative link to the lived experience of the photographed moment. Berger's ideas help in understanding how photographs on Facebook can be a particular kind of emotional disclosure, routed in the interpersonal. This also draws attention to Facebook connections who are not invested in their friends' photographs, who are not part of these private spaces, but can nevertheless look in on them.

Photographs capture scenes and freeze them in time with an uncanny sense of reality. Evincing connections between 'reality' and 'authenticity', Pempek and colleagues (2009) find that Facebook users utilise photographs to express their authentic identities. Photographs are also entangled with our recollection of the past. They materialise memories (Berger 1982) and act as a prosthetic extension of our ability to remember (Lury 1998). Also, as Barthes (1981) eloquently explores in *Camera Lucida*, memories and images are powerful emotional catalysts.

When photographs mobilise this duet of light and thought they are able to 'prick' and 'bruise' with emotional poignancy. The role of photography in establishing intimacy on Facebook is thus an important but still under-researched one. How do these factors influence the negotiation of intimacy on Facebook? How does the intimacy embedded in photographs relate to other forms of disclosure? I return to these issues throughout this book.

A central question animating SNS scholarship asks why users publicly disclose intimate self-aspects. One explanation involves surveillance. While discussing the diagrammatic power relations of the panopticon, Foucault (1977) illustrates how a subject's internalisation of an invisible watcher's gaze produces his or her subjectivity through a process of normative self-discipline. Building on this, Albrechtslund (2008) argues that SNS users welcome the surveillance of their peers as a chance to engage in identity construction. Likewise, Westlake views peer surveillance on Facebook as an opportunity for empowered self-presentation. Departing from Foucault, this form of surveillance does not produce 'docile bodies' but encourages expressive behaviour, drawing on social rather than disciplinary norms which value interpersonal affection, play, and fun (Mallan 2009; Sas et al. 2009). These arguments are often directed toward youth cultures. Hence they connect with the notion that youths capitalise on SNSs as spaces where they can experiment with self-construction while developing into adulthood (Christofides, Muise, & Desmarais 2012).

Another less 'self-focused' explanation argues that intimate disclosures accrete from the interpersonal sociality which occurs on Facebook. Park and colleagues (2011) explore the relationship between self-disclosure and perceived levels of intimacy on Facebook. Out of their sample of university participants, those who engage in a large amount of positive self-disclosures – defined as relating positive, pleasant aspects of oneself – experience a strong sense of intimacy. Research conducted by Sas and colleagues (2009) connects a similar conception of positivity to social interaction. Based on data from diary entries on memorable Facebook experiences completed by a group of twenty-something Facebook users from the United Kingdom, the authors find that participants primarily value experiences in which they share positive emotions with friends online. When users express something positive, their friends capitalise on this by responding with affection, appreciation, and the like. Because these exchanges occur on Facebook they can be preserved, fondly remembered, and re-lived.

This said, not all disclosures are positive, and both Park et al. (2011) and Sas et al. (2009) discovered evidence of users relating negative experiences. A potential explanation for this is that users turn to Facebook for positive reinforcement when feeling down. This is evidenced by the panoply of psychometric empirical literature which correlates Facebook use with elevated self-esteem. For example, Christofides and colleagues (2009) find that users with low self-esteem maximise the visibility of their disclosures so as to increase their popularity and, hence, heighten their self-esteem. In a similar study, Forest and Wood (2012) find that people with low self-esteem are motivated to use Facebook because they perceived it as a comparatively safe, risk-free arena in which to express themselves. However, they tend to make more negative self-disclosures than do people with high self-esteem and, consequently, come across as less likeable. Contrary to the above studies, the authors hypothesise that this may harm the ability to foster interpersonal intimacy online and, hence, make Facebook an ultimately unrewarding social space. Again, these ideas paint Facebook as a kind of 'psychotherapeutic milieu', where online disclosures are intended to have a 'healing effect' (Valesco-Martin 2011).

If disclosures are indicative of interpersonal processes in which people seek to build intimacy through revealing their inner selves, than they should reflect a certain desire for authenticity. However, various studies have questioned the 'authenticity' of disclosures online (Rosen 2007; Walther et al. 2008; Mallan 2009; Ibrahim 2010; Bateman, Pike, & Butler 2011). For example, based on questions such as, 'I do not always feel completely sincere when I reveal my own feelings, emotions, behavior or experiences in Facebook', Park and colleagues (2011: 1977) find a lack of correlation between honest disclosures and the presence of intimacy. They conclude that it is 'quite obvious that FB is not a place where truthful and deep relationships can be sustained' (2011: 1981).

> It is notable that Facebook is a 'social' network site where more and frequent interactions and more positive personal information may facilitate intimacy, while sincere and carefully intended personal information may not be much valued. (2011: 1980)

This puts into question the idea that authentic interpersonal relationships are being maintained online. It is cognate with theorists who view Facebook as an inauthentic space where people mobilise intimacy to garner attention and satisfy narcissistic urges (Rosen 2007; Ibrahim 2010; Aboujaoude 2011; Turkle 2011). However, empirical work which interrogates 'honesty' and 'sincerity' should be taken carefully. 'Honesty' is a problematic category, especially when considering the way in which Facebook may influence the *performance* of intimacy. Rather than seeing 'dishonesty' as antithetical to genuine interpersonal intimacy, the concept of authenticity should be encountered as an open issue, playing out on a novel and often problematic stage.

In this respect, the limits of deductive social psychology reveal themselves, as this methodology tends to neglect performance-related notions of selfhood, and often constructs measures based on empirical work done in completely different social situations. On the one hand, this demands that we move beyond this framework and probe the nature of intimacy on Facebook in a more open-ended manner. On the other hand, it demands that we understand the cultural significance of this psychological, self-disclosure-based construction of the subject. What 'cultural model of intimacy' is at play here?

Public intimacy

When considering why SNS users publicly reveal intimate personal information online, some look to cultural causes. For example, Blatterer (2010) links this voluntary publicity to 'reflexive individualisation'. One version of this thesis put forward by Anthony Giddens (1991) argues that, due to the decay of traditions and entrenched modes of subjectification, people are burdened with self-realisation through personal psychological quests. Giddens gives a familiar historical account of how the rise of urban life complicates social relations; how processes of globalisation open up localities to international flows of culture and people; how liberalised labour markets uproot citizens in search of competitive jobs; and how new consumer cultures bring people together in non-traditional settings. Due to these processes, community, kinship, and family begin to lose their influence on the formation of interpersonal bonds and identities. As well as the loss of these 'embedding' structures, increased individual mobility causes relationships to become ephemeral and fragile. Partly in response to this, psychotherapeutic 'expert systems' permeate academia, popular culture, and everyday life. These discourses valorise the need for a specific kind of intimacy based on voluntary relationships, emotional self-disclosure, mutual knowledge, love, support, and commitment, in order to gain psychological well-being and a sense of self. This is welcomed, given the way in which life is perceived to be full of risk and potential psychic harm. People become self-reflexive regarding the health and authenticity of their identities and see intimate friendships and romantic relationships as a way of securing these qualities and as a buffer against unforeseen contingencies. Selfhood becomes inextricably tied to intimacy.

Importantly, many of these themes – voluntary relationships, reflexive self-construction, mobility, emotional self-disclosure, and therapeutic healing – are reflected in much of the SNS scholarship discussed above. However, Giddens has a distinctly privatised view of intimacy. For a pure relationship to succeed, its locus must be private life. Hence, Giddens says little about how these bonds may play out in public. However, as Blatterer (2010) notes, SNSs reflect a growing tendency for reflexive self-construction to happen in public. Now, cultural theories of *public* intimacy also look to the widespread dissemination of psychology. However, critics such as Illouz (2007) and Bauman (2007) additionally examine how these processes combine with changes in the nature of modern capitalism so as to implode the boundaries between private and public life.

Illouz (2007) writes with particular cogency in this field. Looking predominantly at American culture, Illouz argues that twentieth-century capitalism influenced the emergence of an 'emotional style'. 'Culture', she argues, has become 'preoccupied with emotional life' (2007: 6). This is driven largely by institutions which utilise psychotherapy for profit. For example, Illouz examines how Freudian ideas enter public workplaces, where managers turn to therapeutic techniques to increase worker happiness, improving inter-workplace relations and, hence, productivity. Similarly, she examines how therapy enters public media spaces so as to tap the psyche market. Consider, for instance, fashionable television psychiatrists such as Doctor Phil. Finally, Illouz also traces the popularisation of therapeutic knowledge, from psychoanalysis via early paperback books and magazines through state investment in psychiatric health to sexual liberation and feminist movements to contemporary spectacles such as the *Oprah Winfrey Show*. Modern culture becomes saturated with therapy, a state which De Vos calls 'psychologisation', the 'phenomenon of how the psy-sciences became a hegemonic discourse delivering particular signifiers and discursive schemes for looking upon oneself and upon the world' (2010: 528). These processes lead people to believe that it is both legitimate and important that they discuss their private, personal issues in public.

Along with this belief, a set of valued ideologies and practices emerge. These include 'equality, fairness, neutral procedures, emotional communication, sexuality, overcoming and expressing hidden emotions, and centrality of linguistic self-expression' (2007: 29). These values are instituted in public spheres such as 'support groups, talk shows, counselling, rehabilitation programs, for-profit workshops, therapy sessions, [and] the Internet' (2007: 48). Within these spheres people are asked to identify and rationalise their intimate troubles. Emotions are named and categorised, fixed in place as if outside the body. In contrast to their ephemeral nature, emotions become like texts, able to be manipulated and thus supposedly repaired. Consider online profile creation, which involves a 'mode of self-apprehension in which the self is externalised and objectified through visual means of representations and language' (2007: 76). In many cases this requires that one's identity be represented through 'fill-in-the-blank' emotional categories of 'taste, opinion, personality, and temperament' (2007: 78).

The exteriorisation and objectification of intimacies, argues Bauman (2007), produce a specific kind of object, namely, the commodity. We are so immersed in markets, argues Bauman, that we have internalised their logics and, hence, seek to transform ourselves into commodities. For example, the young have internalised the practices of celebrities and carry out their lives in public as if they are celebrities. The blurring of subject and commodity parallels that of private and public. Once commodified, our private lives are free to circulate through public spaces like other commodities. Yet this transformation is hidden from us. Youths, for instance, view the public manifestations of celebrities as representations of real people, rather than marketing strategies. Bauman calls this 'subjectivity fetishism', an appearance of subjectivity which hides its deeper corruption. Bauman argues that, just like commodities, our identities and relationships have a limited shelf-life. Relationships are easily discarded when they become unfashionable or conflict with a newly adopted persona. Unlike Giddens, whose notion of the 'pure relationship' involves intense commitment, Bauman believes modern individuals are quite capable of discarding friends and lovers.

Critics who apply these ideas to SNSs express deep worry about public intimacy online. Rather than expressing genuine concern for others, SNS users are only concerned with themselves, with their own intimate problems and therapeutic needs. Rather than seeking interpersonal fulfilment from social connections, they leverage these ties as an audience to hear their confessions and mirror their vanities. Rather than seeking 'I–thou' relationships, they seek 'I–it' connections. A friend is an 'it', a mirror, a means to an end. These are not authentic identities, but rather they are empty and ersatz.

In this vein, Facebook and like services seem emblematic of a 'culture of narcissism'. This phrase finds its popular origin in the work of Christopher Lasch (1979). Looking at American culture, Lasch argues that a pathological form of narcissism has become normalised, one of weak ego requiring constant validation. According to Lasch, the incursion of therapy culture into family life causes the enervation of oedipal processes responsible for the formation of a strong super-ego. Simultaneously, the rise of individualism and consumer culture isolates people from meaningful relations and habitual, role oriented identities. The resultant psyche has little self-esteem or strong social bonds and, hence, must solicit from weak ties what can only be shallow recognition. Lack of fulfilment is inevitable, perpetuating a hopeless, continual desire for attention. It is important to emphasise the social deskilling which is implied here, because turning inward accommodates the degradation of social skills and conventions which facilitate 'other-concerned' sociality.

Lasch has been critiqued for failing to produce empirical evidence (Kilminster 2008), for misreading 1960s emancipatory movements as symptomatic of narcissism (Tyler 2007), and for superimposing clinical dispositions on American culture proper without regard to the heterogeneous cultural groups constitutive of this broader space (Valadez & Clignet 2005). Nevertheless, his ideas have taken hold and seem relevant to how SNS users supposedly beseech recognition from weak ties through public, intimate disclosures.

Sherry Turkle (2011) continues her ongoing and influential critique of cyberculture in *Alone Together*, in which she turns her attention to SNSs and narcissism. Like Lasch, she considers this narcissism does not reveal 'people who love themselves, but a personality so fragile that it needs constant support' (2011: 177). Services such as Facebook, argues Turkle, encourage this phenomenon by providing, on the one hand, the ability to judiciously control and broadcast self-presentations, and on the other, an immediately accessible audience from which to garner self-validation. With these options at hand, users neglect a much more mercurial but ultimately more rewarding source of self-discovery, namely, interpersonal experience. For Turkle, this is an experience defined by proximate, face-to-face sociality. Turkle's fondness for the non-mediated can be traced back to *Life on the Screen* (1995), in which she critiques the self-invention which occurs on Multi User Domains because it allows people to sidestep processes of social mastery which allow mature, capable, psychically stable identities to form. Likewise, she believes Facebook provides a kind of false mastery, as it negates the necessary development of social skills that are based in genuine interpersonal engagement. Hence, users fail to grasp what this engagement involves and, hence, turn to publicising their intimacies with the hope this will yield social fruit and self-validation.

Again firmly routed in psychotherapy, Aboujaoude's (2011) reflections on Facebook echo Turkle's. Social networking bestows excessive control over how we present ourselves, hence, encouraging our vain and self-gratifying traits. It seduces us with the instantaneous gratification of sound-bite sociality, while we neglect rewarding interpersonal bonds. Aboujaoude laments how this erodes social mastery:

> Why put up with some character weaknesses when we can pretend to be omnipotent? Why struggle to advance at our job if we can be the reigning boss of our little corner of the blogosphere? Why work hard to socially integrate if we can count five hundred friends between MySpace and Facebook? (76)

Once more, a kind of false mastery is evinced, a seductive omnipotence which Aboujaoude calls 'god mode'. Interpersonal intimacy is dead. Signed, God.

Rosen (2007) delivers a particularly potent critique of narcissism online, taking her cues from adolescent MySpace users. According to Rosen, MySpace suggests no more than a search for 'parochial celebrity'. She mourns the transformation of intimacy from an interpersonal aspect of friendships into a tool for garnering attention.

> '[F]riendship' in these virtual spaces is thoroughly different from real-world friendship. In its traditional sense, friendship is a relationship which, broadly speaking, involves the sharing of mutual interests, reciprocity, trust, and the revelation of intimate details over time and within specific social (and cultural) contexts. Because friendship depends on mutual revelations that are concealed from the rest of the world, it can only flourish within the boundaries of privacy; the idea of public friendship is an oxymoron (2007: 26).

Cognate with Bauman, Rosen imagines friendships to have become secondary to the constitution of self as celebrity. Rosen writes:

> The creation and conspicuous consumption of intimate details and images of one's own and others' lives is the main activity in the online social networking world. There is no room for reticence; there is only revelation'. (2007, 24)

This resonates with what Bauman (2007) terms the 'confessional society', in which social participation requires and demands complete self-publication. Although Facebook's affordance for carefully tailored self-presentations seems to suggest an empowered 'sovereign consumer', refraining from these publications would entail social death. Hence the subjectivity fetishism which hides the impossibility of life outside of commodification.

Rosen closely parallels Frohne (2002), who explores the way in which post-modern media collapse private boundaries and encourage the public theatricalisation of private life. Frohne deftly combines an analysis of how both media content and *form* determine a narcissistic condition. 'Medial self-realisation' has come to dominate cultural narratives which advocate modes of being. For example, reality television's focus on 'nobodies' convinces people who 'do not embody exceptional stories or careers that they can achieve this form of celebrity' (2002: 254). Also, these *vérité* psychodramas use intimacy to code reality and interpolate their viewers. They suggest that public audiences – rather than, say, a good friend or an actual psychiatrist – can act as a therapeutic mirror through which a person can come to know himself or herself.

Meanwhile, cameras and photographic self-expressions are increasingly becoming a significant part of everyday life. These cultural and practical experiences of the camera gaze cause a particular kind of self-awareness. The camera requisitions poses. Like a physical mirror it mobilises an externalised, visual self-awareness. Of course, self-awareness has always resulted from being mirrored in someone else's attention. Frohne's point is that the attentive gaze has shifted away from 'stable social relations' such as family members. Now the 'role of "reflexive self-assurance" has been delegated unconsciously to the media' (2005: 271). The anticipation of mediation becomes automatic. The camera gaze takes on a panopticon character, internalised in its absent potentiality. A complete subjectivisation of the 'medialised view of oneself' sets in – a constant assertion of the media mirror and, therefore, the narcissistic desire to see oneself 'reflected in media reality' (2002: 260). Intimate aspects of people's lives become 'theatricalised' as if they are under media surveillance. 'Under these conditions the exhibition of private life for the unhindered observation of an unknown other has become a popular fascination' (2002, 260).

These ideas fit with many aspects of Facebook. In certain cases, people do seem comfortable under the online gaze of invisible watchers. They seem to revel in the participatory panopticon, disclosing private information and circulating private images. Certainly, the ubiquity of photographs on Facebook connects with Frohne's contention that photographs are now intimately tied to self-understanding and are determining a 'medialised view of oneself'. Is Facebook the latest incarnation of a pattern of media narcissism, the genealogy of which can be traced back through reality television and photography?

Unfortunately, cultural critics offer little empirical evidence when seeking to connect 'SNS culture' with narcissism. Other, more empirically grounded, scholars have investigated Facebook narcissism from a clinical perspective (Buffardi & Campbell 2008; Mehdizadeh 2010; Ong et al. 2011). This research is grounded in trait psychology, which views narcissism as 'a highly inflated, positive but unrealistic self-concept, a lack of interest in forming strong interpersonal relationships, and an engagement in self-regulatory strategies to affirm... positive self-views' (Ong et al. 2011: 181). These studies, however, merely ask how narcissists make use of SNSs and correlate behavioural questions with items that measure traits. Narcissism is not linked to technological, social, or cultural structures. In fact, with no causal elements at play, these studies say nothing about SNSs. Essentially, they discover that narcissists behave narcissistically, a tautology which could have permitted any case study: say, narcissism in Saharan poaching subcultures.

Moreover, empirical research cautions against an overt acceptance of the narcissism thesis. For example, in their investigation into the relationship between publicity and self-disclosure on a hypothetical SNS, Bateman and colleagues (2011) find that perceived publicity limits the amount and intimacy of self-disclosures. Similarly, a host of privacy-related research discerns that users do not always willingly accept the invisible gaze and take steps to curtail their levels of exposure (Dwyer, Hiltz, & Passerini 2007; Lenhart & Madden 2007a, 2007b; Livingstone 2008; Strater & Lipford 2008; Debatin et al. 2009; Madden & Smith 2010; Raynes-Goldie 2010; Stutzman & Kramer-Duffield 2010). This literature, discussed further in the following chapter, suggests that users are concerned with interpersonal life, and that the relationship between self and others online involves the development of a whole set of new social skills. Again, this points toward social life becoming more laborious, toward *intensive intimacy*. What are the socio-cultural dimensions of this intensive intimacy? How can we grasp an everyday, qualitative understanding of this phenomenon?

I think the critics mentioned above are fastened to a constrictive assumption which curtails an understanding of intimacy on Facebook. For instance, both Giddens and Bauman, although disagreeing on certain things, assume that privacy and intimacy are inseparable and, hence, public intimacy is inauthentic. 'Intimacy is the other face of privacy, or at least only becomes possible (or desired) given substantial privacy' (Giddens 1991: 94). This assumption demands a definition of privacy, which is itself a slippery concept (Bennett 2011). The above critics imply a dyadic, rigidly bounded privacy, and this will be questioned throughout this book. More importantly, however, I believe the public intimacy 'contradiction' requires deconstruction, such that an analysis of intimacy on Facebook does not circumscribe its conclusions *a priori*.

Arguably, modern intimacy was produced through the 'privatisation' of personal relationships. Jamieson (1998) critically explores this process. Though sceptical of sharp historical divides, Jamieson proposes an analytic distinction between pre-modern and modern personal relationships. Existing up until the onset of industrial capitalism and urbanisation, 'pre-modern' bonds centred on obligatory relationships with kin and family. These lacked privacy, being relatively open to the closely knit communities they depended on. Communities were stratified, and marriage and children were often the product of economic contracts. The church demonised sexuality, and daily struggles for survival restricted autonomy. Intimacy based on private self-disclosure, moral and sexual equality, love, and freedom were in short supply.

Through the latter part of the Enlightenment, and culminating in the nineteenth and early twentieth centuries, industrialisation and urbanisation significantly changed the nature of social life, fracturing community bonds. In his seminal work, Tönnies (1963) portrays the death of traditional community (*Gemeinschaft*) at the hands of a society of cities (*Gesellschaft*). In this drama, intimate private life forms in reaction to the anomie of the industrial metropolis. Likewise, Sennett (1977) explores how successive market booms and busts ravaged the newly industrialised centres of nineteenth-century Europe.[1] Provoked by this insecurity, people sought safe haven in the home. Bellah and colleagues (1985) trace similar connections, looking specifically at the onset of industrial urbanisation in America. As with Europe, people sought to escape into the solace of private life. Believing that the separation of a sentimental private sphere from a rationalised sphere of work would maximise productivity, industry assisted in the privatisation of personal relationships. 'Domesticity, love and intimacy increasingly became "havens" against the competitive culture of work' (1985: 43). This determined the evolution of polar human traits, of public utilitarian and private *expressive* individualism. Hence, the privatised home bore the germ of emotional self-disclosure. Giddens (1991) is likewise adamant that intimacy is born out of the mutual construction of private and public realms, and from this dichotomy our expressive capabilities are generated.

Bellah and colleagues also argue that friendships have undergone a process of privatisation. That is, friendships came to be influenced by the same 'expressive individualism' fostered in the home. This echoes Giddens' view of friendship as a form of pure relationship, a private, emotionally expressive bond. However, Allan (1998) argues that 'private' friendships were, for most of the twentieth century, enjoyed solely by the middle classes. Working class people constructed friendships in particular public spaces, such as pubs and sporting clubs, which were ritualistically separated from private life. Likewise, it is important to recognise that friendship formation was constricted by gender divisions. Through much of the last century the kinds of voluntary associations open to men were closed to women, who were constrained by a division of labour within the home (Jamieson 1998). In more recent works, though, Allan (2001, 2008) recognises the way in which voluntary, mobile, and emotionally expressive relationships have cross-cut these structures.

Overall, the reality of the 'privatisation thesis' has been questioned because it provides too general a concept for understanding complex processes having to do with domesticity and social structure (Pahl & Wallace 1988), and because it neglects how leisure pursuits between friends often happen publicly outside the home and, hence, cannot be adequately considered 'privatised' (Allan & Crow 1991). However, I argue that those who detect narcissism online are implicitly influenced by this privatised concept of personal relationships. This perpetuates a false dichotomy. Private, intimate life is juxtaposed against public life, which is viewed in terms of 'community'. That is, in terms of sociology's great tragedy, the loss of community and, hence, its great goal, the regeneration of community. This image of community is rooted in classical ethics and makes little room for intimacy. It can be traced back to Aristotle, who, in the *Nicomachean Ethics* (1998), distinguishes between virtuous friendships, friendships based on utility, and friendships based on pleasure. Aristotle favours the virtuous kind, in which each party altruistically wishes good for the other. He imagines that, from this moral attribute, moral societies can form. That is, from virtuous friendships come virtuous communities: from the interpersonal 'good' comes the common good. Hence, virtuous friendships are central to Aristotle's ethical conception of civics and the polis.

In contemporary times, private intimacy is set against this civic ideal. Giddens views intimacy as the opposite of community, as taking shape against civics. Hence, intimate and virtuous friendships are at odds. Other writers attempt to reconcile this divide, to understand how private relationships can take on virtuous aspects and transition into the community. For example, reflecting on Aristotle's tripartite definition of friendship, Bellah and colleagues write: 'In a culture dominated by expressive and utilitarian individualism, it is easy for us to understand the components of pleasure and usefulness, but we have difficulty seeing the point of considering friendship in terms of common moral commitments' (Bellah et al. 1985: 115). These writers wish to connect with a 'traditional view' of friendship, in which 'friendship and its virtues are not merely private: They are public, even political, because a civic order, a "city", is above all a network of friends. Without civic friendship, a city will degenerate into a struggle of contending interest groups unmediated by any public solidarity' (1985: 116). A similar concern is present in Putnam's influential work, Bowling Alone (2000), in which he imagines how social capital may be used to regenerate community life.

If friendships are to be public, is this their only course? Is it either private intimacy, or public community? No in-between? Can we discover more nuanced, contextual, multifaceted understandings of public sociality which move beyond this limited dichotomy? These questions, I argue, should guide an analysis of Facebook. The cultural critiques of public intimacy discussed above are limited by this privacy/community dichotomy, a limitation best expressed when Rosen declares public friendship an oxymoron. Rather than accepting this limitation, I begin by being open and sensitised to the possibility of public intimacy which remains interpersonal and socially skilled. SNS research suggests that these attributes exist, albeit in a problematic state. This, in turn, suggests they are changing, and this change is significant. Hence, intimacy online should be considered *virtual* rather than virtuous. That is, as something *becoming*.

2
Frameworks: Privacy, Performance, Social Capital

Facebook provides various social benefits for my participants. However, it also concerns them by making intimacy problematic. In response they develop novel solutions to these problems. I seek to theorise these problems and solutions through mobilising appropriate conceptual frameworks. Three fields already prevalent in SNS scholarship help in this regard: 'privacy', 'performance', and 'social capital'. Each provides a particular way of thinking through these issues. In what follows I tour through literature which explores these frameworks, suggesting points of critical synthesis which will be taken up in the empirical chapters to come.

Fuzzy privacy

In the previous chapter it became clear that privacy is significantly related to intimacy. Sociologists, psychologists and cultural critics put credence in the idea that intimate relationships are nurtured through private interactions. Privacy has been a key issue for SNSs, and Facebook has been particularly scandalised in this regard (boyd & Hargittai 2010).[1] Privacy is a fuzzy concept and has been applied in various ways in different disciplines. In a legal sense, privacy is founded on the 'right to be let alone' and is routed in protecting the domestic sphere from state and media intrusion (Warren & Brandeis 1890). Privacy rights are ideologically associated with individual rights, the right to control *personal* spaces and information and, hence, emerge with modernisation and liberal individualism (Katsh 1989). Alongside a discourse of 'rights' is one of control and agency. Privacy can be defined as the ability to control access to oneself and one's information (Westin 1970). However, this position problematically neglects the social entanglement of both people and information. Altman (1983) argues that privacy involves both closing and opening up access and, hence, can be thought of as controlling the relative boundaries of a social space. For Altman, privacy involves both individuals and social groups. Burgoon and colleagues (1989) introduce further complexity, suggesting four kinds of privacy: psychological, physical, social, and informational. Certain theorists place explicit focus on social privacy, on social relations and situations. For example, Nissenbaum (2004) proposes a concept of privacy based on separating social contexts from one another by controlling norms of information distribution. In curtain cases, 'surveillance' may be a more appropriate framework, such as when personal data is given up willingly, though naively, and surveillance systems incorporate one's digital self into a system or institutionalised risk and social sorting (Lyon 1994).

Which framework is best for understanding how privacy, publicity, and intimacy play out on Facebook? Facebook is a complex assemblage of software platforms, sharing protocols, network hierarchies, and business deals. It provides services to various actors who are given different degrees of access to a variety of data. From this complexity a constellation of privacy risks arise. Given that privacy is a variform concept, it makes sense that these different risks will yield different frameworks. Hence, I am sensitised to the kinds of risks and corresponding frameworks which jeopardise intimacy.

Awareness, concern, and agency

SNS scholarship into privacy charts the evolution of a more aware, concerned, and agentic user. It is axiomatic that users will not act to resolve problems if they do not perceive their existence. Hence, the distinction between 'actual' and 'perceived' privacy risk is significant (Blatterer 2010). Early scholarship finds SNS users to be unaware of many of the privacy risks which could befall them. For example, Acquisti and Gross (2006) ask a large sample of American university students about their privacy concerns on Facebook as well as their more 'generic' concerns about things such as government surveillance or stranger danger. The authors discovered a dichotomy between generic concerns on the one hand and service uptake and information revelation on the other. Of surveyed participants who expressed the highest generic concerns, 89 per cent still joined Facebook.

Acquisti and Gross propose 'peer pressure', 'unwariness of exposure', and 'trust in the service' as reasons for this dichotomy. Peer pressure, they suggest, could explain why users reveal personal information even though they feel strongly about privacy – a desire not to be excluded from an online social world. 'Unwariness' was supported by a significant amount of users who underestimate who can view their profiles and who are unaware that Facebook provides privacy settings. Trust is evinced by users who do not think it necessary to read Facebook's privacy policy and do not believe Facebook collects their data.

However, in comparing Facebook's privacy issues with 'generic' ones, I think Acquisti and Gross make a methodological error. 'Privacy' is in danger of conceptual over-simplification if thought of 'generically' rather than in terms of specific risks and social contexts.

Certain positions hold that Facebook users are aware of risks but are not concerned about privacy. Ibrahim has defined SNSs as 'complicit risk communities' (2008: 248), referring to how users willingly submit themselves to potential privacy threats. One reason for this has already been discussed, namely that Facebook users welcome the invisible gaze, using it as a mirror for narcissistic self-gratification. Another explanation, proposed by Mark Zuckerberg and his acolytes, is that people are no longer concerned about privacy when weighed up against the benefits of connectivity (Kirkpatrick 2010).

However, both of these explanations lack solid empirical evidence. As research has progressed, scholars continue to find that SNS users are increasingly aware, concerned, and agentic toward risks (Joinson 2008; Livingstone 2008; boyd 2008a; Madden & Smith 2010; Raynes-Goldie 2010; Stutzman & Kramer-Duffield 2010; Bateman, Pike, & Butler 2011; Christofides, Muise, & Desmarais 2012). For example, based on a large telephone survey of American Internet users, Madden and Smith (2010) find that most SNS users engage in privacy behaviour of one sort or another. They change their privacy settings, unfriend connections, remove comments, and use self-searches to identify their digital footprints. Interestingly – and contrary to popular opinion – young adults are found to be most concerned with managing personal information. Young adults are also learning in this respect, becoming more adept as they grow older.

As mentioned in the previous chapter, research suggests that self-disclosure is moderated by how public an SNS is perceived to be (Bateman, Pike, & Butler 2011). Madden and Smith (2010) also discover this correlation, finding that those who consider their visibility to be high are most active in attempting to curtail this visibility. Bateman and colleagues (2011) argue that this goes against the idea that perceived publicity encourages the disclosure of personal information. Before recognising this injunction, it should be noted that these authors investigate publicity as it relates to the Internet as a whole. This is rather amorphous and fails to identify 'risk contexts'. It is important to understand how perceived visibility in the eyes of, say, good friends affects behaviour differently than exposure to, say, governments, corporations, or predators.

Scholars have discovered a host of factors which condition the capacity for people to become aware, concerned, and agentic. One such factor is *trust*. Certain studies find that users express a naïve trust in Facebook to protect their privacy and, hence, engage in excessive self-disclosures (Acquisti & Gross 2006; Fogel & Nehmad 2009). However, other research finds users withhold personal information precisely because they do not trust their SNS (Schofield & Joinson 2008; Shin 2010; Christofides, Muise, & Desmarais 2012). Boyd and Hargittai (2010) find that users became less trusting of Facebook in the wake of controversial privacy upgrades in late 2009. They discuss how negative media attention and privacy campaigns influenced this corrosion of trust and caused a subsequent user engagement with privacy settings.

However, these studies, although informative, do not adequately distinguish between trusting one's SNS service as opposed to trusting the relations one has used that service to connect with. This book goes toward addressing this gap, contextualising issues of trust in terms of intimate interactions within public spaces.

As well as trust, boyd and Hargittai (2010) find that regularity of use, skill, and confidence also influence whether Facebook users act on privacy concerns. Regular users more frequently change their privacy settings. The authors attribute this to greater experience, which leads in turn to greater perceptions of publicity. Skill at privacy setting is related to experience and, hence, regularity of use, but also to overall Internet literacy and, interestingly, gender. Confidence as to whether one's privacy setting behaviour will be successful is, in turn, positively correlated with a higher skill level. The authors find that women tend to change their privacy settings more often, although the relationship between frequency, skill, confidence, and gender is nuanced. Also, participants with more confidence and skill change their privacy settings more than once. If an attempt at privacy setting behaviour proves to be unsuccessful it can weaken people's confidence. This research goes against the idea, discussed in the previous chapter, that a phenomenon of social deskilling is occurring. Rather, people are developing new social skills by enhancing their technical expertise.

Deferment of risk expectations onto others and the reutilisation of media use can also influence the taking of privacy into one's own hands. Based on in-depth interviews with American undergraduates, Debatin and colleagues (2009) argue that Facebook users put risks out of mind through two processes, the 'third person effect' and 'ritualised media use'. The former entails the expectation that privacy risks are visited upon others. The latter describes the way in which Facebook becomes a habitual part of everyday life, whereupon the safety of one's personal information is taken for granted. This can continue until a user personally experiences privacy problems. This makes sense, as habitual behaviour is by definition unreflective and often people require an unexpected contingency to transform something tacit into something problematic. How does ritualistic use and deferment of risk expectations influence the negotiation of intimacy on Facebook? I address this question in Chapter 8.

Time spent using Facebook seems to significantly influence privacy-related behaviour. Boyd and Hargittai reveal how time leads to experience, which positively influences privacy. However, Debatin and colleagues suggest that time leads to habitualisation, which negatively influences privacy. Likewise, Christofides and colleagues (2012) suggest that time spent using Facebook normalises public disclosure. Obviously there are nuances here which require further investigation. Strater and colleagues (2008) look at how the passage of time relates to social contexts. When people first join Facebook, they argue, they are active privacy regulators. They focus on growing their networks and take account of the various social contexts they connect with. However, over time people come to interact with a regular group and forget about the other social contexts which may be watching. The authors thus imply that time spent on Facebook reduces the awareness of social context-related risks. In Chapters 7 and 8 I propose a different position. I argue that the progress of time both multiples and eventually reveals risks to people, sometimes through the experience of contingencies, thus leading to a more reflexive stance.

Certain scholarship argues that users pragmatically balance privacy concerns with the social and self-expressive benefits of visibility. For example, Livingstone (2008) finds her adolescent participants think carefully about their revelations while often also exercising studious reticence. Furthermore, her participants manipulate privacy settings and express a desire for more graduated settings that are capable of accommodating different levels of interpersonal intimacy and different social contexts. Influenced by Giddens, Livingstone thus argues that online adolescent self-construction constitutes a balance between opportunities for self expression, risk taking and risk avoidance.

Studying American university students, Tufekci (2008a) similarly finds MySpace and Facebook users attempt to optimise the balance between revelation and reticence. For example, users delineate virtual boundaries by using nicknames only certain friends can identify. 'Students *do* try to manage the boundary between publicity and privacy, but they do not do this by total withdrawal because they would forfeit a chance for publicity' (2008, 33). Drawing on her ethnography of twenty-something Australian Facebook users, Raynes-Goldie (2010) discovers similar techniques. Aliases can be a powerful form of privacy on Facebook, where finding and friending people involves putting names to faces.

Overall, scholarship reveals evolving concerns and competencies that are moderated by various factors. This suggests a sociological privacy framework which is sensitive to forms of agency and struggle. Yet much of the above research lacks a clear explanation of the relationships between different privacy risks, contexts, and concerns.

Social privacy

As SNS scholarship has progressed, the need to distinguish between amorphous risks, such as those posed by clandestine agencies, and more immanent risks, such as those posed by known social connections, has influenced the way in which privacy has been conceptualised. Based on an ethnography of Facebook users, Raynes-Goldie (2010) argues that people are more concerned with 'social privacy' than 'institutional privacy'. The former relates to the way in which known ties can take possession of personal information while the latter relates to 'how the company behind Facebook...and its partners might use [personal] information' (2010, n.p.). Making a similar distinction, boyd argues that 'when people talk about invasions of privacy on sites like Facebook [they're] talking about how people – including and, especially, people that they know – can hold power over them in a particular moment' (2011: 505).

People articulate heterogeneous social spheres on Facebook, each regulated by different norms, each with its own expectations regarding self-presentation, and each with its own collection of in-group secrets. SNS scholarship is thus concerned with what happens when spheres overlap, potentially exposing abnormal behaviour, undermining well-cultivated identities, and leaking interpersonal secrets (Besmer & Lipford 2009; Lipford et al. 2009; Binder, Howes, & Smart 2012; Marden, Joinson, & Shanker 2012; Vitak et al. 2012). Much of this scholarship finds that users engage privacy settings, utilise aliases, create multiple accounts, moderate their disclosures, and de-friend connections so as to avoid these contingencies (Livingstone 2008; Tufekci 2008a; boyd 2008a; West, Lewis, & Currie 2009; Raynes-Goldie 2010; Vitak et al. 2012).

These social risks become apparent, argues Raynes-Goldie (2010), through everyday interaction with Facebook. For example, Facebook users often seek out information on their connections which would be impossible or inappropriate to access in other mediums due to the separation of contexts. Having experienced this subversion of privacy first-hand, users come to expect similar behaviour from others, thus becoming concerned about their own social privacy.

While Facebook users may find it hard to define some of the agencies capable of viewing their information, they are capable of defining who they have intentionally friended. After all, these people are inventoried in their 'friends lists'. It follows that these friends can also be defined as unwanted audiences (Hull, Lipford, & Latulipe 2010; Stutzman & Kramer-Duffield 2010). The News Feed's controversial introduction in 2006 attests to this. Fearing the News Feed had exposed them, users mounted a sizable backlash. In response, Mark Zuckerberg argued that all the News Feed did was aggregate information that was already publicly available. As boyd (2008b) argues, this misinterprets the contextual nature of privacy. The News Feed broadcasts personal information according to hidden protocols, allowing audiences who may not have cared to navigate to a person's profile to stumble upon his or her content. That is, the News Feed acts to re-contextualise information such that the likelihood of observation by unwanted audiences is felt to increase.

Nissenbaum (1997, 2004) has integrated these ideas into a sophisticated critique of modern privacy. Nissenbaum argues that traditional privacy theory emerges out of legal discourses which view the private realm in terms of personal and familial spaces (such as the home) as well as in terms of intimate and personal information. Such a position assumes there is 'a category of information about persons that is perfectly public (public in a normative sense), which is 'up for grabs' for anyone with an interest in and use for it, and for which 'anything goes' (1997: 213). In turn, this assumes that public places are by definition areas where people feel comfortable expressing 'non-personal' information. However, as Nissenbaum rightly argues, all information is loaded with subjective and intersubjective meaning. This imbues it with preciousness and responsibility, and circumscribes the context in which it can be appropriately expressed. She argues, therefore, that it is important to reject a universal 'private/public' dichotomy and any correlate concepts such as 'generic privacy'.

> A promising alternative rejects the relevance of the dichotomy to information about persons in favor of the idea of a multiplicity of contexts. Information learned in one context belongs in that context and is public *vis à vis* that context. We do not have a dichotomy of two realms but a panoply of realms; something considered public in relation to one realm may be private in relation to another. (215)

Nissenbaum's (2004) valuable contribution lies in her theorisation of how the integrity of contexts is governed by norms. Echoing Erving Goffman, what Nissenbaum calls 'norms of appropriateness' are constitutive of the roles people play in line with a particular social situation. 'Norms of distribution' describe the responsibility a person has with regard to the disclosures he or she is privy to. For example, 'friends expect what they say to each other to be held in confidence and not arbitrarily spread to others' (2004, 124). These ideas have influenced SNS scholarship. Facebook negates contextual integrity by occluding the flow of information between contexts (Hull, Lipford, & Latulipe 2010). Facebook makes awareness of these 'contextual gaps' difficult. This makes it easy to undermine 'norms of distribution', say by posting photographs which depict friends in an unflattering light. Based on a series of focus groups conducted on Facebook users, Besmer and Lipford (2009) find that users are often distressed at the lack of control over the circulation of their photographic self-portraits. This nicely illustrates how norms of distribution become problematic online:

> It would generally be considered acceptable for someone to take a photo at a party, and show that photo to all of the others who were also at that party. Yet, the person would then not send that photo to all of the families and work colleagues of everyone at that party. So photos appropriately shared in one context, may not be appropriate in the context of the entire social network. (2009: 986)

While people can *untag* photos, Besmer and Lipford's participants found this unsatisfactory. It took time, and people remain 'cross-linked' to photographs via their relationships to others who may stay tagged in them. Participants asked posters to take down photographs, although this was not always successful. Posting photographs of friends online raises questions as to who has the ownership and rights to remediate these performances, and these issues connect with 'norms of distribution'. In Chapter 8 I explore how my participants develop new norms of distribution to handle these contingencies, and I argue that 'social capital' can be a very powerful way of conceptualising these processes.

Overall, SNS literature which deals with privacy has yet to thoroughly consider the relationship between privacy and intimacy and, hence, produce a privacy framework which is appropriate for thinking about intimacy problems online. Looking at privacy in terms of social contexts is useful because problems involving interpersonal intimacy are routed in social relations. Importantly, though, not every context problem need involve intimacy. However, in Chapter 7 I argue that intimacy is centrally problematic for my participants because of the indeterminate nature of social contexts and selfhood on Facebook. In Chapter 8 I reinforce existing literature in showing how participants circumscribe social contexts to protect intimacies. However, they also desire public, emotional, interpersonal interactions; hence, they also *perform* intimacy in a particular way.

Cyber-Goffman: reconfiguring the 'situation'

Writers apply performance frameworks in order to understand the public sociality and self-expression which occurs on Facebook. The kinds of public spaces Facebook affords are seen to challenge performances of self. Performance is a central aspect of the grounded theory presented in this book. Consequently, I examine how performance-related literature suggests avenues for understanding the performance of intimacy.

Two general frameworks are relevant here, one situational, the other textual. The former recognises the way in which performances occur within everyday social interactions, or 'situations'. In this sense, 'performance' is utilised to understand how social structures and contexts demand we play a particular role in a particular situation. The work of Erving Goffman (1959), a chief proponent of this analysis, has undergone a widespread resurgence in social media scholarship. Goffman is influenced by pragmatist philosophers such as George H. Meade, John Dewy, and William I. Thomas. These thinkers view social situations as phenomena in which actors pragmatically interpret the meanings given off by their co-present fellows and act according to these interpretations. This describes the basic formula of 'symbolic interaction' (Blumer 1969). Likewise, Goffman argues that when people come together they monitor each other's expressions in order to 'define the situation'. They look for cues which could allow them to glean how others expect them to behave. These cues manifest broader structures – in particular social status. This repertoire of expected behaviour can be thought of as a normative domain of acceptable roles. These roles are dramatised through 'personal front', an aggregate of voluntary and seemingly involuntary expressions, manners, costumes, props, and invariable characteristics such as age and ethnicity. A central concept of personal front describes the way in which involuntary expressions are actually a strategic way of coding the credibility of a performance, making one appear as if naturally suited to the role.

Heterogeneity is implicit in this dramaturgical model: different situations will have different normative definitions and, hence, require different roles. Goffman understands identity as situationally contingent. If one takes 'situation' as a simile for 'context', Goffman's work is closely allied with Nissenbaum's theory of contextual integrity.

Goffman argues that people attempt to actualise their own personal goals while conforming to situational norms and, in doing so, reach a compromise with those around them. In grasping for this 'working consensus' people engage in impression management. This involves a regulation of the impressions one gives off in accordance with how one observes and abides the definition of the situation. Impression management also protects roles through monitoring of both self and other. For example, if a comrade slips out of character an astute observer will show 'tact' in ignoring or helping to cover up this *faux pas*. In so doing the situation's normative framework remains uninjured. In most situations people act in 'teams'. Continually monitoring one another, a team will come to the aid of a struggling compatriot if necessary. Overall, then, situations are created through team-supported dramatisation of context-specific norms and roles and are maintained through a reflexive circuitry of careful observation and performance. Note, then, how actors take on the dialogical roles of both performer and audience. This dialogical position, at the heart of situational performance theory, is apt in understanding how, say, Facebook users respond to each others' posts and form threads. However, as I later show, it also poses some real problems.

In explaining these processes, Goffman often goes into the performer's mind, articulating his or her motivations, embarrassments, second-guesses, and observational practices. Goffman is a social psychologist of sorts. His theory of identity describes a cognitive, reflexive social agent strategically attempting to optimise his or her social position. However, Goffman argues that people are limited in the degree to which they can slip 'out of character' – contrary to social structures. Hence, the purpose of his foray into the mind is to show the laborious mental processes that are undergone to make sure the right masks are worn.

According to Goffman it is common to see social life separated into relative 'back regions' and 'front regions'. In general, Goffman considers front regions to be public: workplaces, restaurants, elevators, reception areas, and the like – while back regions are comparatively private. Front-region behaviour involves careful attention to a performance, to the maintenance of 'face' through various standards of 'decorum', 'manner', and 'appearance' in accordance with the social norms expected by one's audience. On the other hand, back-region behaviour involves relaxing and 'stepping out of character', as well as rehearsing for future front-region performances. Hence, back-region performances 'knowingly contradict' that of the front region 'as a matter of course' (1959: 114). Because of this, it is crucial to manage impressions such that back-region behaviour is fully circumscribed from, and invisible to, front region personae.

Goffman's ideas are apt in theorising how SNS publics are constructed out of social situations and how users embody the dialogical role of both performer and audience. However, Goffman's theories are based on 'co-present interactions.' Therefore, because SNS publics are technologically mediated, they demand to be reworked. In this vein, boyd (2008a) argues that SNSs are 'networked publics' in which performances broadcast out toward invisible audiences and are able to be digitally edited and reproduced. With this in mind, I now turn to literature which probes how SNSs transform performances and social situations, still within a Goffmanian framework. Following this, I focus on the weaknesses of a Goffmanian approach and propose a more textual theory of performance to augment it.

Controlling the self and the situation

For Goffman, how people comport themselves with a 'personal front' – including especially how they give off both intentional, and seemingly unintentional, expressions – is crucial to the performance of self. Scholars explore how SNSs replace or remediate traditional equipment used in this endeavour while affording more self-conscious control over performances. 'Facebook users', writes Westlake, 'employ the static text of the profile in tandem with the more immediate and fluid text of messaging and poking to manage an image of self presented to other users' (2008: 27–28). Such static elements involve things like descriptions of tastes (displayed in the 'info section' of a person's profile), which have been analysed in a Goffmanian fashion in accordance with how they appeal to the social norms of an expected audience (Liu 2008). These constitute what Zhao and colleagues (2008) refer to as an explicit form of first-person, narrative-based self-creation. Photographs are also crucial sites of visual performativity on Facebook. Van House (2009) explores the way in which collocating photographs online – arranging them so as to tell a particular story – constitutes a novel mode of narrative performance. Sas and colleagues (2009) characterise vetting photographs as a form of backstage rehearsal. Selecting, editing, tagging, and arranging photographs constitutes a performative ritual emblematic of the way in which digital photography is becoming a more potent, dynamic, and ubiquitous tool for self-construction (Van Dijck 2008; Mendelson & Papacharissi 2011). Strano analyses Facebook 'profile pictures', images which appear in the corner of profiles and attached to posts. Strano argues that these photographs often evince a spontaneous character which remediates the 'unintentional expressivity' Goffman finds central to the way people code the credibility of their performances. Van Der Heide and colleagues (2012) argue that profile pictures are central in cuing others as to key personality traits, such as one's level of extroversion.

Performances also play out in more fluid situations, such as through conversational threads. More can be said about these dialogues, a gap this book addresses.

Facebook allows people to choose carefully what they disclose on their profiles, judiciously selecting photographs, drafting self-descriptions, and tailoring tastes and interests. 'A user may employ these tools to emphasize the characteristics that person feels best express his or her nature: that the user is funny, serious, studious, creative, fun-loving, popular, deep, or committed to certain beliefs, ideas, or institutions' (Westlake 2008, 27–28). Note the empowerment implicit in these words. Profile creation, argues Illouz (2007), instigates a process of self-reflection which results in a careful exteriorisation, textualisation, and objectification of self-aspects. Unlike in co-present interactions, Facebook allows users to see their own performances mirrored back at them from the screen. This may instigate a kind of media self-awareness. However, in seeing one's performance of self as separate – and hence as capable of being edited – interesting questions are raised with regard to the relationship between subjectivity and objectivity. Does Facebook allow us to produce ourselves through first objectifying ourselves? How does this relate to intimacy? How can intimacy become a *performance object*? I explore these issues in depth in Chapters 6, 8, and 9, mobilising new concepts such as 'prosthetic intimacy' and 'intimacy capital'.

However, Facebook users do not enjoy limitless control over their self-presentations. Facebook networks are typically composed of 'anchored relationships' with shared social biographies (Zhao, Grasmuch, and Martin 2008). These ties have public access to each other. A public based on shared biographies, a *biographical public*, has the capacity to discredit the self-claims a person makes if they stray from what others believe to be 'true'. Claims take on a 'warranting value' (Walther & Parks 2002). People are obliged to perform in accordance with the norma- tive expectations fostered over the course of their relationships. Hence, biographical publics act as a normalising force. Facebook is a kind or 'participatory panopticon' (Albrechtslund 2008), in which users will- ingly submit to the 'policing and establishing of normative behaviour' (Westlake 2008, 35).

At first glance, this nicely fits within Goffman's theory, as these shared histories are used to 'define the situation' (boyd 2008a). However, people connect with a range of different social contexts on Facebook. Prior to the instigation of privacy settings these are subsumed within a singular, public performance space. If each context cues a specific situation and each situation demands a specific role, how does a user choose which role to play? While studying university-aged users, Tufekci responds to this problem:

> Students now find themselves in an environment in which the norm is to publicly articulate one's social networks and some of the inter- actions therein...Such norms of disclosure are having an effect that is the opposite of some of the early predictions about the impact of the Internet. Instead of being able to experiment with multiple identities, young people often find themselves having to present a constrained, unitary identity to multiple audiences, audiences that might have been separate in the past. (2008, 35)

In medical parlance, the self is a cell unable to divide: identity in a kind of 'mitotic arrest'. Goffman explores a similar problem when he looks at what happens when back and front regions implode. Joshua Meyrowitz (1985) famously investigates how electronic media lead to such implosions, looking at television in particular. For example, chil- dren may witness adult programming on television, receiving insight into the secret lives of their parents. Here, exposure to adult discourses (which were previously obscured) engenders an implosion of social contexts. Meyrowitz argues that television's distribution of information beyond situational boundaries creates a 'middle region' in which public and private life are blurred. Likewise, the articulation of both weak and strong interpersonal bonds on Facebook may engender a kind of intimacy middle-region, in which extremely private and personal intimacies are excluded, while more convivial emotions are included. While the specific nature of such a middle region requires further research, SNS scholarship has examined how the merging of back and front regions has led to negative consequences such as the exposure of secrets, contrary roles, and the fostering of out-group enmity which, in turn, burdens impression management (DiMicco & Millen 2007; Tufekci 2008a; Sas, et al. 2009; Skeels & Grudin 2009; Binder, Howes, & Smart 2012; Marden, Joinson, & Shanker 2012). Again, these ideas suggest that the performance of self is laborious and, hence, can be considered in terms of intensive intimacy. Also, in recognising the implosion of roles, contexts, and regions, it is important to question the idea of 'authenticity'. One role may appear authentic in the presence of a specific audience while appearing inauthentic in the presence of another. Hence, the need to move beyond a conception of intimacy which is wedded to the inner, authentic self. These notions – the nature of an intimate middle region, the intensification of impression management, and the performance of authenticity – are taken up in Chapter 8.

While heterogeneous social contexts may harm self-presentation when these contexts are perceived to be audiences, they are also dangerous when they join in with performances. Facebook allows numerous different people to contribute to posts. For example, Timelines are spaces in which both the profile owner and his or her connections can post content (depending on privacy settings). Walther and colleagues (2008) find that the impressions which people form regarding a user's attractiveness are influenced by those of the people who post on his or her page. Hence, on Facebook people are 'known by the company they keep' (2008, 29). From this perspective, control over a performance is subverted by the fact that sociality on Facebook is publicised outwardly in a *group-to-many* fashion, such that other social connections can observe. This is compounded if a user does not wish certain friends witnessing his or her interactions with other friends from, say, a different social group (Binder, Howes, & Smart 2012).

However, before fully decrying the social subversion of performances, it is important to signal that SNS users welcome and exploit the opportunity to perform their identities in a relational context. This is perhaps best seen in photographic performances. Concerned with how youths construct their profiles and perform their identities on Facebook, Mallen (2009) interviews a large sample of Australian secondary school students. Mallen finds that youths often display themselves in group photographs. She writes, '[This] may suggest that young people are developing an understanding of their identities within the context of their social networks' (2009: 57). Likewise, Mendelson and Papacharissi (2011), who qualitatively analyse the photographs of young-adult Facebook users, discover ubiquitous depictions of dyads and groups socialising. For these participants, relationships 'are the dominant subject matter in all photographs' (2011: 259). Based on a small sample of in-depth interviews, Livingstone (2008) illuminates aspects of online identity construction for adolescent SNS users. Livingstone finds that early adolescents engage in performances she classifies as 'identity as display'. A profile of this kind is "visually ambitious", and 'frequently remixes borrowed images and other content to express continually shifting tastes (2008: 402). However, as adolescents grow older they change their mode of self-presentation to what Livingstone terms 'identity as connection'. 'On this alternative approach, elements of display are excised from the profile, replaced by the visual privileging of one's contacts, primarily through links to others' profiles and by posting photos of the peer group socializing offline' (ibid).

Analysing downloaded profiles of a large sample of college-age Facebook users, Zhao and colleagues (2008) uncover similar themes. They categorise a continuum identity performances. On one end is placed 'implicit' self-presentation, which involve photos and wall posts. These performances 'show without telling' and express relational identity. Most photos, for example, show people with friends. On the other end is explicit self-presentation, which includes direct autobiographic statements. These performances evince a 'narrative', 'first-person self'. Importantly, the authors find that most performances are of the 'implicit', relational kind.

> [Users] were more likely to showcase themselves indirectly through friend lists, photo albums, and wall posts; and they tried to avoid making explicit self descriptions, such as the 'About Me' blurb. In this way, the visual possibilities of Facebook mean that users offer a mediated interaction to their audience, one that requires the audience to pay equal attention to the social milieu of the individual. (2008, 1831)

These findings aptly illustrate how performances of self are mediated by social groups and novel forms of content. The above research indicates that users welcome this social negotiation of identity for the rewards it brings, such as group-identification and collective self-esteem. Mallen (2009) argues that 'sharing' is an essential logic of SNSs and, hence, so too is the notion of 'sharing yourself'. In this light, photographs which depict various people can be seen as 'shared artefacts' (Lipford, et al. 2009). Performatively speaking, this can be thought of as 'sharing a stage': these are 'our-spaces' rather than '*MySpaces*'. This form of sharing, continues Mallen, resembles a form of post-structural collaboration. 'The collaborative approach to identity construction undertaken in SNS or other Web 2.0 enabled spaces is similar to the creative process of the *bricologe*, as it draws on a diverse set of materials and tools' (2009, 54). Such ideas are provocative and demand an investigation of just how this form of collaboration takes place. What norms are relevant? What other processes and problems are significant? What roles do other technologies and forms of content play?

The mediated self: acting without author

Goffman's performance theories are concerned with dialogical spaces. That is, with spaces in which performers are aware of each other and are contemplating and acting toward each other through a reflexive circuit of observation, interpretation, and performance. As with Buber, Goffman investigates physical social spaces. Nevertheless, one can think of certain Facebook interactions as dialogical. For example, I argue that comment threads form a kind of dialogical space. However, this is transformed and mediated in peculiar ways. People are not co-present; interactions are a-synchronous – it is unclear who will become part of the space and, hence, its spatiotemporal and social bounds are generally fuzzy. Theorising such a space makes up a large portion of this book.

Within a dialogical space each person takes on the dual roles of performer and audience. However, many people may observe performances on Facebook without reciprocating. They remain separate from dialogical space and occupy only one role: the spectator. Rather than a situational theory, a textual theory of performance is more appropriate for understanding this asymmetry – that is, a theory which views performances as sign-systems which are inherently mediated beyond the moment of authorship. Here, Derrida's understanding of signification, which is founded on mediation, is useful. Derrida (1976) famously critiques the idea, to which Buber is aligned, that signification cannot be understood beyond the presence of an intentional consciousness. Against this notion of *presence*, Derrida argues there is always a breach between what is intended and what is conveyed. It is the capacity of the sign to exist beyond the moment of speech, illustrated through writing, which constitutes its true character. Writing is by nature an embodiment of *absence*, that is, the ability to be split from its moment of production and go beyond it. Because of this ability it is characteristic of signs that they take on new meanings over time when used in different contexts, a quality Derrida terms *différance*. Hence, the meaning of a sign is always deferred into the future, toward an endlessly iterative, open-ended horizon of resignification. The term 'Facebook' strikes me as conflating presence and absence. To face someone is to demand presence, yet a book embodies writing and, hence, absence.

Judith Butler (1990, 1993) has notably fused Derrida's ideas with notions of performative identity and gender. Critiquing essentialist divisions between gender and sex, Butler follows Althusser and Foucault in arguing there is no aspect of identity beyond discourse. The subject does not exist until interpolated through language. All identity is performative, and performances are learned and perfected through constant repetition over time. Like signs, performances have a future-oriented, iterative quality. They are open-ended and, hence, are able to be resignified, ironically cited, and subverted. Like Derrida, Butler refuses to couch the meaning of performances in the moment of performance. This differs from Goffman, who is centrally concerned with how subjects produce performances. Inversely, Butler argues that performances produce subjects. They are scripts which social structures compel people to learn and constantly enact.

These ideas introduce some interesting problems when thinking about the relationship between intimacy, the interpersonal, and performance. Intimate interactions are thought to be those in which each party expresses emotional concern and validation for the other (Reis & Shaver 1988). Intimacy is routed in emotional motivation (Inness 1992; Prager 1995). Such ideas work well with Goffman, whose theory abides an understanding of motivation and, hence, how intimacy can be performed. But how can we understand intimacy if it is detached from the moment of emotional motivation? How do intimacies become texts in a realm such as Facebook? Are these texts read by others to suggest emotionally motivated subjects or are intimacies resignified such that they lose their subject orientation, becoming objects? If they are objects, artefacts, what use do people find in them? How do people manipulate them for their own gain? Moreover, how do those who perform their intimacies feel about these intimacies becoming detaching and moving beyond the self? These constitute some of the key questions which drive my research and which I use to understand the concerns of my participants.

Social capital and the moment of exchange

Research interest into SNSs and social capital is broadly summarised by Ellison and colleagues (2011), who write:

> Social capital is embedded in the structure of social networks and the location of individuals within these structures ... Because [SNSs] have the potential to reshape social networks and lower the costs of communicating with (and thus contributing to and extracting benefits from) this social network, SNS use may have social capital implications. (2011: 1)

This reshaping of networks has been investigated in terms of the relationship between strong and weak ties. In particular, SNSs are seen to allow users to capture and maintain both kinds of ties within an online personal network (Ellison, Steinfield, & Lampe 2007; Ellison, Steinfield, & Lampe 2011). As has been argued, Facebook users predominantly connect with people with whom they share a pre-existing relationship. However, many of these connections may be loosely knit and geographically and culturally diffuse. In point, they may move beyond one's local life-world, their social resources becoming inaccessible. Facebook allows users to digitally materialise these ties, making the resources they offer 'ready to hand'.

Investigating the relationship between different tie strengths and social capital, SNS scholars are influenced by Robert Putnam (2000), who argues that strong ties provide 'bonding social capital', while weak ties provide 'bridging social capital'. Putnam is influenced by Granovetter (1973), who found that employment seekers who leverage weak, diffuse networks are more likely to succeed in finding jobs. While a person will exhaust the resources his or her strong ties possess, weak ties occupy different social spaces and, hence, can provide novel resources – in this case employment opportunities. Keeping with the simplistic notion that social capital amounts to the connections people possess and the resources they can claim from them, Putnam wants to distinguish between the kinds of resources strong and weak ties make available, and to delineate what positive outcomes come with claiming them.

Bonding social capital makes resources available which usually exact heavy costs on the resource giver. These include scarce resources such as money, reputation, or a person's emotional energies in the form of intimate support. Bonding social capital usually delimits the boundaries of strongly tied groups and, hence, leads to insularity, or 'out-group antagonism'. However, this kind of group membership allows people to 'mobilise solidarity' by, say, energising group support for a personal project. On the other hand, bridging social capital makes resources available, such as new information, diverse perspectives, and the feeling of being part of a broader community. People who possess bridging social capital, Putnam argues, are usually outward looking and come into contact with a variety of others.

In an influential early work, Ellison and colleagues (2007) investigate the relationship between the 'intensity' of Facebook use and the perceived social capital of a large sample of university students. The authors are sensitised to how Facebook use affects bridging and bonding social capital as well as a third category they term 'maintained social capital'. This refers to resources associated with connections which have moved out of a person's immediate life-world due to significant 'life changes'. In particular, the authors focus on the migration from high school to college, a salient aspect of their participants' biographies. Although they seem to correlate maintained social capital with both bridging and bonding elements, Ellison and colleagues remain unclear about what maintained social capital actually is, how it works, and how it relates to different types of connections. For example, the authors do not touch on how a strong tie who has moved away may provide both emotional support and novel information drawn from his or her experiences in a different locale.

Ellison and colleagues construct a quantitative item which measures intensity of Facebook use, consisting of scales which measure average time spent daily on Facebook, the emotional component of Facebook in everyday life, and the number of Facebook 'friends' a participant has. These measures are correlated with an adaptation of the Internet Social Capital Scales developed by Williams (2006), whose work concerns the relationship between social capital and online–offline dynamics. Drawing on Putnam's definitions of bridging and bonding social capital, Williams constructs survey propositions with accompanying Likert response sets. So, for example, in addressing the notion that bridging social capital is associated with diverse perspectives and feeling part of a broader community, Williams formulates the following types of propositions: 'Interacting with people online/offline makes me interested in things that happen outside of my town ... Interacting with people online/offline makes me feel connected to the bigger picture' (2006: 602). Most of Williams' scales measure the outcomes of social capital, such as 'feeling connected'. Likewise, Ellison and colleagues' method deduces social capital from outcomes. For example, the authors measure for elevated self-esteem, a supposed outcome of social capital. Overall, survey results correlate intensity, social capital, and self-esteem items. The resulting 'social capital/intensity' method has been influential to many of the later social capital inquiries into Facebook (Joinson 2008; Steinfield, Ellison, & Lampe 2008; Valenzuela, Park, & Kee 2009; Burke, Marlow, & Lento 2010).

The results of Ellison's and colleagues' research suggest that intensity of Facebook use is linked to both bridging and bonding social capital, although bridging social capital shows a higher correlation. This makes sense if one assumes that people tend to maintain a relatively stable set of strong ties while often forming acquaintances with an expansive set of weak ties. Ellison and colleagues suggest that many of these may be activated 'latent ties', people known well by a friend but not known well directly.

Much of the research in this field looks at how Facebook's affordances for increased social capital can lead to elevated psychological well-being. As Valenzuela and colleagues (2009) argue, life satisfaction is determined in part by social connections and the ability to claim support and other positive resources from them. Hence, they hypothesise that 'people who actively participate in Facebook are more likely to experience connectedness and feel happier' (2009, 878). Various studies argue that people actively search out connections on Facebook to increase social capital and thereby increase well-being and life satisfaction (Ellison, Steinfield, & Lampe 2007; Steinfield, Ellison, & Lampe 2008; Zywica & Danowski 2008; Barker 2009; Valenzuela, Park, & Kee 2009; Burke, Marlow, & Lento 2010; Mehdizadeh 2010). Self-esteem is mobilised as a salient psychological trait through which to measure these outcomes.

However, these studies lack a theorisation of how social capital actually plays out through everyday Facebook-related activities. Instead, they focus on outcomes: that is, on the consequences of possessing social capital, such as self-esteem or civic engagement (Valenzuela, Park, & Kee 2009). Often, they utilise perceived consequences as a way of inferring types of social capital. Moreover, in considering social capital in terms of bringing and bonding types, the concept is associated too much with particular kinds of connections. Something crucial is ignored, namely the actual exchange of resources. This moment remains an 'empty X'. However, without actually knowing what resources are claimed, who they are claimed from, and in what context they are claimed, a link between connections and consequences is evidently incomplete. Overall, these methods cannot tell us much – for instance, about how social capital relates to something as essential as people socialising around a photograph on Facebook. How can this be considered an online exchange of social resources?

These studies define social capital in terms of networks and resources, or of types of connections (bridging/bonding) and consequences (self-esteem). Instead, I argue, social capital must be viewed as a *process* with various elements, each with its own quality but all interdependent. Hence, this affords an understanding of how social norms influence the exchange of resources and how these resources are reinvested into groups to reproduce social norms.

The above frameworks – privacy, performance, social capital – are used throughout the following pages to understand how my participants negotiate intimacy on Facebook. They all help to understand a particular moment I call the 'performance of connection'. Here, social resources are claimed and exchanged, a relationship is performed, and a private space is established. Also, they assist in comprehending how my participants negotiate the intimacy needed to engage in social interactions and to prevent these interactions from harming themselves or others due to their public nature. Participants learn what social resources can be claimed in public and how they should be exchanged. In this way they also manage impressions to protect their private intimacies and *perform private intimacy* in a 'safe' manner.

3
Methodology

The study of Facebook and SNSs in general has yielded a large amount of deductive methodologies. Although qualitative and ethnographic research exists, it remains in the minority. Consequently, a collection of disparate, often discrete, concepts has been produced. There remains a need for inductive research and theory. I do not seek to prove or disprove specific hypotheses under exclusive conditions. Instead, I combine ethnography and Grounded Theory so as to produce a collection of qualitatively grounded concepts which are theoretically related. I recruited a small group of Facebook users in early 2010, interviewed them numerous times both face to face and through email, and spent a period being a participant observer as their Facebook 'friend'. I continued to communicate via email with each participant into mid 2012, saturating my grounded concepts and updating my ideas as Facebook changed.

Participants

In early 2010 I recruited a group of six participants, using advertisements at a Victorian university. Penny was 20, female, Australian, and had recently graduated from high school and begun studying at university. Sally was 25, female, Australian, and had recently moved from her home state to conduct further study at a new university. Odette was 25, female, Australian, and worked as a journalist. Flash was 31, male, Australian, and was an early career researcher. Bret was 33, male, from New Zealand, and worked in art management. John was 47, male, from New Zealand, and had recently completed postgraduate study.

This group either lived, worked, or studied in the inner northern suburbs of Melbourne, an area known for its student lifestyle, live music, and subcultural enclaves. They often expressed affection for this area and identified as being part of the inner north. More broadly, their Facebook profiles strongly exhibited a sense of cultural 'place' based around Melbourne and what it means to be a Melbournian. This said, some of them were from other parts of Victoria and Australia, and Bret and John were from New Zealand. Hence, the prevalence of place was tied up with their mobile biographies, an issue I shall return to. They enjoyed using Facebook for a variety of pursuits, such as playing Farmville and joining political groups. They used Facebook to connect with distant friends, to observe others, and to playfully socialise, usually around photographs, pithy status updates, and links to humorous content found elsewhere on the Web. My participants valued this public social interaction most of all. It has a playful, gregarious quality which participants find interpersonally rewarding and is quite unique to Facebook. Participants used Facebook both on their computers and phones, with the latter becoming more prevalent over the last two years.

Ethnographic and Grounded Theory methods

When first meeting my participants I had them review a plain language statement and sign a consent form. We talked about the kinds of things I would be viewing when I became their Facebook friend. The first meeting with each participant also involved a one-on-one in-depth interview which established a great deal of rapport and sensitised me to various key issues. Shortly after this I became Facebook friends with my participants by sending them a friend request. I engaged in digital ethnography for a period of 12 weeks in total, in which time I also conducted follow-up interviews. After that period I continued to stay in contact with my participants by email. Data persists on Facebook, hence I was also able to look back at performances which had occurred prior to my gaining access to my participants' profiles.

As well as constantly taking field notes and writing memos, I recorded online data in various ways. I took screen shots of photographs, threads, personal info, page and group affiliations, and more. I noted links to other content on the Web as well as Facebook pages, which I would revisit. I copied and pasted status updates and comments into Microsoft Word, along with the dates, times, and authors of the posts. I found the qualitative analysis software MAXQDA useful for coding data. Copying threads into Word allowed me to then convert these documents in to Rich Text files which I could then import into MAXQDA.

Facebook provides the opportunity to examine some novel ethnographic 'objects'. Some of these are user-generated performances, such as photographs, status updates, links to other media, 'pokes', 'likes', 'tags', page and group affiliations, applications, social games, 'recent activity' summaries, stories or 'notes', and more. There are also other, 'non-human' objects, such as Facebook's interface design and functionality. Some objects, such as privacy settings, are invisible. However, like gravity, their effects can be felt.

Facebook profiles (now Timelines) are hyperlinked to websites all over the Internet, and connect with hundreds, if not thousands of social ties. The search for significant content in a dynamic virtual world can be seen as 'tracing connections' rather than 'inhabiting space' (Hine 2000: 60). Although the latter is traditionally ethnographic, it seems ill fitted to the unboundedness of the Internet. Hence, Hine discusses a method which she terms 'flow-field' ethnography.

Ethnographers might start from a particular place, but would be encouraged to follow connections which were made meaningful from the setting. The ethnographic sensitivity would focus on the ways in which particular places were made meaningful and visible (2000: 60).

As well as collecting and analysing ethnographic objects, I experienced performances and interactions unfold. One of the chief insights I gained from this was how a performance may 'hang in wait' for a response, in a state of dialogical suspension. The mode of consciousness that accompanies the space between address and response is significant. When asked, my participants talked at length about the expectations and anticipation which palpably linger in this space. I discuss this mode of consciousness in Chapter 7.

I often turned to a form of discourse analysis when analysing posts. I 'read' the various objects described above as texts. Specifically, as performances 'written' by some agency or cooperation of agencies. I let my interactions with my participants guide my analysis, although – as I will shortly discuss – the search for context was not without problems. I looked at what particular performances were trying to do/say, as well as where they were relationally positioned. Every performance has a rhetorical function (Rose 2001). It may argue a position, respond to an attack, deny an affiliation, affiliate with an idea, and so forth. I continually asked myself questions such as: What role domains are visible? What evidence is there of my informant acting counter to these roles? What rhetorical strategies are evident in this participant's performances? What are these strategies trying to persuade an audience about this participant? What common themes arise in public wall posts? What common themes arise in other forms of content? Do the 'richest' performances occur in public spaces like the wall, or are they hidden away in other vistas? Do performances get many comments? If not, why not? How drawn out in time are social interactions? What do inter-actions and performances leave out? What causes these absences? Are they the result of social forces or my own position as ethnographer?

Photographs provided a particularly interesting site for discourse analysis. As Rose (2001) argues, photographs are intertextual and make references to many things beyond the light captured. Some of these I could make sense of, based on interviews. However, much was opaque to me. This considerably shaped my experience, as I realised that I was not included in these 'private photographs' (Berger 1982). That is, I was not part of that private group which could give intimate meaning to the moments depicted. Being unable to make a personal narrative out of these images, I was particularly sensitive to their privacy. Participants had informed me that they had also experienced this while observing the photographs of some of the weaker connections they had made. Hence, I realised I was reflexively experiencing what it was like to be a weak tie on Facebook, a potential voyeur.

Photographs have material meanings which are also significant, such as the way they capture and freeze moments with such uncanny, yet ambiguous, accuracy. Furthermore, one must take into account the sites and modes of production and consumption of photographs. Hence, in analysing these artefacts I was conscious of their reality effect, the scenes they depicted, what participants had told me abut how they had been taken (say, on a mobile phone), and how they were collocated in a specific way on Facebook, surrounded by various interface affordances and other forms of text.

Rather than producing 'thick description', I use Grounded Theory techniques to generate a more conceptual ethnography. Through constant comparison of relevant data, Grounded Theories seek out patterns which can be conceptualised in terms of common properties and variable dimensions (Glaser 1998). When conceptualising these patterns the 'story' of the data is fractured. However, core themes begin to emerge which weave this story back together through a set of hypoth-eses, creating a theory. These hypotheses, or 'theoretical codes', delimit shapes, causal mechanisms, and different processes. These can include: 'basic social processes', such as 'learning curves'; 'paired opposites', such as 'in-group out-group antagonisms'; 'cumulative scales', such as the evolution of a story; and 'boundary zones', such as 'limits of tolerance' (Glaser 1998: 170–173). To clarify by example, in my research a theoretical code – 'the performance of connection' – started to crystallise. This concept is a 'mutually constitutive binary', and speaks to how people on Facebook simultaneously socialise and perform their relational identities. It is also a 'basic social process', as it can be found everywhere in social life, though it takes on novel characteristics on Facebook.

Eventually, a core concept emerges which organises every other concept. Glaser (1998) argues that the 'core concept' conceptualises how participants resolve their main concern. This concern, whatever it may be, mobilises the most significant forms of action in the world under study. I discovered the primary concern of my participants to be the 'performance of connection'. However, achieving this goal on Facebook can be problematic for various reasons. My participants resolved these problems by negotiating intimacy. The 'negotiation of intimacy' is the core concept which explains the majority of the behaviour my participants engage in.

Online ethnography provokes complex ethical issues (Eynon, Fry, & Schroeder 2008). In particular, the Internet renders classifications of what is public and private problematic. Facebook – a service which can be closed off to the Internet as a whole, but be public to one's friends – provides a case in point. This requires heightened sensitivity with regard to what a researcher feels he or she can observe, record, and describe. Informed consent was acquired before the first interview began for online data gathering. Participants read a plain language statement explaining the kind of information that would be viewed. Certain participants also wished to discuss in greater detail exactly what would be observed and recorded. Following Eynon and colleagues (2008), who argue that sensitivity toward private information can be obtained by building a rapport with users, I utilised personal conversations to guide my judgements as to what my participants considered private and public, and what revelations they would condone.

Importantly, as well as participant information, I also observed the expressions of my participants' friends who chose to post on their profiles. To protect the identity of both my core participants and these 'unintentional participants' I changed all names to pseudonyms. Where I have though that information could potentially lead to revealing someone's identity I have either redacted the information or, if it is not significant (such as an address), changed it to something false. With regard to exchanges that are particularly personal, I take three approaches: not using the data at all; using only a sample of the data; fragmenting and merging data. Data is always taken out of context and put in a new context when writing ethnographies (Markham 2004). In fragmenting and merging certain descriptions, I hope to convey the essence of what I am conceptualising while protecting the identities of those I am researching.

I did not seek permission to show participant photographs. Photographs have a particular intimacy to them which, combined with their accurate depiction of bodies and settings, can be highly exposing. Hence, instead of reproducing photographs I have chosen, in the style of Barthes (1985), to describe through text both what they denote and what I interpret them to connote. There is definitely something lost in this translation. However, I am confident that my analysis of photographs supports and enriches the arguments given.

In becoming 'friends' with my informants I also had to face some impression management issues of my own. Participants could potentially access my profile and trawl through my own archived identity on Facebook. I did not want to seem hypocritical or intimidating by blocking my informants from seeing my information. However, I had to be sensitised to their values and concerns. For example, Penny conveyed her dislike for 'stupid' status updates. I realised that some of my own updates reflected what she meant by this. Witnessing these could have made her feel self-conscious and undermine my authority as researcher. Hence, I removed these posts.

Ethnography attempts to achieve 'holism'. That is, the ethnographer becomes completely entrenched in the culture he or she is studying. Hine (2000) has critiqued this project, arguing there are always things an ethnographer cannot access. Furthermore, constructionists reject the positivist notion that ethnography understands social worlds transparently, and they argue that the ethnographer's subjectivity interfaces with those he or she studies in the interpretation and construction of a world (Holstein & Gubrium 2008). There are various parts of the worlds I studied which I did not see. These include participant News Feeds, which could only be accessed by logging on as a participant; posts participants made on other peoples' walls, which would require getting access to these profiles; and certain sociality in offline life. In regard to each of these I have attempted to use conversations with my participants to fill in the blanks. However, future ethnographic research would benefit from thinking about how to become immersed in these zones while retaining ethical standards.

This study does not focus on issues such as those relating to gender and ethnicity. This is partly because of small participant numbers, which could say little if anything predictive about demographic traits. It is also because the path this research took naturally focused on other sociological issues, while working with the limited resources on hand. I believe, however, that the ideas put forward in this book would be made substantially richer if they were to be correlated with an in-depth investigation of identity categories such as gender, ethnicity, sexuality and so forth.

Facebook is an incredibly large, global phenomenon, and the cultural position described above may differ from those users who occupy different socio-cultural spheres. Hence, it may not be the case that, for example, the reflexivity shown by participants in this study, which could potentially be linked to education, would be evinced by Facebook users who are less educated or less Internet literate. This will be discussed further in the conclusion. The benefit of a Grounded Theory is that further researchers can take the concepts I have provided in this book and continue to build on, modify, or refute them in different domains, either through further theoretical sampling and comparison or quantitative testing.

I now turn to the presentation of the novel research mentioned above. I begin with a discussion of my participants' central motivation for using Facebook: the performance of connection (Chapter 4), connecting with distant ties (Chapter 5), and gathering information (Chapter 6). Chapter 7 presents the various problems people face in achieving these goals, and Chapter 8 explores how my participants resolve these problems.

4
The Performance of Connection

My participants use Facebook to make connections, perform connections, and gather information on connections. 'Connecting' is the first act required of a Facebook user. This involves finding others and sending and accepting 'friend requests'. Once friends, people have public access to one another's Facebook Timelines. When a person addresses another person or interacts with another person's content, he or she is 'performing connection'. For example, commenting on a status update is a performance of connection. On the one hand, performances of connection are private social exchanges aimed at social gratification through the mobilisation of interpersonal intimacy. On the other hand, they constitute the public performance of social relationality which projects out toward a bounded public, garnering a form of recognition which strengthens social connections. This should be understood as a mutually constitutive duality which acts to reproduce social connections.

That people are primarily motivated to use a social network in order to socialise seems like an obvious point. In fact, the performance of connection is what Grounded Theoreticians would term a 'basic social process' (Simmons, Hadden, & Glaser 1994) common to most, if not all, areas of public social life. People come into each other's presence and form a social space: they connect. They then interact with one another, 'performing' this connection and changing the nature of this space. However, the performance of connection on Facebook takes a novel form and offers novel rewards. It allows for new forms of interpersonal intimacy and for the reproduction of relationships through a process of self-reflexive public identification.

Dialogical focus

SNS research has been predisposed toward the study of profile elements such as descriptions of tastes, 'about me' sections, autobiographical information, friends lists, pages and groups, and so forth (Hearn 2008; Kolek & Saunders 2008; Liu 2008; Zhao, Grasmuch, & Martin 2008; 2009; Pempek, Yermolayeva, & Calvert 2009; Papp, Danielewicz, & Cayemberg 2011). There is a general lack of research which examines how social interactions play out when users post on each other's Timelines and leave comments on each other's posts, sometimes starting long conversational threads. My participants overwhelmingly emphasise the way in which they value Facebook for interactions. As Odette succinctly states: 'The main motivation is social interaction. ... If I was to disconnect, I feel my social life would be decreased'. Certain content, though, is more amenable to interaction than others. Status updates provoke interactions, changing one's 'religion' or 'high school' – personal information tucked away in the 'info tab' – usually doesn't. Hence, I want to focus analysis away from 'inert' content to content which anticipates dialogical spaces.

While researching an object-oriented Multi User Domain (also known as a MOO), Sundén reflects on the difference between people's inert character descriptions and their online conversations:

> Character descriptions are relatively stable pieces of text, which are written beforehand but can nevertheless at any moment be modified, transformed, erased or rewritten... A character description is like a snapshot, a picture of a textual body, whereas MOO dialogues come closer to the logic of a motion picture. (2003: 19)

Like Sundén, I want to focus on performative sites which anticipate sociality and, hence, have a certain motion to them. Here, people's feelings, opinions, desires, values, and reflections are not only expressed but left in dialogical suspension, waiting for recognition. I find this quality of expectation/anticipation/suspension, this desire for social dialogue (rather than one-way presentation), to be crucial to Facebook.

It is customary for people to 'fill in' their inert profile elements at the beginning of their Facebook careers (Strater & Lipford 2008). However, my participants understand that this information is, on its own, relatively useless at conveying the kind of identity they wish to produce on Facebook.

> I don't really go onto people's profile 'cause I know them, otherwise I wouldn't have added them, so I know where they are, where they

live, who they are, how old they are, like it's just I don't go flipping, some people go flipping through peoples' profile – I just think it's boring.

Penny

Sally echoes this position. She ritualistically began her Facebook career by filling in her profile in detail, but soon began to care less and less about this information, stating that 'it did feel a bit like people should already know it'.

Describing the info tab, Penny remarks: 'I just think it's a bit of a superfluous page because really you could just get to know me if you talk to me'. Penny indicates conversation as her preferred medium of self-presentation. Both participants suggest that dialogical sites are capable of providing the kind of non-redundant, dynamic information they and others are interested in. This information is *immanently social*. It constitutes social identity as it plays out through social, symbolic interaction.

Participants preferred Facebook over other SNSs because of its affordance for this form of sociality. Flash compares Facebook to Twitter, stating that he found the latter 'very impersonal'. This is the result of Twitter's limited affordance for dialogue.[1]

140 characters, it wasn't – there was no warmth to it. I'm not saying Facebook's a particularly warm and cozy site. But there is a sort of intimacy there that you don't get with Twitter. ... You know, there – you can have multiple threads like people commenting on someone's status, you comment and then they comment, then you comment.

Flash

Flash appreciates Facebook's affordance for long threads, relating this to a sense of intimacy. Confirming the 'interpersonal model' discussed in Chapter 2, Flash describes how intimacy emerges from social interaction. Connecting this to Facebook's interface, Flash continues:

Aesthetics are a lot more appealing [on Facebook]. I found Twitter a bit cold, and MySpace a bit: 21 and let's go down to, you know, the club after we've had a UDL, yeah.[2]

Flash contrasts MySpace's lack of maturity with Facebook's aesthetic. The former is a social ethos, a culture. Hence, the latter should also be read in social and cultural terms. Facebook creates an uncluttered space which focuses on threaded interactions rather than the glamorous self-exhibitionism associated with MySpace, and on young teenage users in particular (Livingstone 2008; Robards 2012). Flash nicely exemplifies how interpersonal intimacy and interfaces are socio-technically and culturally entangled.

Moving the analytic focus away from Facebook's inert elements to its dialogical elements forces a reappraisal of overstated individualising theories. It no longer makes sense to talk about 'individuals' who exist at the centre of personal networks in such a way as to constitute the former in its singularity and the latter in its instrumentality. Instead, I will talk about people who exist within and through connections as well as in front of them.

Identification through the performance of connection

As discussed in Chapter 2, scholars have explored the importance of relation self-presentation on Facebook and like SNSs. For example, Livingstone (2008), Mallan (2009) and Zhao and colleagues (2008) discovered a predominance of photographs which depicted social groups. This 'visual privileging of one's contacts' constitutes what Livingstone calls 'identity as connection' (2008, 402). These authors suggest a paradigm in which people seek to identify with each other through the signification of their social relationality. While this work is suggestive, there is more to be done in rigorously exploring how this process plays out through online interactions. What differences are there, for instance, between remediated interactions presented through photographs and those which occur in conversation threads? Also, if these interactions are forms of identification, why are they publicised beyond the scope of those implicated in them? Indeed, why are they publicised out toward an audience of both weak and strong ties?

Identification is a *process* of simultaneous alliance and differentiation. Similarity and difference, inclusion and exclusion, these mutually constitutive binaries are how identity functions. Jenkins writes: 'To define the criteria for membership of any set of objects is, at the same time, also to create a boundary, everything beyond which does not belong' (2004: 102). Hence, identification is also a form of spatialisation. Social identification produces social spaces, although, as will soon become apparent, these are not rigid and impermeable.

My participants reveal how identification and spatiality go to the heart of what they find rewarding about Facebook. For instance, Odette encounters her roommates everyday in face-to-face situations.

Despite these regular private, face-to-face interactions, Odette play-fully attempts to embarrass her roommates by posting jocular remarks on their Facebook walls. Asked what she values about this, given her regular co-presence with these people, she replies:

> Um, oh yeah, like I said it's to annoy them on a public forum really, um, it's like a joke. ... It's a way to annoy them on a public forum that other people are going to see on their wall.

Odette

Odette receives a different kind of gratification from communicating with her friends publicly rather than in the private confines of their share house. On Facebook she not only communicates with her friends, she allows others to recognise that this communication has taken place and, in the jocular warmth therein, she and her roommates share a close friendship. She allows her connections to be identified through their performance. Sally echoes this point:

> It's a common joke with the Facebook friends: 'you're not really friends until your Facebook friends'. Cause people then know you're doing stuff together, people know, um, you've got kind of the in jokes going on – it's very cliquey in a way, I think, 'cause it doesn't really ask people to discuss those things that you necessarily, um, that you're doing. It's just putting it out there, that, you know, these two hang out.

Sally

Like Odette, Sally recognises that communicating on Facebook allows people to identify her connections. Audiences constitute the relational identity of performers. Moreover, she also suggests that this has a constitutive effect on the performers themselves. That is, in having others recognise her relationships, she receives a kind of external confirmation. Mirroring a relationship in the eyes of others allows for its self-recognition and self-identification in the eyes of those who share it. Bret expounds further:

> There's a bit of titillation, or there's a bit of extra thrill in knowing that other people who don't know you are getting insights into you. ... this weird kind of territorial stuff that happens, or you can kind of try and prove how – how good – how well you know someone

by disclosing intimate details in a public forum, ... um, because it's a way of kind of going 'I'm – I'm your really, really good friend and I'm going to let everyone know it while I'm talking to you'.

Bret

Bret suggests that public recognition induces pleasure, 'titillation'. Importantly, he relates this to 'territorial stuff'. When identifying publicly, people not only allow others and themselves to constitute their relational identities, they create a territory which signifies to others and to themselves that they possess something scarce and valuable, namely, unique friendships and shared social histories. Knowing that others are excluded from this territory emphasises the pleasure of this possession, *the pleasure of belonging.*

Identification involves recognising and representing similarities and differences. Social identification between good friends constitutes similarity through shared experiences, through a social history. Signifying similarity and shared history are the chief methods participants use to perform connection on Facebook. Performances which appeal to similarities and shared histories mobilise 'in'-formation, as they seek to form an 'in' group which excludes the broader public.

[S]ome status updates I think are just for general fodder. And then some status updates are for your friends. They're in jokes, they're things that are a bit more witty and you guys know what's going on with it and you can be included in that.

Sally

An 'in' joke is something tailored to the shared history, cultural lexicon, domain of interest, and shared sense of humour of a particular group. As well as defining an internal similarity, it defines external difference: the broad public who do not share in these social and cultural elements. Sally explains:

Whereas, say, if that was an in joke with a friend I'm not that close to and I can see their discussion I can't be included in that.

Sally

Taking the position of a public onlooker, unfamiliar with the social group in question, Sally illustrates how in jokes also exclude. Note the figuration of a boundary, reified nicely in the term 'in joke' itself. An 'in' group necessarily implies an 'out' group.

Observe how 'in'-formation plays out in the following thread:

Penny
Awkward situations; Jake Crow creates them.

Jake Crow
It's what I do.

Sarah Motley
And Sarah Motley doesn't salvage them in time :P

Penny
Lol!

Note how this thread reflexively circumscribes a social space through the play of name-dropping. A name, a direct signification of relational capital, is a powerful kind of 'in'-formation as it will immediately attract the attention of a specific person. This exchange is carried through with mock sarcasm and light-hearted humour. In part rhetorical function, this emotionality signifies to others that these people share a history, and that this history has imbued their relationship with positive emotion.

Goffman (1971) argues that when people seek to publicly alert others as to the nature of their relationship they utilise 'tie signs'. For example, romantic partners may hold hands in a public space so that others treat them as 'a couple'. The primacy of performances of connection on Facebook is reflected by Facebook's affordance for what I term 'functionalised tie signs', or 'tie functions' for short. The central purpose of these functions is to allow a connection to be identified, often in an incredibly simple form. Two chief examples of these are 'likes' and 'tags'. If someone finds a friend's post interesting, and wants to signal this approval, he or she can click the 'like button'. Correspondingly, this content will now contain an additional piece of text which states 'X likes this'. If someone uploads something – say, a photograph or status update – he or she can 'tag' another person to this piece of content. Correspondingly the content will now be associated with that person's name. In each of these cases a function allows the connection between two people to be performed such that one of the parties need not actually contribute any substantive content. Substantive, reciprocal communication is bypassed. Instead, the connection itself is reified as a function which in turn acts to signify it.

Sally explains 'liking' as a 'very good way of, kind of, not interacting too much but kind of agreeing with people'. Semantically speaking, likes are immediately composed of a person's name and very simple, implied 'predicate', which can be conceptualised as 'positive affilia- tion'. On this immediate level the performance of connection, in and for itself, is emphasised. However, liking also infers a secondary level of affiliation. To illustrate this, take an example in which Bret has posted a link to a B-grade horror movie clip, to which he has attached his own commentary, and which has been 'liked'.

Sonya Bell 'likes' this

Bret: amazing. this film is playing at 7.30pm at the Astor. i'm gagging for it.

Content: Wake In Fright: Have a Drink, Mate
www.youtube.com
A memorable scene from the sort-of lost Australian film 'Wake In Fright' ('Outback') (1971).

Immediately, Sonya Bell performs her connection with Bret. However, on the secondary level of affiliation, Sonya identifies with the cultural content of Bret's post. Hence, Sonya invisibly states that she 'likes' *Wake in Fright*. Moreover, she indicates that she shares a taste for the cultural macabre, B-grade movies, Australian film, and even indi- cates a certain place-based subcultural identity, evinced by the Astor theatre, a cult local. On the one hand there exists a simplistic signi- fication of social similarity, on the other a complex signification of cultural similarity.

Tags also contain this socio-cultural duality. However, a primary difference between liking and tagging must be noted. While an audience attaches his or her 'like' to a post after it has been posted, performers alert an audience to a post by 'tagging' them to it at the moment of posting. For example, Penny tags her best friend Carry to a post which reads 'a tune and start to swoon; My life would seem complete ... I'd take my foot ... '. Because this tag takes the form of a direct, personal address, a dyadic logic comes into play. This example illustrates what Simmell (1950) refers to as the innate 'secretiveness' of the dyad. Dyadic inti- macy, Simmell argues, is expressed through knowledge which only the dyad possesses. The expression of this knowledge circumscribes a space for two, and no more. Penny's theatrical post is opaque to an outside observer, although in tagging Carry it is apparent that Penny expects her best friend to 'get' it. Hence, the mysterious cultural content of this post combined with the dyadic logic of the tag suggests that Penny and

Carry share a close friendship. On Facebook, tie signification is a lot more complex than holding hands.

Because a tag is an address, it encourages a response. Hence, Carry reciprocates by taking up the joke, and writing: 'I've got to get back to Hogwarts got to get back to school'. Now a substantive interaction is taking place. Tags are an important mode of performing connection because they can facilitate both simple affiliations and in-depth inter-actions. Also, because Facebook is a mediated public, it is felicitous to be able to make audiences aware of content through tags.

> Instead of writing on someone else's wall, I tend to write a status and tag them. Can also tag multiple people and get a conversation going in a thread, which happens quite a bit.
>
> Sally

Here, Sally simultaneously evinces the usefulness of tagging, not only to achieve personal recognition, but to engage performances of connection. That is, the desire to engage in conversations.

Many other tie functions exist. There are basic 'pokes', which one person sends to another, appearing on a person's profile as 'X poked you'. This indicates, again, the existence of a social connection with little substantive interaction. There are also forms of reification which are facilitated by third-party applications. For example, the 'super-poke' application, which affords a more detailed cultural connotation, such as 'X gave you a bear hug'. A similar example can be found in the many different gift giving applications available, in which a comical 'virtual gift' can be sent to a person's profile along with the name of the sender. Such applications embody a norm which is present in most perform-ances of connection, namely, reciprocity. Drawing on anthropological research into pre-modern groups, Mauss (1969) argues that gifts are rarely given without the expectation of reciprocity. The act of giving is woven through a history of ritualised obligations. Moreover, gift giving has a social function. Gifts are loaded with identity and culture. They are never alienated from the giver, as they carry a trace of his or her social and spiritual aura. Fulfilling gift debts thus affords the creation of a social bond in which people reproduce their socio-cultural posi-tions and relationships. My participants receive likes from friends and, in response, usually 'like back' their friends' posts. In doing so they perpetuate reciprocal obligations of identification, as well as their social and cultural similarities.

My participants also identify themselves as different to many of their connections and find themselves feeling excluded from certain performances of connection which they witness on Facebook. To illustrate, Flash explains his reaction to those he terms 'exhibitionists':

> In some ways it makes me uncomfortable, but I can't look away. In some ways it makes me feel, uncomfortable, you know. I – maybe because maybe I am being a bit judgemental, because I don't express myself like that.
>
> Flash

Flash is both drawn to and repulsed by these people for, simultaneously, he realises he is different from them and yet is able to constitute himself as different by observing them. Experience with being both the public audience and the different outsider on Facebook allows people, while performing themselves, to project an imagined, expected audience who are engaged in identifying and categorising them as part of their own project of self-identification. I term this an 'audience of constitutive difference'. Participants imagine a 'mass audience' in this regard. 'It comes back,' remarks Odette, 'to sort of showing other people, your mass audience.' This is a broad space where 'hundreds of people can wander' across one's information.

The imagining of an audience of constitutive difference must be understood pragmatically. Whether an audience actually exists or not does not matter. Participants pragmatically assume the existence of such an audience when they perform their connections in order to reap the benefits therein. However, as I argue in Chapter 7, participants also take on another mindset, one in which they are concerned with defining just who their audiences may be. In this case the publics accessed via Facebook are transformed from mass audiences to problematic 'grey areas' whose characteristics, differences, and similarities demand to be defined. In Chapter 8 I argue that participants come to define an audience of people whom they interact with regularly and rely on for performances of connection.

To summarise, performances of connection are modes of identification which operate by defining themselves against a broad public, assumed to be a mass audience of constitutive difference. When people publicly perform connections they take them as objects of thought and labour. Self-identification occurs, constituting and strengthening connections and, in this process, imbuing the pleasure of belonging. Facebook publicity should be understood in this light. One of its chief values is in reproducing relationships through reflexive representation. It acts as a social glue. Certainly, any kind of publicity will have this effect on groups, and groups have always interfaced with public life as a way of constituting their identities. 'A secret group', Jenkins writes, 'would have a very limited presence in the human world' (2004, 83). Sally echoes this: 'It's almost like you're not friends until people know you're friends'. It seems obvious that Facebook, in affording broad, heterogeneous, networked publics within which social connections are constantly embedded, amplifies this process. Facebook, remarks Bret, 'kind of enables this kind of stuff to happen on a massive scale'.

Social capital in performances of connection

Performances of connection are social capital exchanges. When people perform connection they claim on social resources. This process of claiming, combined with the reinvestment of resources, acts to reproduce and strengthen connections.

In Chapter 2 I argued that SNS research which looks at social capital has yet to account for moments when social resources are exchanged online. Understanding exchanges involves understanding social capital to be a *process*, like performance and identification. In general, Bourdieu considers capital to be that which can reproduce itself and hence 'persist in its being' (1986: 81). In a simple sense, Bourdieu argues that social capital functions through social connections and social obligations. Note the temporality implicit in 'obligation'. Bourdieu extrapolates:

> Social capital is the aggregate of the actual or potential resources which are linked to possession of a durable network of more or less institutionalised relationships of mutual acquaintance and recognition – or in other words, to membership in a group – which provides each of its members with the backing of the collectivity-owned capital, a 'credential' which entitles them to credit, in the various senses of the word. (2011: 86)

Unlike cultural capital, which is institutionalised in education, or economic capital, which is institutionalised in financial markets, social capital is institutionalised in relationships and groups. Cultural capital is objectified as cultural goods such as fashionable clothing. Economic capital is objectified as money. Social capital is objectified as social resources which can be both material, 'such as all the types of services accruing from useful relationships', and symbolic, 'such as those derived from association with a rare, prestigious group' (2011: 87). Importantly, these resources may or may not be claimed. Hence Bourdieu's use of 'potential'. For example, just because someone is a member of a club does not oblige him or her to patronise it (although it may oblige other forms of patronage which vouchsafe membership). The point is that they *can* be claimed, and in this sense social capital is like 'credit'. This potentiality confers temporal dimensions on social capital and begins to reveal its nature as a process.

Failing to understand this nature can often lead to theoretical confusion, as various different phenomena such as norms, connections and resources become subsumed within one static concept. Portes (1998) critiques Coleman's (1988) famous conception of social capital for this reason. Capital suggests something possessed, something solid and quantitative. 'The confusion over the meaning of this term, then', write Bankston and Zhou, 'is a consequence of a metaphorical confusion of a substantive quantity (capital) and a process that takes place through stages (embedded, goal directed social relations)' (2002: 286). That social groups are in motion, acting toward goals and embedded in broader networks, institutions, norms and cultural structures is something clearly present in Bourdieu's analysis. In this figuration, the elements of social capital cannot just be thought to exist together but relate to each other through causal stages. I read Bourdieu's argument to suggest that this process has five elements: socio-cultural structures; relationships and their shared histories; norms and expectations on resource-giving; exchanges; and the reinvestment of resources. This process is cyclical in that each element may become both cause and consequence. In this way social capital is reproduced.

Bourdieu considers groups in terms of their social temporality, their 'social power over time' (1984: 71), in order to explain how they accumulate capital. Social capital comes about through a shared history of social exchanges. Bourdieu writes:

> The existence or a network of connections is not naturally given...It is the product of an endless effort at institution...In other words, the network of relationships is the product of investment strategies, individual or collective, consciously or unconsciously aimed at establishing or reproducing social relationships. (2011: 87)

This shared history becomes 'institutionalised' when mutual knowledge systems form that allow group members to recognise and behave appropriately toward one another. That is, when norms are produced. Based on shared histories and norms, people form expectations that they will be able to claim resources from their connections. On Facebook, the shared histories of concern are primarily those of friendships and friendship groups. The norms produced by these histories determine a sensitivity regarding what information can be claimed and expressed in public. Driven by various interpersonal properties (explored fully in Chapter 8) these are norms concerning the protection of contexts and the negotiation of intimacy.

Histories and norms crystallise in exchanges when resources are claimed. Bourdieu argues that social capital is 'endlessly reproduced through the exchange' (1986, 52). These exchanges are themselves governed by 'the symbolic constitution produced by social institution' (ibid), namely, shared histories and resultant normativities and roles. Portes illustrates the anatomy of an exchange, which involves: '(a) the possessors of social capital (those making claims); (b) the sources of social capital (those agreeing to these demands); (c) the resources themselves' (1998: 6). Participants in my research make claims of other friends when they perform connection on Facebook. The resources they claim can be broadly placed into two camps: (a) knowledge and emotions which imply others or directly concern others; (b) the expectation that others will 'join in' the performance and create a social space.

Recall the thread presented above, which begins by Penny writing: 'Awkward situations; Jake Crow creates them'. Here, Penny is engaged in more than a simple signification. Penny is claiming on the right to express Jake's name as well as an affectually loaded (albeit sarcastically humorous) judgment regarding him in public. Consider another example. Lupé leaves a public message on Sally's wall which reads: 'I'm starting to get myself all excited about next year! giggidy! how's melbourne? uni? life? xoxo'. Here, Lupé claims on the right to publicly express information regarding her and Sally's upcoming trip overseas. Again the post evinces the friendship the two share, framed with eager emotion, punctuated with the affect-coda 'xoxo'. Consider what happens also when a friend posts photographs depicting his or her other friends. Physical bodies reveal a terrain of intimacy and identification which is, when taken out of context, sensitive to exposure. Posting photographs is more than a mere act of signification. It is a claim on the permission to reveal physically exposing information regarding others, a claim which is expected to be agreed to based on the shared histories and norms people develop through interpersonal experience.

However, the information which people convey through their performances of connection need not directly reference another person. It can merely imply the interest of others by appealing to similarities such as shared interests, tastes, experiences, and emotions. These performances are claims on social capital because they seek to provoke a response and hence allow for a connection to be identified. 'I want to provoke discussion,' remarks Flash. This equates to the desire to have another come and identify with oneself and to form a social space. By way of analogy, think of a street protest. People who wear certain colours may cue others as to their common group membership. These people come together and become identified in public. By mobilising a specific resource, the signification of similarity through clothing, they have exercised social capital in order to come together and be recognised. When people perform connection on Facebook, one of the primary resources they claim on is the willingness of others to come together in such a way.

Hence, to return to the example of Sally and Lupé, Sally responds to Lupé's post, writing: 'me too! travelling the world via seabikes is more appealing as each day passes. Melbourne is treating me well, how is the affair with the coffee boy going?' Now Lupé and Sally have engaged in a fully fledged performance of connection, and Sally has 'given' the resource of 'joining in' and creating a social space. Notice that Sally in turn claims on the right to publicly express personal information regarding Lupé, namely, the 'affair with the coffee boy'. Now Sally and Lupe are reciprocally exchanging claims and resources.

Bourdieu argues that social capital resources are in some way reinvested in the social group, either through reciprocal social favours or through resultant cultural, symbolic or economic capital. Crucially, the act of exchange itself reproduces the group through a process of signification:

> Exchange transforms the things exchanged into signs of recognition and, through the mutual recognition and the recognition of group membership which it implies, reproduces the group. By the same token, it reaffirms the limits of the group...Each member of the group is thus instituted as a custodian of the limits of the group. (1986, 52)

This formulation of social capital exchanges as moments of 'mutual recognition', which allows people to identify the groups they are a part of, resonates profoundly with what occurs in the performance of connection on Facebook. As with the spatial logic of identification, the group is reproduced by reflexively delimiting its boundaries – a kind of reproduction through differentiation – and imbuing in its members a sense of responsibility with regard to the upkeep of these boundaries. Hence, social capital exchanges and identification are intimately linked. The act of exchange itself has the capacity to reproduce groups and, hence, reinvest social capital.

Looking at the disclosures which occur on Facebook in terms of performances of connection and social capital exchanges helps elucidate a problem I set forth in Chapter 2. Does Facebook encourage the social subversion of control over performances or do people socially collaborate in their efforts at self-authorship? I think both accounts are true to some extent. However, just how the latter operates is made evident in the operation of reciprocal social capital exchanges, a mutual effort at public identification. Thinking of collaborative self-authorship in these terms identifies the benefits therein, namely, social identification and the reproduction of connections. It also affords an understanding of how this works, namely, through norms of social capital exchange relative to the shared history of specific friends and friendship groups. I will add, however, that it is not just the self being authored. Rather, this mutual effort is also aimed at authoring connections. Its successful end product is the categorisation of a connection or group and a person's place within it.

Figurative private spatialisation

When participants perform their connections the sociality in which they engage has a private quality, particularly when juxtaposed against their broader Facebook publics. This private quality is evident in the contextual interpersonal knowledge and emotion which specific interactions reveal. Through performances of connection, participants enact a process of identification which differentiates them from their broader publics, creating a figurative social space. It follows that this is figurative private space. Here, I employ 'figurative' in two senses. First, in the metaphorical sense of representing something through another thing. Social connections are represented through a concept of spatiality. Second, in the objective sense of standing apart from something in order to represent it. Private space on Facebook is annexed public space. It get its boundary, its 'figure', by standing apart from and in juxtaposition to this public space and the audiences which inhabit it. Odette expounds:

> So you know other people aren't really going to understand what you're talking about but even if it's just one person that understands,

like my best friend. It's sort of, yeah, it's like a private, um, joke that you are communicating on this public forum that you know other people don't get but as long as you've got that connection then that's meaningful to you.

Odette

Odette describes how her relationship with her best friend has a quality that is only meaningful to them. In keeping this meaning secret they circumscribe a private social space which, when juxtaposed against their broad Facebook publics, allows them to become conscious of the significance of their relationship. *Knowing others 'don't get it', emphasises just how meaningful 'it' is.* Odette continues:

I guess it's to intrigue other people really, get them thinking about what you might be talking about but you're not really going to tell them what you are talking about.

Odette

Dyadic relationships have a 'secretive intimacy' to them. This heightens the exclusivity of the private space they occupy while simultaneously making them a mystery that draws others in. It emphasises the boundary of identification and the anticipation of an intrigued audience whose imagined purpose it is to constitute this boundary. This is not an intimacy made of revelations. Paradoxically, it is an intimacy made of reticence and secrets. 'You have some sort of mystery,' remarks Flash. This dyadic example nicely illustrates, then, how the performance of connection on Facebook utilises privacy as a way to simultaneously allow connections to be constituted, strengthened, and reproduced, as well as protected. In this case, privacy is performed rather than permeated.

One of Sally's photographs elucidates this point. It is positioned within a photo album dedicated to Sally's travels. Sally is lying down, smiling but looking tired, across two other people in what looks like a waiting room, suitcases nearby. The viewer is given the impression of an exhausted traveller, making a comic bed out of her companions. However, this connoted message does not seem to flow contiguously into the comment Sally leaves below the photograph, which reads: 'hahahahahaha now our games of hide and seek are public knowledge'. I, like many of Sally's hundreds of Facebook friends, am unable to link this joke to the nature of the image. This is because it is an in joke. It is meaningful only to those pictured or to the people who know Sally well enough to have been part of such games. The statement is thus wholly ironic, as what Sally means is not public knowledge at all. It remains mysterious and private.

However, performances of connection do not enact private boundaries without conceding them to some extent. As Flash remarks: 'You know there is a sense of ambiguity. You're giving away something but you're not giving away everything.' Participants usually make some disclosure or express some kind of emotion which 'invites people in'. For example, photographs often reify the figurative spatiality of performances of connection through the material layout of the scenes they depict, such as private homes. Examples of images taken within private homes abound on Facebook. Sally provides an apt example, a photo album entitled, 'Welcome Home Pete'. The album title anticipates a domestic motif and, given that Pete has long since returned, is really welcoming the viewer into Pete's home. The viewer observes images of a small group of close friends, enjoying a convivial dinner. These are excellent examples of what Berger (1982) calls 'private photographs', the meanings of which are intimately tied to interpersonal histories. If not a part of this group, if absent from these histories, the viewer is incapable of understanding their meaning except at a general level, and in this way is not included in the private space. It is the conviviality of the group pictured which is truly what is private about these images, but the homestead in which this takes place serves to literally illustrate that a private boundary has been crossed. Photographs of homes literally image what is figuratively imagined in all performances of connection: the enticements of privacy. The viewer has been 'invited in' to the emotional play of characters, gestures, glances and so forth and is free to do with this information what he or she desires, however opaque it may seem. To summarise, then, private spatialisations on Facebook both hide and disclose. They invite people into a kind of antechamber where certain information slips through, but which is nevertheless separate from a core, secretive zone.

In a work which was written long after *The Presentation of Self in Everyday Life*, Goffman (1971) begins to supersede his notion that actors attempt to separate back and front regions at all costs in order to maintain the definition of the situation. Goffman studies how what he calls 'anchored ties' – those with a degree of shared history and intimacy – cue their relationship status to 'anonymous ties' in public through the deployment of tie signs. Through such a mechanism anonymous ties know how to behave toward anchored ties and avoid awkward missteps. Tie signs allow for a connection to be named. For instance, Facebook provides a 'relationship status' function which allows two people to assign categories to themselves, say as in a romantic relationship. Also, tie signs transmit the strength of a connection. This strength is conveyed, argues Goffman, as a sense of intimacy, which emanates from the fact that both parties seem to have licence to access each others 'territories and preserves' (1971: 192). These are physical, figurative, and cognitive spaces in which an individual can exercise certain private rights and customs. For example, 'personal space' describes 'the space surrounding an individual, anywhere within which an entering other causes the individual to feel encroached upon' (1971: 30). Hand holding, for example, claims license to personal space. Hand holding is thus 'an open declaration to third parties that they are in the presence of a relationship' (1971: 195). Crucially, Goffman thus theorises tie signs in terms of a public exteriorisation of private space. He writes, 'squeezing a held hand and declining to let one's hand be found for holding (or once released to be regrasped) are signs ordinarily designed for the [relationship's] private consumption' (1971, 196). Therefore, rather than having two separate realms, Goffman conceives of how back-region private life is, in fact, transformed into a performative public tool. Actors instrumentalise private contexts as a form of impression management.

This phenomenon cannot be understood through a mere private/public dichotomy. Rather, that which is private must be understood as something flexible and performative. Moreover, it must be understood as something which acts to impinge on public space whenever it is enacted. When my participants perform connection on Facebook they annex public space and use it to build private space. The expansion of a thread which grows to accommodate more posts and posters can be understood in this way, as a private space which utilises, occupies and excludes public space. This departs from an understanding of privacy solely in terms of closing off access. Altman (1983) speaks against this paradigm, arguing that privacy is a boundary-regulation process which involves both closing off and opening up. That is, both restricting and seeking interaction. Altman conceives of these opposing processes dialectically. Hence, sometimes access is sought out and seclusion is unwelcome and, at other times, seclusion is sought out and access is unwelcome. The implication is not only that people often desire not to be left alone and that too much privacy can be an unhealthy thing, but that different gradations of privacy can exist and that these are shaped according to people's social desires. Günter Burkart (2010) engages with this notion, making distinctions between four shifting 'levels' of privacy. These include: the first level, the 'inner world of the subject', which delimits inner, psychological privacy; the second level, the 'personal sphere of individuality, autonomy, and free will separate from social relationships', or 'individual privacy'; the third level, 'the sphere of intimate relationships', including that of 'sexual privacy' and 'shared secrets'; and the fourth level, 'the domestic sphere of family community (household privacy) separated from the whole world outside the family' (Burkart 2010: 25). Burkart's levels of privacy are, I believe, limited and conservative, especially in their domestic focus. However, they engage with the notion of privacy as involving an opening up of access. That is, 'we have, from level to level, an extension of the private sphere at the cost of (a diminishing) public sphere' (ibid). When participants perform connection on Facebook they enact the expansion of private space and the diminishment of public space. Isomorphically this can be understood as the inclusion of a set number of people who occupy a personal network, and the exclusion of the remainder.

Given that the spatialisation in question is the result of identification through social capital exchanges, it can be understood through social capital. These spaces can be thought of as private inasmuch as only those who possess the correct social capital can access them. Furthermore, identity is a not a static form; it is a process, hence the verb 'identification'. Identity is always in a state of becoming, specifically of becoming affiliated with something or someone. Similarly, social capital is a process – a process acting to reproduce social connections in which shared histories condition norms, which condition claims, which condition exchanges, which condition the appropriation of resources, which are reinvested. Likewise, the spaces people create on Facebook are processes. These spaces are always in a state of becoming; they are always being constructed to accept and reject people. This happens through social capital exchanges and the reinvesting of symbolic resources. Because of this 'processional' nature, social spaces on Facebook do not have predefined boundaries and are always subject to mutation and calamity. Space is a fluid, relational, informational, immaterial, symbolic construct.

The creation of a figurative private space is the result of interpersonal sociality, and the disclosures participants make in such spaces, I argue, can be thought of as intimate. In most cases, they reveal the intimacy of a friendship or a friendship group. If such spaces are the result of social resources being exchanged, then intimacy is one such resource, mobilised within a performance. If this resource –intimacy – is credited by a response, it creates a social dialogue. If this dialogue is positive and affectionate, then intimacy has been reinvested. Even in its dialogical form, intimacy remains performed, as it signals the strength of the connection being performed. Concurrently, intimacy is an instrument as much as it is the emotional accretion of sociality. In terms of the former, intimacy is given its meaning and intensity by the spatial juxtaposition mentioned above.

Prager, reflects on this logic:

> Two friends laugh together about a private meaning that may or may not be understood by others who are present. These are intimacy's modal characteristics, the first to occur to scholars and laypersons alike when they are asked to define intimacy. (1995: 12)

Here, Prager understands intimacy as the product of a private meaning, imbued with positive emotion, being voiced in a public space. It follows that the nature of those who occupy this public space – the purpose behind their gazes, and the information being disclosed – all cooperate to give dimension to intimacy as a resource and a performance (discussed more in Chapter 8). However, given that intimacy speaks to a realm of significant meaning and emotion, its mobilisation as a performative tool is a dangerous affair. The vulnerability of intimacy depends on the above factors: Who is included in a space and who is excluded? What is the perceived purpose behind the gazes of those who are excluded? What is the nature of the information being disclosed? What other performance contexts and equipment influence this information?

In this chapter I have reviewed how participants are motivated to use Facebook to reproduce their interpersonal connections through the performance of connection. This involves socialising in an intimate way while, at the same time, mobilising this intimacy as a form of performance which signals the strength of a connection. I now turn to another key motivation: connecting with distant ties. In discussing these connections I continue to develop the concept of performing connection, as this takes on important properties in this respect.

5
Distant Intimacy

Participants value Facebook as a means of connecting with people who have moved out of their immediate life-worlds. These ties have become 'distanced', although this term can refer to different kinds of 'distances'. For example, people may become geographically distanced; they may remain geographically proximate but exist in different social spaces – say, different workplaces – and they may become distanced in time. Old high school friends are a common example of temporally distanced, 'estranged ties'.

Resolving distance entails two contingent processes: reclaiming connections and sustaining connections. When a distant tie is connected with, he or she is 'reclaimed'. However, making a connection on Facebook is not the same as performing a connection. A connection may be forgotten or may, perhaps, become the object of conspicuous observation. A connection is 'sustained' when those who share it regularly engage in performances of connection. 'Sustaining' entails giving a relationship 'sustenance' through the emotional participation of each party and the intimacy this generates. Whether a connection is reclaimed or sustained depends on a number of issues, such as the strength and meaning of a tie and what form of distancing has occurred. Finally, it is common that ties are reclaimed but interacted with only on occasion. These connections are meaningful, just not as meaningful as those which are actively sustained. They are not looked to for regular confidence, perspective, support, conviviality and the like. Instead, they are just meaningful enough for people to value Facebook's affordance of 'keeping a foot in the door'. In what follows I explore how these different kinds of connections influence intimacy.

Facebook as 'trans-mobile' space

The distances bridged on Facebook result from the *movement* of social ties into different spaces and life-worlds. Hence, 'mobility' is a useful concept with which to frame these processes. Sheller and Urry (2006a) identify a 'mobility turn' in the social sciences. This involves 'putting social relations into travel and connecting different forms of transport with complex patterns of social experience conducted through communications at-a-distance' (2006: 208). Sheller and Urry emphasise the different layers of focus within this paradigm, shifting from global to local flows – from, say, migration to urban transport. Mobility is often related to processes of globalisation which involve the movement of people, goods, culture, and capital, but which nevertheless rely on immobile infrastructures, networks, and sovereign legal frameworks (Castells 1996; Sassen 1998). Mobility and globalisation are viewed as the consequence of post-modernity, flexible accumulation and post-Fordist time–space compression (Harvey 1990), the rise of tourism as a leisure industry (Hall & Williams 2002), the existence of migrant communities and diaspora (Blunt 2007), as well as the economic liberalisation of the labour market and, concurrently, an increase in job competitiveness and precarity (Bauman 2000; Beck & Beck-Gernsheim 2002). Framing these processes is the argument that human social experience has moved beyond the 'little boxes' which characterised dense early twentieth century urban life, and has become embroiled in trans-local social networks, predominantly distributed along tangents of shifting labour relations in which competitive jobs seem inherently migratory (Putnam 2000; 2002; Wellman 2002; Urry 2003). Competitive labour markets compel actors to move beyond familial spaces in order to achieve various levels of specialised education so as to become an attractive labour commodity (Beck and Beck-Gernsheim 2002). Roderick (2010), encounters these themes in her grounded ethnography of university students, finding that there is considerable pressure to 'commodify the self' which drives peoples' movement through tertiary stages. These ideas reverberate with my participants' who, being picked from various stages of their tertiary education, have experienced forms of mobility associated with attending university.

As well as global mobility, people are on the move within regional locales and urban spaces. Concurrently, people increasingly rely on wireless networks and mobile devices to socialise and organise their social lives at a distance and in transit. This requires complex understandings of how spatial ecologies are produced and transformed through mobile people and technologies (Sheller & Urry 2006b). For example, much has been said about the way in which mobile phones implode spaces, allowing private space to impinge on public space (Campbell & Park 2008; Hampton & Gupta 2008). Moreover, as smart phones converge with Web 2.0 technologies and locative media systems, they further extend our embodied capacity to access information, guide ourselves through physical space, and merge physical and virtual social cartographies (Richardson 2007; Hjorth 2008; Goggin 2011; Gordon & de Souza a Silva 2011; Bilandzic & Foth 2012). Consider locative social media such as Facebook Places, an application which, among other things, announces where one is physically located whenever one posts a status update.[1] Status updating has become location updating. Mobile phones are now used as a portal through which to access the comparatively 'fixed' online space of Facebook while on the move (Goggin 2010). Hence, I argue, rather than a 'trans-local' space, Facebook is more of a 'trans-mobile' space.

Certain scholars take a pessimistic view of our increasingly fast-paced, mobile and dispersed world. Beck and Beck-Gernsheim (2002) argue that mobility is part of a broader process they call 'individualisation'. Mobile lifestyles individualise people by preventing them from forming strong relationships. The authors offer a bleak appraisal of modern society which, according to them, has lost its sentiment for enduring friendship or kinship, and is likewise apathetic toward paradigms of commitment, such as marriage. Similarly, Putnam (2000) argues that mobility is corrosive to 'bonding social capital' – the social resources exchanged in the upkeep of strong interpersonal relationships – as it creates distances between close ties which hamper the exchange of such resources.

A contrary view finds relationships, in particular friendships, to be 'flexible' rather than fragile (Allan 2008; Becker et al. 2009). People invent 'mobile methods' to remain in contact with important others (Larsen, Axhausen, & Urry 2006). In this regard, they come to rely on ICTs to facilitate a kind of 'virtual travel' (ibid), sustaining interpersonal intimacy at a distance (Duck 2007). As mentioned in Chapter 1, Facebook networks support 'personal communities'. These are not defined by shared location, so much as by an 'individuals biography' (Pahl 2005). That is, these communities make sense from a person's unique perspective. They result from an individual's mobile lifespan, moving through different social spaces. Recalling Castells (1996: 440–459), Facebook is a kind of 'flow space' which allows various 'place spaces' and mobile spaces to integrate. In talking about Facebook's affordances in this regard, my participants mention various spaces and materials – mobile phones, laptops, hostels, Internet cafes, wireless networks, and so forth. 'Distant intimacy' is sustained through such an assemblage. I now turn to how my participants experience this kind of intimacy, its benefits and pitfalls.

Defeating loss

Connecting with a *strong* tie who has moved out of one's immediate life-world provides emotional rewards which cannot be overstated. These emotions stem from the fact that these ties may have otherwise been lost. John extrapolates:

> It – it has changed my life in the way that, um, there was a lot of people that I would have lost contact with and – and they were really important at one time in my life and because we're all geographically scattered, um, that has really, I – I feel that – that it's – it's enabled a connection that I would have lost and I think that I would have been – I mean I think that my connections would have been poorer because of that, um, and I guess that's partly, you know, an aging question, you know, as – as you get older you do lose contact with people and how amazing that this technology has come along.

The loss of a friend can be a tragic affair. John experiences the prevention of such loss as momentous, life changing. Good friends and family are interwoven through our personal biographies. The negation of a social tie is thus also a negation of self. Hence, the prevention of loss has existential dimensions. Reclaiming ties on Facebook is an existential process. It chooses being over nothingness, presence over absence. The emotions which accompany reclamation accrete from the existential success of defeating loss.

Wrapped up with the prevention of loss, Facebook offers the seductive possibility of 'return'. John continues:

> I've been in a number of different cities I've got a number of those quite close groups which if I've stayed in one city I wouldn't have had, um, and I'm just about to start looking for the group that I worked with [in] Minneapolis when I worked in the States. So that will be quite an interesting time because it was a very intense and possibly one of the best times of my life, um, so it would be nice to kind of make some connections with them and see – see what's happening.

For estranged ties in particular, the desire to 'return' is a powerful one, imbued with nostalgia. However, it would be a mistake to think that this nostalgia is only a negative emotion, a yearning for the past, and a dissatisfaction with the present. In this respect I agree with Sedikides and colleagues (2004), that nostalgia can be a positive/bittersweet emotion which serves an existential function. Nostalgia is an affect-laden temporal ordering of the past which stirs up happiness, pleasure, joy, and the like. The past is, in one sense, lost and, hence, this can also be a bittersweet experience. However, as Sedikides and colleagues argue, nostalgia also provides a sense of biographical continuity. This 'soothes the self from existential pangs by solidifying and augmenting identity, regenerating and sustaining a sense of meaning, and buttressing and invigorating desired connectedness with the social world' (2004: 206). Hence, Nostalgia additionally acts to bolster the worth of the present. When nostalgia is triggered by the reclamation of social ties, it serves to knit these ties back together. This 'reignition of meaningful relational bonds satisfies one's need for interpersonal belongingness' (Sedekides, Wildschut, & Baden 2004: 207).

John echoes these themes. When asked about the value of his reclaimed ties, he replies:

> I think they mean a certain sense of consistency for me, um, a continuing presence, um, that there have been some values in rela-tionships that have held from when I was in my 20s to now, so that's now 27 years, um, that these people are quite similar to me in many ways.

John reflects on his and his friends' identities as they were 'then' compared to how they are 'now'. He derives positive nostalgia from not only the analysis of what 'has been', but the ability to continue to iden-tify with these meaningful others. The recognition of shared similari-ties which have, in a sense, defeated loss simultaneously solidifies social identity and biography. This existential process can now proceed to a dynamic 'being with':

> [W]e care about each other enough to have kept that relationship over a very long time, um, that we've, um, I suppose there's a level of support in it as well in that some of the things that just outrage me about the world in terms of war, treatment of women, treat-ment of children, um, the entire sort of drift to a meaningless, um, consumer society that winds me up, um, it's – it's really nice to have

a supportive community in some ways to circulate information and ideas around with.

John

Having recognised a field of similarity and re-identified with his distant friends, John is able to socialise with them online. John illustrates how these performances of connection are social capital exchanges – claims on support and perspective – which strengthen bonds.

The accumulation of many known ties into a public space gives participants a sense of community. The reclamation of multiple distant ties is thus seen as the success of community in a world which seems corrosive to it:

> [W]here [Facebook's] huge value, ah, and positive value comes in, partly is through, ah, helping you stay in touch with people that you haven't done so well with that, either because they're in different countries or cities or even just different suburbs or what-ever...So Facebook has kind of, um, definitely I think filled a need or responded to this lack of community, um, that I think to a large extent the fact that we are living in this very kind of mediated cyber world, Facebook has managed to kind of recuperate a lot of that and create this wonderful space, which is amazing.

Bret

Here, the prevention of the loss of multiple ties is experienced as the resuscitation of community. In communities people and groups are autonomous, and yet nevertheless are implied in each other's activities and can be grouped together. Likewise, people accumulate many distant ties – meandering through different walks of life – who are grouped together on Facebook.

> Occasionally people surprise me, you know, someone I haven't heard from for years just suddenly decides to respond to my post. ... How do I value that? ... it's a sense of community. It does give you a sense of being amongst people.

Flash

Flash describes how even ties that he does not actively sustain can 'surprise' him. This is the positive emotion which comes from knowing this tie has not been lost. Even if, like a community, they do not always interact with each other, they are still 'among' one another. Bret provides a similar example:

> I enjoy having a fairly easily updateable thing where people can, where I can have that presence, where I can make – turn my life into little aphorisms and get these – these responses and it's kind of especially good and nice in random when you say something and you, you know, it will be like Shelly Bracken likes this and it's like Shelly is my second cousin from New Zealand who I've seen four times in last decade or whatever but I – I really like to hang out with her when I see her.
>
> Bret

Note how this indeterminate social recognition and consequent feeling of community is rather unique to Facebook. It is the product of a broad, heterogeneous public audience, composed of people whom one can easily forget and, hence, be positively reminded of later. More will be said about the positive and negative aspects of this 'indeterminate publicity' in the following chapters.

To summarise, then, reclaiming distant ties creates emotions derived from the prevention of the loss of these ties. This is an existential phenomenon which prevents the negation of both the other and aspects of the self. The reclamation of multiple ties gives the feeling that one has maintained one's social world in a collective sense: that is, a feeling of community.

Mediated publicity and distant intimacy

Facebook offers opportunities for intimacy with distant ties which other mediums do not. The characteristics of Facebook's mediated publicity are salient. First, Facebook affords constantly connected profiles and hence a-synchronous communication.

> It is a great tool in that I can chat to everyone, no matter where they are in the world, what tertiary institution they go to, etcetera, without having to worry about time and location to meet up.
>
> Penny

Facebook empowers connection by making synchronous presence irrelevant. Furthermore, it largely reduces the cost and effort involved in connecting and communicating.

I think that a real gift of Facebook is that you can keep alive a relationship much easier than you can just by phoning, um, I mean it's got a bit better in that I have an international mobile that I dial internationally on but I don't always have it with me, um, it's not always convenient because of the time zones.

John

Connecting via posted letters or telephone takes effort and costs time and money. Also, such connections have a relatively short lifespan. People must eventually 'hang up'. Conversely, Facebook freely connects people such that they are continuously, publicly visible to one another. Other research has confirmed that Facebook offers an attractive mode of connection because it is easier than picking up a phone (Pempek, Yermolayeva, & Calvert 2009). There is a sense that Facebook 'takes up' the work of connection, becoming like a human agent:

[Having] Facebook tell you what people are up to is really lovely, and having these photo albums pop up that are tagged, and you can go, 'ohh wow', you know, 'ohh, my friend's birthday party in New Zealand, look at the photos, beautiful'. And it kind of looks after, you know, it's kind of like a you know, um, there is a sense that it's a – a really active community member, or active family member that's really interested in keeping people in touch.

Bret

The agency Bret describes manifests prominently through the News Feed, the digital materiality of which consists of hidden protocols which aggregate peoples' activities into a live streaming reportage. The News Feed takes up the work of connecting. Its replacement of human labour allows it to possess human qualities, such as the ability to 'surprise' and 'remind' people. Above, Bret describes the positive emotionality of such moments, using words such as 'lovely' and 'beautiful'. It is important to keep in mind that such moments are predicated on publicity. The News Feed is an interface in which a large mass of public information has been egocentrically contextualised for the eyes of a specific person. Publicity has a peculiar effect on intimacy where distant ties are concerned. John explains:

I do think that there's – there is, it might be a false sense of intimacy but it is a – it is a sense of – it's a more immediate and regular intimacy than there was in the old days of letters.

In this key response, John suggests that publicity negates one kind of intimacy, and yet a new kind – empowered by immediate, regular, publicity – rises in its ashes. When information is posted publicly it becomes easily, regularly accessible. Low cost, low effort, and continual connection gives such information a sense of immediacy. Regular, immediate access to the information concerning someone a person cares about, therefore, opens up novel opportunities for interpersonal emotion.

Publicity also encourages intimacy between distant ties on a group level:

> If you didn't get a handwritten letter you felt a bit gipped, um, now look, you know, honestly if everyone reads the information against the photos we all feel included.
>
> John

Publicity affords one-to-many performances. It offers the opportunity to 'include' a meaningful social group. Inclusion fosters group intimacy, emotions of belonging, and collective interpersonal history. These resonate when distant group members can come 'back into the fold' through a medium such as Facebook. Also, consider the importance of photographs in the above examples. Being able to access friends in this regular, immediate, social way serves to compound the intimacy which already exists when people interact with private photographs.

> Here, I can actually look at their photos, I can see, you know, they've got kids now, they've got relationships, they've new jobs, um, you know, gone are the days of getting the bulky envelope with the six photos in it that someone had to go and print each one, cost a lot of money, cost a lot of money to send.
>
> John

'Kids', 'relationships' – these are the intimate aspects of someone's life. They hold meaning for the social connections this person is emotionally bonded to. These connections, in turn, delineate a kind of private space beyond which such meaning does not exist. Only those within this space can 'fill in' the private narrative which exists between frozen moments and subjective observations. Furthermore, photographs emphasise this private meaning by the manner in which they transmit intimacy through the eye. That is, the way in which they visually denote 'reality'. Penny reflects on this:

I'm able to put names to faces and I can get a better understanding of what, you know, what Betty or what Chris was talking about when they were here, what they were saying to me, and they're like oh you have to go to this place because of this, and like I can see it and what they were talking about when I couldn't when they were here 'cause they didn't really think to bring photos. So that sort of stuff, I think, its good to sort of place what they were talking about. Especially when people go overseas...you can actually place it and you can get your own sort of value for it, and you can sort of feel with the image.

Penny

Photographs are the residue of frozen moments. They have a being that is defined, in part, by distance in time and space. Yet, their accurate representation of reality also imbues them with a peculiar form of presence. This opens up channels of information and emotion which other media lack. Hence, when Penny is able to associate photographs with the stories her friends have told, a new form of intimacy is produced as she 'feels with the image'. The photographic embodiment of distant presence, therefore, is fortuitously beneficial in sustaining distant ties.

To summarise, Facebook allows distant ties to connect with each other in a low-cost, low-effort manner, and remain continuously connected such that a-synchronous, mediated information exchanges can occur. This affords distinctive forms of personal and social communication and information gathering, the regularity and immediacy of which produces a novel form of intimacy. Photographs convey intimate information in this fashion, although photographs are particularly potent sites of intimacy because of their 'private' nature, and their ability to denote reality, overcoming distance and imbuing a sense of presence.

Occasional identification and the role of triggers

Participants frequently accumulate distant connections whom they do not actively sustain, but may show an occasional interest toward. These ties are meaningful, but, to use a term of Penny's, they are 'outstretched'. Flash provides some description in this regard:

[O]ld school friends, old work colleagues, people you've known years ago – you might occasionally communicate with them on there, but you might even catch up with them once-in-a-while, but they're not people you would see a lot. And they're not people who would be a major part of your life.

Yet, these connections are not friended haphazardly. Flash stipulates that in order to become Facebook friends with such people he would 'have to like them as a person. I'd have to ... I'd have to have no ill feeling towards them'. Penny echoes this sentiment:

> You don't want to lose contact with them because you – like, to friend someone you obviously think that they're a nice person otherwise you don't friend them ... it's sort of saying that you haven't forgotten them ... like 'it's I haven't forgotten you', it's more like 'I think that you are someone worthwhile enough that I don't want to lose contact with you'.

Such connections share a modicum of meaning and good will. They are 'worthwhile enough' such that their loss would be negatively felt. This degree of meaning makes such ties occasional objects of interest. Facebook affords such interest by allowing people to 'keep tabs' and 'keep track' of these ties through conspicuous observation, without feeling obliged to interact with them. 'I think it's more of a means for me to keep in contact with a lot of people very easily', remarks Penny, 'and I can sort of keep in contact with them at my own discretion'. This process, Penny continues, is akin to 'keeping a foot in the door':

> [In keeping] my little foot in the door ... I can see that one of them is at uni and they're doing this subject and they really like it or another one has just got their licence really recently, so I'm happy for him to get his licence. So even though in a daily context it wasn't relevant, it's still cool to know that you know 'oh Drake got his licence, that's awesome you know good for him' sort of stuff, even though I'm not going to go on there and say 'hi, how was your day' that sort of stuff.

Keeping a foot in the door suggests retaining access and being able to 'peek into' someone's life. Penny takes a certain comfort in this ability. Again, I believe this comfort can be attributed to the defeat of loss. In being able to peek into the lives of meaningful ties people are reminded that they remain among one another. It is evident that for this to occur people implicitly grant public access to each other's profiles. Certainly, this is the case with all ties who have been consciously friended.

However, this reciprocal visibility has a specific function with regard to distant connections. Penny expresses this while talking in general about how she feels when reclaiming a distant tie:

> I'd like to keep in contact with you because I think that you're a nice person, you know eventually if it happens it would be great to get to know you a bit more but if it doesn't I'm content to just chill out and see what you're up to and, you know, see what's going on in your life, and you can see what's going on in my life, you know, we can keep tabs on each other in that sort of way.

Two contingent expectations are running through Penny's mind here. First, she hopes that they will be able to 'get to know' one another, that is, to perform this connection in the future. Second, she hopes that both she and her new connection will 'keep tabs' on each other, both peeking into each other's lives. Interestingly, this promise of reciprocal observation acts as a condition on future performances of connection. To illustrate, weak others who have no routine interaction with one another will usually only come into contact when, by seeming happenstance, something of mutual interest draws them into dialogue. 'I think there has to be sort of like a trigger to talk to them, if not, if there's not a trigger then I won't bother' (Penny). But this cannot occur on Facebook unless both parties can see into parts of each other's lives.

As has been argued, the News Feed aggregates an egocentric reportage of the activities of one's Facebook friends. The News Feed has the capacity to remind people about their friends, and sometimes these reminders act as 'triggers' for performances of connection.

> I like to think that it – I am a bit more connected, or I make an effort to be – stay more in touch. 'Cause you know you're regularly reminded that that person exists sometimes. Which I wouldn't normally, ah, have, I guess, in my regular life. It kind of broadens my regular life scope.
>
> Sally

Triggers can take the form of anything which appeals to the shared histories, affections, and socio-cultural similarities of the ties in question. In this way triggers allow for people to 're-identify' with distant others. Hence, triggered interactions, as with all performances of connection, operate according to the logic of public identification and create a figurative private space. Introducing the social capital component, a performance is a trigger if it makes claims on a resource which a distant tie is able to credit. In the following post, for instance, Sally evinces her background as a person who has lived in Perth (a city in Western Australia), while utilising the Perth floods in 2010 as a cultural moment, a form of cultural capital, with which to attract sociality:

| **Sally** |
| Don't worry about flooding Perth, I have a ShamWow. |

This post acts as a trigger, attracting the interest of a distant friend who is travelling overseas.

| **Helen** |
| omg hows the storms there i saw it on the news x |

| **Sally** |
| haha it made it to the news in the UK? |
| I'm fine – I'm in Melbourne, but the photos from Perth are crazy |

| **Helen** |
| ye they showed massive hail and a tree nearly falling over it looked like a hurricane lol |

Interestingly, while observing participant profiles I found triggers often accompanied what I term 'occasions of pride'. These are events which a person can be happy and proud about, such as trips, birthdays, personal achievements, and so forth. These capture distant ties because of their simultaneous appeal to something cultural and personal. Getting a job, for example, is something most people can identify with. But it also serves as a personal token which can be capitalised on to reassert an interpersonal connection. John explains:

> [Facebook] allows me to expand my network to people that I don't have to write to all the time to keep connected with. I can just kind of keep a sense of connection and then write to them when I see something of interest, like they've got a new job, so I write and say 'congratulations, it's really great, you know, this is what I'm up to'.

A birthday celebration is another example of a cultural and personal token, an occasion to be proud of which acts as an excellent trigger. Sally attracts these responses when her birthday is announced on Facebook:

> Happy bday!!!!!
> I'm soz i never got to see you!!! I have been thinkin about ya heaps.... so u must fill me in. Where are u and what r u doing??????????????? Will you be home anytime soon! I gotta see ya... its been far too long!!! loads of hugs [Sally] you crazy hipster lady awesome gurl, person who is far away in awesome town [doing] awesome cool things with herselfs!!! Happy Bdays ! *hugggies*

Notice the positive emotions in these posts. Occasions to be proud of attract esteem in the form of congratulations, honour, admiration, and the like, and this has a positive, interpersonal emotionality. In these examples this is overlaid with the affect imbued by distance, evident in comments like 'its been far too long!!!' Esteem and distance are performed as two forms of social intimacy, negotiated in public. Performances which anticipate esteem thus make an excellent trigger, as they catalyse the cultural and the intimate in a relatively innocuous fashion, which explains the commonality of such moments.

However, although triggers re-instigate interpersonal connection, they are also the product of norms which act to limit overt personal engagement and intimacy. Triggers operate according to the logic of response, rather than address. This is understandably desired, as directly addressing a person who has not been actively sustained can expose the distance between two ties.

> I think when you meet someone that you haven't seen in ages you sort of admit how, like not openly but you sort of demonstrate how far you've gone apart because you know so little about them... And it sounds really awkward because you sort of, through questioning them continuously you're sort of admitting how little you actually know about them and that's just, I don't know, it's sad. Yeah, so it's a lot better when someone posts something that's interesting and then the other person can give their comments to it because you feel as though you're connected to them although you don't have to have, like you don't have to be 100% up to date with exactly what's going on in their life. So it's sort of like an interaction that's not dictated by context but more of content.
>
> Penny

What constitutes an interaction, driven by what Penny calls 'context', with a relatively weak, distant tie? Penny astutely implies a person's 'life context', personal details which are a mystery to such ties. Hence, such 'context-driven' interactions would reveal a lack of intimacy and intimate knowledge. Intimacy is implied in negation; it hangs awkwardly between the two parties. The absent presence of intimacy prevents the formation of a true interpersonal space, a space of real identification. Triggers allow interactions to focus, as Penny explains, on 'content': tokens which reveal points of socio-cultural similarity. Through a focus on 'content', a real space of identification can form. Hence, triggered interactions paradoxically negotiate intimacy away from the personal in order to reinstate the interpersonal. Such interactions constitute a new normativeness which structures the performance of connection on Facebook and which arises out of the nature of the mediated, heterogeneous publics people form therein.

Distance, identity drift, and conflict

Sometimes participants reclaim distant ties in a well-meaning fashion but find little opportunity to perform these connections. In this way, without at first realising it, they accumulate connections who differ significantly from themselves. If the occasion arises when such a tie becomes of interest and a performance of connection ensues, these 'identity drifts' may become evident, causing conflicts. In such moments the performance of connection breaks down.

Take Flash's description of his encounter with a controversial comment, posted by an acquaintance from high school:

> About two years ago I had a friend from – well, a former friend from high school, I hadn't seen him for many years. And he – I get the impression he's a very bitter person – had a lot of very controversial comments...and generally I would, these days, I would just not react to that. I did, and I was quite angry in what I said to him, and he cut me off.

Flash describes how he felt uncontrollably provoked to criticise his 'former friend'. Flash's combatant 'cut him off', meaning he was 'unfriended'. At the heart of this conflict is a change in values. Flash's values have become radically different from those of his former friend.

Identity drift can even occur between ties who were once extremely close. Bret explains how an ex-girlfriend perceived his 'identity drift' and felt forced to unfriend him.

> [T]his ex-girlfriend from New Zealand, Zoey, who, I mean we broke up years ago but that was a four year and pretty intense relationship and

we became Facebook friends for a while and then she just stopped. And she told a mutual friend, I think Craig was asking her, because I'd realised that Zoey had de-friended me and she was like 'yeah, it's just too weird for me seeing all these pictures of you in weird fancy dress type costumes with strange girls'. And so I think for her she just went 'yeah, out of sight out of mind' again.

Zoey's inability to identify with Bret is painful given the past they shared in which their identities were so closely united. Facebook's affordance of public, conspicuous access to Bret's life is experienced negatively. Such a virtual presence will inevitably conflict with distance and differentiation. In both examples something which stabs at the heart of relationships and identities is exposed and intimacy is mobilised. Differences between how people are 'now' compared to how they were 'then' force reappraisals of relationships, resuscitating intimacies long past. In the first example the intimacy of a broken friendship is manifest as rage and offense. In the second the intimacy of a broken romance is manifest as discomfort and jealousy. Bret furnishes another example:

> I think there was one time where I kind of, I put up this kind of short, two line update that was just 'sad guy', and I got a couple of hits to that. Um, but I didn't – and it was fucking weird 'cause one of them was this girl who like, you know, I went to primary school with and we were almost boyfriend and girlfriend but we were twelve, so what is that anyway? She lives in Adelaide, I haven't seen her for twenty odd year – I don't know – eighteen years. And so this girl Rebecca, ah, replied to that post saying 'what's the matter Bret' and I was like, 'what the fuck am I gonna say to that', you know? Like what – what possible – you know obviously it's nice, she, on some weird level, is concerned. But we were twelve and she was so shy when we went out and she didn't say more than two words to me *then*.

Here, Rebecca capitalises on Bret's comment as a trigger to interact with him, but the comment is too much on the level of personal intimacy for Rebecca's desire to perform connection not to come off as awkward. This is caused by a lack of interpersonal intimacy between them which carries through to the 'here and now'. Intimacy remains the cause of conflict, though here it is mobilised in negation. However, this form of identity drift is not needlessly evident 'after the fact'. Bret makes a claim on social capital, on the bonding resource of emotional support. Only those who can credit this social capital, by virtue of their relevant shared history with Bret, can appropriately respond. Bret is frustrated by Rebecca's naivety regarding this fact. This example also nicely illustrates how identification, social capital, and the negotiation of intimacy go hand in hand. This is a failure at identification which could have been prevented if Rebecca had negotiated intimacy with more savvy, which in this case would have meant abstaining from crediting a resource she was not entitled to give.

Overall, these conflicts can be viewed as moments in which intimacies are uprooted in a negative way. Hence, avoiding these moments, where possible, means negotiating intimacy. Bret's experience with Rebecca made him change his impression-management strategies. That was the last time he posted a call for personal support in public. Hence, Bret has taken steps to prevent moments such as his experience with Rebecca occurring again. Also, based on conflicts of this type, people learn to be more circumspect with regard to who they friend. Friending conditions are techniques for negotiating intimacy. These and other strategies will be the purview of Chapter 8.

So far I have argued that the primary motivation participants have in using Facebook is to perform connection. When participants do this they take their connections as objects of thought and labour, mirroring them against an imagined public of constitutive difference. This reproduces and strengthens connections. In this process they reap the benefits of interpersonal intimacy and the pleasure of belonging. Connections are performed by claiming on, and crediting, social capital. This, in turn, creates a figurative private space and, therefore, delimits the spatial contours of an intimate exchange. These processes take on special dimensions in relation to distant ties. The ability to reclaim and sustain these ties is another key motivation for using Facebook. Reclaiming these ties has existential dimensions, the emotional resonance felt when negating the loss of meaningful others. Performances of connection with these others carry a peculiar intimacy, as they have long been distant, hence the ability to easily and regularly receive rich information about them is highly valued. Ties which are reclaimed but do not carry much meaning require some form of trigger to engage the performance of connection. This is a way of negotiating intimacy such that interpersonal communication can centre around positive identification. Reclaimed ties often go through changes in their identities such that the performance of connection causes conflict. In such cases there is a breakdown of identification and interpersonal intimacy, and one party has credited social capital he or she was not entitled to.

So far I have primarily discussed online interactions. Now I turn to how social surveillance relates to these performances of connection, and consider how Facebook's affordance of mediated surveillance is one of its most alluring and multifaceted aspects.

6
Prosthetic Intimacy

In this Chapter I discuss the various social surveillance practices my participants engage in on an everyday basis while using Facebook. I emphasise the role of intimacy and social context in structuring how and why surveillance takes place, and what consequences result. I build up to a discussion of voyeuristic 'spying' and the way it 'steals' intimacies from weak ties in order to morally and biographically articulate the self. Because of its distinctly artificial qualities, I term this process 'prosthetic intimacy'. It can be contrasted with the more natural, 'symbiotic' intimacy which is produced from watching and interacting with close friends. Finally, I discuss how Facebook affords a kind of subjective truth-giving, constituted through the mediated gaze, which I term first-hand judgement. This becomes significant in the following chapter, as this gaze can often make participants feel objectified and dissatisfied with Facebook.

Forms of surveillance

When referring to how they engage with Facebook, the most common word my participants use is 'look'. Facebook appears as a visual interface on computers and mobile devices. It is an 'ocular public' which privileges visual surveillance. Though Facebook offers a convergence of media which appeal to other senses, such as links to music videos, these do not account for the Facebook experience in either a necessary or sufficient manner. The social worlds on Facebook arrest and seduce a person through the eye. Below, I explore the general forms this surveillance can take. These forms in turn act to frame an understanding of the different social contexts within which observational practices occur. Observation can take the form of a tacit routine, an indeterminate moment, or a self-conscious endeavour, although these modes are not discrete, and often direct and enfold one another. After exploring each of these forms, special attention will be paid to self-conscious observation, also known as 'spying', which constitutes one of Facebook's most seductive temptations.

Surveillance as tacit routine

Here, by 'tacit' I refer to routinised behaviour in which a person is not self-conscious of the activities in which he or she is engaged. To understand how observation can become tacit, it is important to recognise just how central it is to 'working with' the Facebook system. When a user logs in, he or she is immediately presented with the 'home page', in which the News Feed streams a reportage of his or her friends' activities. With but the slightest volition a person becomes an audience for the lives of others. Bret explains

> I log on and then it comes up on the home page, I guess, where it has the list of everyone's thing. And I probably, you know, skim my eyes over the page of that, without scrolling down too much, but I probably just scroll over.
>
> Bret

Notice the pre-reflective habit evinced by this 'skimming' of the eyes. The low cost, low effort ritualism of logging on and having information 'just there' makes scrolling through the News Feed one of the basic, tacit routines participants maintain. To get a more detailed picture, consider John and Odette's descriptions of their everyday routines when they log in:

> I go to the home page, I see what everyone's been doing and mostly I'm probably initially looking for people in a different time zone, so UK, America, um, and I follow some of their links. I steal some of their ideas, um, and I guess I just get a picture of where they're up to ...
>
> John

> Um, I pretty much scroll through the News Feed and see what is coming up photo wise and status wise, um, yeah, if there's any events that I've been invited to, I'll look at that, just put – write them in my diary for something of interest and yeah, see if there's any friend requests, any new personal messages ...
>
> Odette

Both examples illustrate how Facebook becomes a tool for keeping up to date with one's social connections. Most of the time, these connections are immanent to one's own life-world. Therefore, this constitutes the routine information consumption which allows people to reproduce their social lives. Sally describes how she will routinely check up on the News Feed every few minutes or so while online. This allows her to see what content has been recently updated – say, photos which have received commentary – as well as what new activities have been reported on.

> [I] go on the home page again after a couple of minutes 'cause it might have been updated. Um, I look at photos, I, you know, check those profiles again, and – and you find that sometimes it, there's just, it links through. So you might be looking at someone's, um, photo album they just put up, and there's someone in it and you're like 'ohh I don't know what they're doing', go on their page, and then there's other photos, or, someone's posted on their wall...
>
> Sally

Observation on Facebook cannot occur continuously. Rather, it is what Christine Hine (2000), referring to the observational practices of the virtual ethnographer, would term 'interstitial'. People roam through different parts of their networks and the Internet as a whole. Moreover, they log in and out of Facebook while performing other daily routines. Hence, this interstitiality, as Sally explains, will often cause routines, such as 'checking up' on particular friends, or returning to a particular thread. Bret describes similar behaviour:

> Usually it'd be, like, maybe do a status update at the beginning of the day and then check it a couple of times during the day to see if anything interesting has happened, or if anyone's responded to my witty, witty updates.
>
> Bret

While Sally discusses checking back every couple of minutes when online, Bret expands this to include regular checks throughout the day. Participants regularly log into Facebook, sometimes multiple times a day. These routines are themselves part of broader, weekly rhythms. They need to keep up to date with what their friends are doing, and to check back on their own posts. On Facebook everyone must cope with each other's interstitial rhythms, making information gathering a constant routine of 'checking back'.

Surveillance as indeterminate vision

As has been discussed already, Facebook seems to have the potential to 'remind' and 'surprise' users about others. To act as if with human agency like a kind of 'community organiser'. This was mentioned in relation to distant ties, although that is just one example of a broader socio-technical effect, namely, 'indeterminate vision'. When a user observes something unexpected, he or she has experienced a moment of indeterminate vision. People accumulate heterogeneous networks on Facebook. Many of these connections carry on their everyday activities beyond the scope of a person's immediate concerns and tacit routines. However, it is easy for a person to encounter these activities, especially through the News Feed, which combines the operation of hidden protocols and the social fact of a heterogeneous network to make such moments inevitable.

Also, recall that every user is at the centre of his or her own egocentric network. Hence, when visiting a friend's profile a person can never be sure what he or she will encounter. This friend will possess his or her own egocentric network which is likely to be composed of connections who are not shared with the visitor. Hence, although when tacitly observing people on Facebook a user may observe things which are relatively expected and commonplace, they may also discover things which may surprise, startle, or even shock, depending on the context. This is the source of various key problems, discussed fully in the following chapter. While it is possible, for instance, to tailor one's privacy settings to control what other people can see of oneself, it is much more difficult to control what one sees of other people. Indeterminate vision subverts the agency of vision with both negative and positive consequences.

Self-conscious surveillance

People also carry out self-conscious, goal-orientated information-gathering practices on Facebook. In such cases they are specifically aware of their own conspicuous gaze. This imbues a consciousness of the subject–object relationship between the gaze and the images on the screen. As Odette remarks, 'you actually come to realise that what you're doing is sitting on a computer and looking at someone else's pictures'. Surveillance is most self-conscious when it gathers information which would be hard and perhaps inappropriate to gather in other social contexts. Such information appears as furtive and auspicious. Its virtual presence is understood in terms of its physical or figurative distance, its public character in terms of its privacy. Observation becomes self-conscious when a person cannot be included in a performance of connection, when he or she does not occupy a domain of appropriate similarity, cannot credit the social capital this makes claims on and, hence, cannot identify with the connection in question. In such cases a person really feels that he or she is outside of a figurative private space, looking in. This mode of information gathering involves many novel aspects of social life on Facebook, and hence warrants further attention.

The contradictions of spying

Conspicuous surveillance is a seductive affordance, to which Odette remarks, 'you're basically spying, you're looking through their photos, observing their activity'. Sally explains:

> It's kind of like knowing something about someone but you know you probably shouldn't. I don't know. Like, you'll find out that, um, an ex of yours [has] gotten married or something, you know? They're probably not gonna tell you, but you know through Facebook.

Spying involves gathering information which would be socially inappropriate to gather in other media. Sally evinces how such information often describes weak, distant ties. As Sally points out, this kind of information would not be disclosed in conversation. Hence, spying emphasises how norms of appropriate information gathering are transformed on Facebook. The same norms which govern information gathering in conversations do not operate here.

Becoming Facebook friends is itself an act which requires people to search out others, identify their profiles and send them friend requests (Lampe, Ellison, and Steinfield 2006). For strong ties this is a relatively unproblematic affair, as such friends often welcome the ability to form a community on Facebook. Yet, there is a sense that, even for weak ties, this kind of preliminary conspicuous observation has become culturally sanctioned where Facebook is concerned. Penny evinces this while describing how she reclaimed an old primary school friend:

> I found her the other day and I was really excited, it was like 'oh it's you, how's it going'. So it's fun to sort of keep in touch with – like, because you couldn't do that beforehand, like it'd be creepy if I got a phone book and just called her. It's like 'do you remember me', it would be like 'who the hell is this, who is stalking me'.

The fact that such behaviour might be considered 'stalking' in offline life is revealing. A different set of cultural norms apply in this instance. Because it seems both socially and culturally sanctioned, spying on Facebook appears as not overly clandestine or pathological. Flash reflects on this:

> I think as humans we're naturally curious. You know, we're curious people. My mother when she was doing the ironing, putting out the washing years ago I remember she would always used to peer over the neighbours fence. She's not someone who would, you know, hide in the bushes, you know. Presumably, she might, I don't know. But um that's another form. I suppose Facebook is the 21st century equivalent.

Here, spying is justified as part of human nature. Importantly, it is also justified against offline stalking, defined as the invasion of a physical private space. Continuing the analogy of his mother's curiosity, Flash remarks:

> Yeah, yeah, I mean its, you know, it's passive. She's not going to set up a web cam in their house, or, you know, stalk them

Again, Flash contrasts Facebook, by analogy, with invading a physical private space. Spying is distinguished from stalking, as the former takes place within a safe, 'passive', culturally condoned online public space, while the latter involves a physical personal space. The latter should be considered not only in terms of a lack of physical materiality, but more importantly in terms of cultural narratives regarding the sanctity of the private home and the frightening threat of physical danger.

The binaries implicit in this discussion – passive/dangerous, curiosity/stalking, normative/pathological – should not be considered in any way immutable, stable, and 'true'. They are pragmatic justifications, symptomatic of changes in culture and social life, and are subject to an ongoing intensive negotiation of intimacy at the level of individuals, groups, and socio-cultural structures. The norms which condone spying are unstable and open-ended. Certainly, despite these justifications and normalisations, people also find spying morally problematic. This is reflected in research conducted by Madden and Smith (2010). Based on a large-sample quantitative survey of American Internet users, the authors find that 'half of Internet users say it bothers them that people think it's normal to search for information about others online'

(2010: 44). Yet, most of this cohort admit to engaging in such practices, revealing how those who play into this new norm also question it. This contradictory process plays out on Facebook.

> Sometimes I feel better about it when I can talk to a friend about it, because you do feel a bit guilty it's like a guilty pleasure. So when you know that a friend does it as well that's a bit better...

> Sally

In order to assuage her moral self-consciousness, Sally must vouchsafe that others also spy. She must take moral refuge in the recognition of a new norm. Yet, the widespread adoption of these practices is often seen as a further sign of their problematic nature. Although I have argued that 'spying' is qualitatively different to offline stalking, the term 'stalking' is often used as a synonym for spying, used in order to emphasise the latter's negative dimensions. Correspondingly, Facebook has been given the widespread cultural epithet, 'Stalkbook', given that, as Sally remarks, 'everyone does it'.

Another similar and frequently used synonym is 'voyeurism', a term I believe is most apt in espousing the moral dimensions of this phenomenon.

> It's a form of voyeurism in some ways, don't you think?...in some ways there's almost a voyeuristic element to it. I'm not going to, you know, look them up in the phone book and go round in their house. That's scary shit. But, you know, in some ways it's a form of curiosity, it's a form of voyeurism. It's a form of watching people, surveillance.

> Flash

Here, Flash justifies the passivity and safety of spying, while simultaneously signalling its voyeuristic characteristics. This is not, I believe, the kind of pathological voyeurism explored in psychoanalytic literature. This discipline views voyeurism as an inherently sexual act, aimed at a private, erotic scene which causes sexual arousal (Freund, Watson, and Rienzo 1988). Similarly, I want to avoid an investigation of this gaze in terms of Freudian scopophilia (Freud 1962). This approach considers the act of taking people as objects of curiosity to have its routes in infant exploration of sexuality and genital absence. Hence, any exploration of such a curiosity is doomed to fall into a psychoanalytic reductionism.

Although spying on Facebook can be sexual – Bret gives examples of 'vetting' possible romantic partners using Facebook – it need not be. Furthermore, even if a romantic interest is at play, this need not lead to sexual arousal. Also, spying is not determined by the cultural sublimation of the male gaze (Mulvey 1975, 11–13). Both men and women engage in this practice, and spying is far more complex than this.

Recall that spying has a 'natural curiosity' which speaks more to the difference between what is present and known, and what is distant and mysterious. Between what is similar and what is different. Hence, this study is allied with theorists who posit a form of voyeurism which is not based purely on sexuality (Clavert 2000). Participants use the term 'voyeurism' because they understand they are circumventing a barrier, gazing into a figurative private space. Their position outside of this space is defined by their inability to credit the social capital which would allow them to be included. That is, they cannot positively identify with their objects of interest in such a way that a performance of connection could proceed.

Yet, when people become Facebook friends they do engage in a kind of social capital exchange in which they tacitly credit each other with the opportunity to watch each other, to gather an informational resource. Hence, social surveillance on Facebook constitutes a form of exchange which derives from the exchange which occurs when people become Facebook friends. Hence, when people spy they 'take' but do not 'give'. They *take* the resource of information, but do not *give* the resource of sociability and identification. Voyeurism describes both trespassing and appropriation.

Deborah Gaensbauer (1987) considers this form of voyeurism in her discussion of the novels of Virginia Woolf. Woolf's 'narrative voice', argues Gaensbauer, 'echoes a trespassing vision' and 'stems from the situation of an outsider looking on, speculatively participating in another's existence in an effort to fill in emotional or physical lacunae' (1987, 194). Here, Woolf comments on the dispossession of feminine identity, crystallised in the moment of feminine voyeurism which attempts to appropriate a social life denied to women. Voyeurism acts as a tragic polemic. As Gaensbauer writes:

> Perhaps what is especially terrible in the act of voyeurism is not necessarily what is being seen or the idea of being seen so much as the need it represents, the incompleteness of the voyeur having to fabricate or 'steal' an existence. (1987: 192)

I do not wish to explore voyeurism on Facebook in terms of the identity politics of gender, although this would provide fruitful research. However, I argue that in 'taking' and not 'giving', Facebook voyeurs 'steal an existence' to fill a lack in their own. This lack should not be overdramatised, as if Facebook users are all fundamentally traumatised. However, this 'lack' is likely the result of specific historical conditions which could be called 'disruptive'. Consider our definitively 'modern' lifespans, characterised by mobility and the precariousness of personal biography (Giddens 1991; Beck 1992; Beck & Beck-Gernsheim 2002). Hence, people seek to buttress their social identities and to experience moments of biographical and moral validation. That is, spying on Facebook takes information here and there for the purposes of increasing the worth of one's own social identity. But, unlike performances of connection, this form of negative identification is not a cooperative process aimed at maintaining or strengthening bonds. Voyeurism is a guilty pleasure because it achieves identification through difference, while maintaining the distance between ties.

In order to understand this process in more depth, I turn to the exploration of a particular 'surveillance context', namely, spying on estranged ties.

Estranged ties and prosthetic intimacy

Out of the distant ties my participants reclaim on Facebook, estranged ties have a distinctive value. Temporal distance imbues a sense of mystery in estranged ties, sparking curiosity as to how different they have become. Of course, similarity is also at play. But whether similarity or difference is emphasised depends on someone's motivations. For example, if a person wants to both reclaim and sustain a tie, points of similarity will be sought out. On the other hand, if a person wants to reclaim a distant tie without the intention of performing connection difference is sought out. Spying on this latter kind of weak, different, estranged tie constitutes one of Facebook's chief values for my participants.

Flash reflects on how Facebook mobilises a desire to connect with estranged ties:

I remember when I first joined in…I had this insatiable curiosity to find people I hadn't seen for years. You know, either because I went to school with them or we'd lost contact or I'd known them years ago and, you know, we'd lost contact and I was curious.

Flash illustrates how temporal distance produces potential novel information, a form of bridging social capital, which in turn rouses 'insatiable curiosity'. In the following example, observe how this curiosity is directed at points of similarity:

> I typed in my school the other day and – and saw these people came out and I suddenly realised that, you know, there were a whole pile of guys who came out who are now gay and, um, you know, and another pile who've done – gone on to do some really interesting things and I thought 'well yeah, it might be interesting to connect with them at some stage', um, I'm sure if I remember them they remember me and I know they've got – we've got friends in common
>
> John

Looking for similarities, John uses Facebook to 'vet' potential reclaimed ties with the intention of both connecting and socialising. Given the potency of sexuality in processes of identification, discovering this point of similarity is highly gratifying. Moreover, John finds that these ties are doing 'interesting things', which can be read as the recognition of shared interests and, hence, a common cultural position. Finally, John discovers aspects of social similarity, pointing out that the ties in question share 'friends in common' with himself.

Participants are also motivated to exclusively spy on estranged ties, and care little about re-establishing friendships. Odette illustrates:

> Well you're not really friends with these people, you're not talking to them, you're essentially looking at their profile without being their friend and you're, um, yeah, you're basically spying, you're looking through their photos, observing their activity. They don't know you're looking at it.

This exemplifies the voyeurism discussed earlier, defined by 'taking' through looking, but not 'giving' anything social in return. This is a sentiment echoed by Flash, who recollects 'friending' people,

> not out of a desire to become friends with them, but more… It was a great curiosity – as well as adding people I was friends with at the time – it was this, you know, it was like a reunion thing. Very much.

'Reunion' is an apt term. It resounds with the fact that many estranged ties are reclaimed from peoples' formative high school years. Also, a 'class reunion' serves as a good general metaphor for what happens when estranged ties are reclaimed. Class reunions are haunted by the memory of high school, of old crushes and conflicts. Grudges are rarely dropped, and old social divisions seem to congeal again. Whoever someone has become is inevitably viewed in terms of who he or she once was. Likewise, this form of 'life-change comparison' is at play when people use Facebook to spy on estranged ties. Sally reflects on this by giving an example of a friend's experience with an estranged tie:

> So obviously the school ... it's quite bogan.[1] It's very, very different. So a lot of my high school friends I'm not in touch with anymore and it's really interesting to see what they're up to. And, um, and one of my friends that went to the same school – and she went – ended up going to uni as well, and there's very few, like, out of 200 graduating class, um, there's about five of us that went to uni. Um, so, and she was just saying, you know, there was this one girl that gave her shit during high school and she could go look on her Facebook page and in her mind the girl probably really likes her life. She's a – she's a mother of two now. And we're only what? Twenty, twenty-three? And so she's twenty-two, and, um, and – and she's like – she feels better about herself, like 'I've done better than her', in that sort of sense, 'she gave me shit during high school'. It allows you to compare your life to other peoples in that sense ...

Sally contextualises the life-world of her school and, hence, the estranged characters which will be drawn from it, as 'very, very different'. The comparative process Sally's friend engages in seems to be driven by an old grudge. Hence, whatever she uncovers, if it displays her enemy in a negative light she will be morally validated. Self-validation through moral differentiation plays a crucial part in this comparative process. This is articulated in the judgement 'I've done better than her'. Difference drives this conclusion. While Sally's friend is embarking on a rewarding education, her grudge is weighed down with two kids, and is implicitly cast as having followed a stereotypical, and morally inferior, 'bogan' path. Odette provides a similar example:

> Yeah, um, I guess I went to an all girls high school, so I wasn't friends with everyone. So the people I was friends with, yeah, I'm sort of friends with them now on Facebook even though I don't really keep in contact with them outside of Facebook but yeah, there's other people that you find out are engaged or have children even. I'm 24

so I guess that's pretty young to be married and having children but yeah, it's interesting to find out yeah, where people are at in life. It's a bit of a social comparison I suppose which can be bad, but um, no, it's still interesting nonetheless.

Here, difference is again discovered in the fact that an old high school acquaintance has married and had kids at a young age. A similar moral judgment is reached: 'I'm twenty-four, so I guess that's pretty young to be married and having children'. Odette sits in brief judgement of herself as voyeur, as taking information at a distance for her own self-validation, which is 'bad'.

Social comparison has been found to play a crucial role in human self-assessment and self-awareness. This theory, as espoused by Festinger (1954), states that human beings necessarily observe others in order to evaluate their own abilities and opinions. For instance, a person may compare his or her own abilities to others to determine how 'good' he or she is. Or, a person may compare his or her opinion to others who share a similar opinion so as to validate it. Festinger argues that social comparisons are aimed at similar people, as self-evaluations would lack accuracy and worth if gauged by those who are radically different. There is nothing valuable, for instance, in remarking that a college student has greater intellectual abilities than a feeble-minded person (ibid: 120). Yet, it is apparent that Facebook users utilise comparisons with different ties in order to assess their own identities. Hence, while difference may not be appropriate for evaluating one's opinions and abilities, it is useful in evaluating other self-aspects. The life-change comparisons in question, I argue, compare dissimilar intimacies and personal histories in order to articulate the self, both morally and biographically.

In the above examples intimate details are focused on: the status of a person's home life, relationships, and family situation. In fact, in comparing these things to themselves, Sally and Odette implicitly articulate the subtext of their own relationships, sexual practices, and even reproductive histories. This comparison of intimacies is undertaken because such details supposedly constitute the 'essence' of someone's life, and are thus apposite markers of change and differentiation. Furthermore, when spying on estranged ties, participants report an engrossment with photographs. As has been argued, photographs on Facebook have a peculiar private, intimate nature. They delimit a domain of people who are capable of 'filling in' the meaning gap which exists between the image depicted and the moment of spectatorship. The photo both excludes those who do not occupy this domain and, yet, seems to entice them and to reveal *something* through its uncanny realism. The intimate details people gather are augmented by this more intimate form of looking. The irony being that this information is gathered in the absence of interpersonal intimacy between the watcher and the watched.

A logical analysis can make the anatomy of life-change comparisons and the role of intimacy more clear. There is the comparison of how a person is 'now', compared to how the person was back 'then'. There is the comparison of this person 'now' to oneself. However, this comparison necessarily involves an understanding of how one's own life has changed. For example: 'since high school she has gotten married while I have not gotten married' requires a reflection on one's own relationship history. Hence, one compares one's own identity 'now' to how it was back 'then'. It is, thus, apparent that comparing oneself to an estranged other means taking a self-reflexive stance in regard to one's own biography. The self's biography is produced in terms of its difference. Thus, such comparisons not only potentially validate the self through moral judgments, but potentially act to anchor the self by producing biography. Given that intimate information is most prized as constitutive of difference, it is really the comparison of intimacies which acts to produce this biography. Returning to Gaensbauer's conception of voyeurism, intimacy is the thing which is 'appropriated' and biography the 'personal lacunae' which is 'filled'.

This mode of constituting biography resounds with what Celia Lury (1998) calls 'prosthetic culture'. Lury identifies a mode of experimental individualism in contemporary times in which selves, and biographies in particular, are constructed through the assemblage of 'prostheses'. This, she argues, is emblematic of an 'I can, therefore I am', rather than an 'I think therefore I am' culture (1998: 3). Meaning that in their own self-projects people are empowered to use and experiment with things, such as the memories of others. In so doing the gaps between 'subject and object... are remedied through an artificial extension of capability, resulting in a transferable potential' (1998, 18). Facebook affords this kind of 'artificial extension of capability', empowering people to reach distant objects and enfold them within themselves. In this sense, I argue, the intimacies and biographies of estranged ties are a kind of prosthesis used to construct one's own biography. This is not interpersonal intimacy, but prosthetic intimacy.

Prostheses are attached, argues Lury, through processes of 'outcontextualisation' and 'indifferentiation'. The former describes taking things out of context, which seems to be Facebook's *raison d'etre*. The latter

describes enfolding difference into the self, in this case different intimacies and biographies. However, indifferentiation does not recontex-
tualise. Lury argues that prosthetic individuals consist of multiple parts,
yet these parts do not make up a whole. Hence, she distinguishes 'prosthesis' from 'synthesis'. Likewise, there is a sense that, on Facebook,
prosthetic intimacies construct a biography which is artificial. Which,
like a replacement organ, refuses to integrate into a natural system. This
form of comparative biography – constructed through difference and at
a distance – contrasts with a lived biography, which is constructed out
of social interactions and shared histories.

Lury (1998) argues that photographs are particularly good at outcon-
textualsing because of the way they freeze moments in time and can be
distributed and reproduced beyond such moments. Photographs are also
good at indifferentiating, as their reality effect imbues a sense of presence and false memory. Hence, photographs depicting the experiences
of others can facilitate prosthetic memories. This process is amplified
by social networks which afford the distribution and public collocation
of photographs. As Van Dijck writes, 'the function of memory reap-
pears in the networked, distributed nature of digital photographs as
most images are sent over wires and end up somewhere in virtual space'
(2008: 58). In this way Facebook allows for dissimilar ties to 'outcontex-
tualise' each other's photos as mnemonic prostheses.

Prosthetic identification, Lury argues, happens through mimesis.
Identities are extended by imitating difference. This is how people
remember the memories of others through their photographs. However,
here I want to depart from Lury while still focusing on the estranged ties
in question. People do not imitate these ties. In fact, they consciously
attempt to do the opposite, to identify in negation. Nevertheless, artificial extensions of capability like Facebook and photographs, are utilised
to achieve this. Therefore, I utilise 'prosthesis' to refer to both 'extensions
of capability' and 'objects of difference' which afford self-construction
through differentiation, not mimesis. The shared social memories of
connections who can positively, mimetically identify with each other
should, thus, not be called prosthetic. In metaphorical contradistinc-
tion they can be called symbiotic, to indicate an organic merging.

Turkle (2011) expresses concern over SNSs because, she argues, they
make it far more convenient for us to treat others as objects. Specifically,
as 'part objects', representations which are not 'whole people' in any
interpersonally rewarding sense. The above discussion seems to
confirm aspects of this thesis. Moreover, the kind of voyeurism at play
here appears to have shades of the kind of narcissism which Turkle and

like critics are concerned about. Estranged ties are not spied on with the genuine interest of forming a social bond. Rather, interest in their lives seems wholly selfish and self-concerned.

Facebook users utilise the intimacies of certain estranged ties in order to understand themselves while never engaging in social interactions with those ties. Yet, for two reasons, I do not believe this is emblematic of a more narcissistic culture. First, spying on these kinds of ties is not the only, nor the most valued, pursuit of Facebook users. People also utilise Facebook to reproduce their social connections through positive identification, carried out via sociable performances of connection. As will be shown in Chapter 8, such performances manifest a 'group ego', are highly theatrical, and purposely negotiate intimacy in such a way that what Sennett (1977: 262) calls insidious and 'intangible tones of feeling and motive' are abstracted.

Also, a person can only reclaim a finite amount of estranged ties. Correspondingly, the amount of novel information which can be collected is also finite. Early on, this novelty is incredibly powerful. Flash attributes the 'initial buzz of excitement' from using Facebook to 'reuniting with all these people'. However, this novelty fades once every tie within reason has been collected. Sally explains: '[B]ack then I think there was a bit more [spying] going on – maybe the novelty of it', whereas, 'now it's a bit more stable. It's the same, you know, everyone's joined'. Likewise, Odette states that 'once you find out what someone is doing it's kind of – I mean I've got better things to do than keep returning to their profile and seeing what they're doing now in 2010 as opposed to 2008'. Hence, while sociality with friends endures, the voyeuristic compulsion toward estranged ties fades.

Second, spying on estranged ties does not always result in positive consequences. Odette illustrates this:

> I guess it's just interesting to see what they're doing but, like, another friend of mine said, she finds that depressing doing that because she thinks 'this person has achieved this and I haven't achieved this'. So I try not to do it too much for that reason.

There is always a chance that the desire for moral self-validation will be disappointed. This possibility 'reins in' Odette's desire to spy on estranged ties. Indeed, my participants commonly unfriend certain estranged ties after being similarly disappointed. They learn from their visual experiences of the intimacies of others. When to spy and when not to spy is learnt as a kind of 'emotional competency'. Here, I want to again draw on Illouz (2007), who investigates intimacy in terms of 'emotional style', 'emotional competence', and 'emotional capital'. Illouz understands emotional style as stratified and differentiated across society, such that certain groups embody emotional style in different ways and to different degrees. 'Emotional competence' describes the degree of embodiment of emotional style, actually quantified and measured by psychologists in the form of 'emotional intelligence'. 'Emotional capital' is the degree to which one's emotional competence can be mobilised to claim resources. The reclamation and surveillance of estranged ties on Facebook unveils a normative patterning suggestive of a culture of intimacy, namely, the acceptability for people to not only observe, but to use each other's distant, intimate details for the purpose of constructing identity. Given that identity, and biography in particular, is affectual as well as cognitive, these personal details can be seen as forms of emotional capital. In learning to deny voyeuristic moments, as these create emotional pain, people learn to refuse the appropriation of this emotional capital. Instead they find the 'emotional competence' to appropriate emotional capital from other, more rewarding, sources (such as social interactions with friends). *This constitutes a reflexive negotiation of intimacy.* Hence, rather than being a narcissistic process, observing estranged ties can be seen as part of a process involving the evolution of emotional competence. Rather than a culture of narcissism, I believe that this points toward a culture of reflexive intimacy.

First-hand judgement

It has now been established how Facebook affords easy access to information which would be technically difficult and socially inappropriate to gather through other mediums. There is also a qualitative difference in the manner in which this information is subjectively received and given meaning on Facebook.

> Oh, it's different from someone saying to you 'oh this person is engaged', but if you actually look at a picture it's the first hand information that you're seeing with your own eyes.
>
> Odette

Odette compares hearing about an event second- or third-hand to seeing images of the event 'first-hand'. There is also an implicit medium comparison. In the former case the channel of information is spoken-word, in the latter photographic evidence. While, in the former case, Odette must depend on the judgement of another, in the latter she can constitute the meaning of something with her own subjective gaze, with her 'own eyes'. Sally echoes this distinction:

> I mean I know that there's a group of my girlfriends back home, where we'd catch up. ... And a lot of it would end up talking about these things. And like I said before you say, 'ohh who are they dating. Ohh I've never met them, tell me about them'. And they'll be like, 'ohh I don't know much'. Someone else in the group might know a bit about them. And – and, um, they'll usually tell you, like, 'ohh she's pretty, she's a bitch', you know, those sort of things. And, like, 'she works here, she studies this'. Those sort of things. So, you usually get it through like second, third hand kind of gossip normally ... And you have to kind of rely on their judgement. And so here it feels like you can make the judgement, 'cause you've seen the photos and stuff yourself.

Sally's explanation helps clarify 'first-hand judgement', the ability to apply one's own subjective meaning in a seemingly direct fashion to some social object. Both Sally's and Odette's examples describe information that comes from outside their immediate life-worlds, 'distant objects'. In both cases, in order to access this information they would normally have to 'catch up' with friends, and those with access to other social spheres could then supply gossip. This was the means of attaining information about weak and distant ties. In affording a new means of gathering such information, Facebook also allows for a new means of judging it, because it is not 'brought' to a social meeting by a 'middleman' and filtered through his or her subjectivity. Facebook empowers 'first-hand subjectivity' when it comes to information gathering. In the previous chapter this was touched on by Penny while describing photographs posted by distant ties: 'You can actually place it, and you can get your own sort of value for it, and you can sort of feel with the image'.

As well as subjective empowerment, first-hand judgment mobilises questions about what is true and what is real. The subjective position becomes a vehicle for seemingly objective judgements. Sally, explaining why she will show her roommate Facebook photographs of people he does not know, comments: 'Facebook is really good to kind of remind you, or give evidence to your friend, that it's actually true'. This can work both ways. That is, people can use their own first-hand judgement to judge the truth of something, and submit their own claims to the first-hand judgement of others. For example, although Sally never would usually post pictures of her partner on Facebook, she has moved to a new state, and now posts pictures of her long-distance boyfriend so that her new, proximate friends can see him, because they 'didn't know what he looked like'. Sally thus submits evidence of her boyfriend to the first-hand judgement of her peers.

First-hand judgment exists as the mode of perceiving many forms of information on Facebook. Hence, if a person witnesses a conversation between two friends contained within a status-update thread, he or she is witnessing it first-hand. In offline life this conversation may have happened outside this person's immediate experience, and he or she would have had to hear about it second- or third-hand. Take another example: If a person navigates to a friend's profile and sees that this friend 'likes' a particular Facebook page, say, devoted to a particular political party, this information is received first-hand. This is different to hearing that 'so-and-so' may be 'right-leaning'.

Interestingly, first-hand judgement takes the photograph as its cardinal object. This is a curious contradiction, because while in the status-update example above the resultant conversation may be said to actually occur on Facebook, photographs capture events which have occurred in some other place and time. They are more mediated, so to speak, than threaded interactions. Yet, no other medium acts so power-fully to 'give evidence' to participants' first-hand judgement about the lives of others. It is understandable, then, why scholars have found that SNS users inevitably seek out photos as the objects which can tell them what is 'really happening' in a person's life (Pempek, Yermolayeva, & Calvert 2009).

Various writers have explored the reality effect which photographs convey (Sontag 1973; Berger 1982; Barthes 1985). Photographic 'real-ness' is attributed to the way they seem to map or index reality without the mediation of any stylistic agency. I am more closely allied with writers who consider the photograph's reality effect in psychological terms. Photographs seem to portray images with the accuracy and complexity of our human eyes (Gunning 2008). Combined with this complexity and accuracy, I argue that photographs achieve their status as first-hand facts on Facebook in a *relational way*. That is, they work in relation to other modes of expression, such as status updates. Flash explains:

> Um, well photos, when you see a photo of someone like when you see them in real life it humanizes them. You know, they become a

flesh and blood creature, you know. You probably had no idea what I looked like before now. You know what I'm saying? You know, they become a flesh and blood creature, you know they – they're in the world, they're a person in the world. I mean of course if you put a status update one would assume you are a person in the world, but um...

Flash

Flash puzzles over the fact that while status updates would seem to suggest an intentionality behind them, and hence a person in the world, they do not transmit this understanding with the forcefulness and evidentiary power of photographs. So much so that photographs seem to carry an ontological capacity which status updates lack. Odette makes a similar comparison:

> I guess it's showing you in a real life event, photos are quite, um, what's the word, they're quite, um, I don't know what the word is but, um, it's different from, you know when you have in your news-feed 'Odette's attend Catherine's 18th birthday' or something it's – yeah, it's more of a tangible, um, look. It's a tangible image where you can actually see that you're at this venue with these people.

Odette

Here, Odette compares a status update to a photograph in order to establish how a photograph is 'tangible' and can evince 'real life'. Implicitly, photos possess an ontic dimension which status updates lack, a dimension with seeming ontological powers, evincing reality and, in Flash's case, 'being in the world'. But what is also important here, I think, is that in order to establish this ontic relationship, Odette makes a medium comparison. This is significant, I argue, because gathering information on Facebook is not a phenomenon composed of discrete moments conditioned by the experiential sequestration of media. Rather, the eye travels from one medium to another, such that each is implied in the other's capacity to give evidence and to evince 'realness'. Hence, the realness of a photograph is understood in comparison with how a similar event, such as 'Catherine's eighteenth birthday' could be depicted in another medium.

To summarise, Facebook empowers a form of subjective truth giving that I term 'first-hand judgement'. This mode of truth giving is subjective, but the subject feels like he or she is giving truth precisely because he or she is witnessing information which was previously obscured or translated through the judgements of others. First-hand judgement is ultimately the product of Facebook's ability to implode distance and presence, to bring heterogeneous, mysterious, far-flung people into the realm of observation. Photographs are the cardinal object of first-hand judgement because of the way they seem to depict reality with such accuracy. However, this reality is also the result of the experiential relationship between photos and other media. In the following chapter I explore how participants project first-hand judgement on others and feel objectified under this gaze. This can threaten them with socio-ontological insecurity, and compels them to produce their identities in a particular way. Hence, it is through first-hand judgement that an understanding of the panoptic subjectifying of Facebook users can proceed.

In the following chapter I discuss the problems people face in relation to the performance of connection and social surveillance. Performances of connection are made problematic, I argue, by contingencies having to do with intimate privacy and social presence. Here, notions of distance, presence, social capital, space, intimacy, spying, prostheses, and first-hand judgement, return – but in a problematic light.

7
When Insecurity Looms

Heterogeneous publicity: removing ties from time

In 2009 the New Oxford American Dictionary anointed 'unfriend' its word of the year. This term encapsulates the contradictory connotations 'friendship' has taken on in the SNS era. One would think 'friendships' involves a degree of commitment. Hence, the notion that a person can be quickly and easily 'unfriended' seems paradoxical. Drawing on her ethnography of Friendster, danah boyd (2006) argues that 'friend' connotes different things when reffering to 'actual' friendships or to SNS connections in general. Flash also explores this distinction:

> I mean, the term 'friend' is a loaded one, I'm not really sure it's a very appropriate one, but – because it presumes a kind of *intimacy* that isn't often there. You know, my mate in year seven who I haven't seen for – how many years would it have been now? – seventeen years, you know, isn't technically my friend any more. We don't know each other on a day-to-day basis.

Flash draws attention to the presence and absence of intimacy on Facebook, contextualised in terms of friendships. In using the example of an old 'mate', he also alerts us to how intimacy and friendship must be understood through reference to social context. Finally, in contrasting this decades-dormant connection with friends whom he shares day-to-day interactions with, he implies that both *space* and *time* are central to intimacy. That is, intimacy is fostered through forming regular dialogical spaces. How are these factors – degrees of friendship, intimacy, context, space and time – influenced by Facebook? Intimacy is made problematic, I argue, because users connect with a heterogeneous amalgam of social ties who posses different gradations of intimacy and hail from different social contexts. People fix these ties in a bounded public space wherein they can access one another. However, this process removes certain ties from time. That is, from the temporality of consciousness, which constitutes awareness of them, and from the temporality of dialogical space, which fosters intimacy between them. In this chapter I discuss the problematic consequences of this, first in terms of intimate privacy, then in terms of social presence. First, though, I address how my participants construct their heterogeneous networks.

When considering these networks, participants use phrases such as 'genuine friends', and 'second and third-tier friends'. I discerned four 'levels' of Facebook 'friend', each qualified in different ways with regard to intimacy. The first, strongest level of friendship, describes friends who often share private, dyadic interactions, are comfortable interacting with one another, interact both online and offline, have a detailed history, and share similar interests and values. Second-level friends are less meaningful to each other, have less of a history, do not necessarily share values, and interact only on occasion, but they nevertheless value Facebook as a means of 'keeping in touch' (recall the discussion of distant ties given in Chapter 5). Third-level connections do not merit the term 'friend' in its intimate sense. They have a modicum of meaning, a general 'liking' and 'good will' based on fleeting encounters, but share no in-depth knowledge of one another, and hardly ever interact. On the fourth level reside ties who are so weak they possess no meaning and have been completely forgotten. Bret describes these as 'dead wood in my social universe'.

Apart from the first 'level', these gradations have the capacity to become a 'grey area' as time passes: a forgotten, undefined audience. This is particularly likely to happen the weaker the tie, and is most definitely likely with 'dead wood'.

Beyond their close friends, my participants describe a host of social contexts from which they draw their Facebook connections. Here, I am not only interested in describing some of these contexts, but also in conceptualising how and why they became Facebook friends. A similar approach was taken with regard to distant and estranged ties in Chapters 5 and 6. Participants friend ties when they 'embed the self', show 'general good will', 'promote cultural production', 'network', 'feel obliged', and 'structure liminality'. 'Embedding the self' involves friending others when one has moved into a new social space, so as to develop new friendships and inculcate oneself in the social experience of a particular locale:

> I've just moved to Melbourne, so, um, a couple of people at uni that I've had decent chats with, you know, like after class we've talked for about half an hour or something, I've gone yeah I'll find them and friend them. Or, um, ah, mutual friends: so people that, like, there's a few groups of friends that I have over here, and as I'm meeting more of the people in those groups, and since I already hung out with them a few times, I'll look for those people cause I think I'm going to see them a few times.
>
> Sally

Participants also report friending people because when they first meet there is a sense of 'general good will'; hence, they return this good will by becoming Facebook friends:

> One of my other friends introduced me to a girl, Shay, who I just added last night and, um, we do literature together and she's doing lit as her breadth and she seems a really nice girl, so I added her, because I've met her and I talked to her for a little bit and she seems really, really nice. So she's been added.
>
> Penny

Both Bret and Odette are professional 'producers', Bret being a dramatist, and Odette a journalist. They utilise Facebook to 'promote cultural production'. Although, this can be a frustrating process, as Bret illustrates:

> It seems like more people that I know, or I – I agreed to be friends with and now they're hassling me about once every six months about some shit show that doesn't actually excite me, and the whole thing feels like a weird marketing exercise. Um, which, you know, every six months to a year I'm guilty of as well if I'm doing a show or involved in something I will bacon people, you know, or spam people or bacon them or whatever. And try and kind of hustle it out that way as well.

Bret friends people in order to promote his shows, and becomes susceptible to the pros and cons of 'bacon', self-promotional advertisements sent by friends through Facebook (a play on 'spam'). Band promotion provides another common example of this phenomenon. Bands drove the early emergence of MySpace when they discovered they could utilise the easy, low-cost access to social capital it provided (boyd 2008a). Today, there are many bands who have Facebook 'pages', and utilise their social networks to promote their music. Facebook affords the conflation of amateurism, professionalism, and casual sociality.

Participants also use Facebook to network with those they share a broader interest with, or can reap professional opportunities from. Sally has friended strangers from a volunteering organisation she is passionate about. Bret networks with fellow artists and drama enthusiasts. Odette networks with others in the media industry. In this sense, Facebook is less like a social network site, and more like a Usenet community, in which likeminded strangers would connect.

Of course, participants connect with people out of social obligation and decorum. For example, Bret describes having to accept certain friend requests in order to remain part of the artistic community on which he relies for social and cultural patronage. Odette provides a more general example:

> If you reject someone's friend request that's got a certain, um, it's going to have a certain impact on the consequence, so sometimes it's easier to just accept them if you don't want to rock the boat, um, yeah, I guess that happens in real life as well if someone wants your phone number and you just give it to them but you don't really – you're not really going to plan to talk to them, be in – be in communication with them so you just accept in that moment to avoid an awkward situation.

Interestingly, Odette suggests that people accept requests that they see as obligatory, even though they are mindful of the fact that they are likely to become dead wood through a lack of future interactions.

A highly common reason for friending others relates to a specific kind of 'liminal' social context:

> You're friends with one or two people and they're going out in a group, and those group things sometimes there's, you know people that you've got mutual friends but you don't really know. You've gone out, you've had a few drinks, you've gone to the pub or something together, but, yeah, you don't have that constant contact with them,

you don't work or study with them, you don't see them regularly. And, um, and yeah, and you might not even see them out again. Or, you know, but you might. And, yeah you just have a good time with them that time so you Facebook friend them.

Sally

Sally meets a latent tie at the 'pub', a locus of fun and social recreation, and they have a good time together. They create the germ of mutual affection which could potentially lead to a more substantial relationship, hence they decide to become Facebook friends. Here, I argue, a liminal scene has played out. Theories of liminality in social encounters have their routes in anthropology and the study of rituals in which spontaneous sociality takes place beyond the influence of traditional social structures (Turner 1969). Here, liminality is defined as sociality at the 'threshold', 'boundary', or 'interstices' of structure. These ideas have been applied to contemporary social groups, in particular to subcultures which utilise 'psychedelic' environments, music, and mind-altering substances to catalyse liminal moments (St John 2006). Conceptualised as spiritual and ecstatic (Rill 2006; St John 2006), these occasions seem much more intense and 'anti-structural' than the quotidian 'nights out' in Melbourne's Inner North my participants enjoy. However, certain theorists argue that post-modernity is partly characterised by the diffusion of liminal enclaves throughout everyday life (Maffesoli 1996). Sociality which occurs at pubs, nightclubs, and parties can be thought of as possessing liminal qualities, such as spontaneous communion between strangers and the forming of proto-friendships. This kind of liminality is arguably empowered by the commodification of such leisure activities and the normalisation of 'making friends' in recreational enclaves.

However, as Turner (1969) argues, liminal moments are by nature transitory and quickly give way to the structured patterns of everyday life. Hence, if one wishes to 'carry on' liminal social connections, they too must be structured. Facebook aids in the 'structuring of liminality'.

The promise to structure a connection through Facebook takes on a ritualistic role at the close of the liminal scene. Odette explains:

I guess it's when you're leaving that party in order to stay in touch with them, it's something you might say in conversation 'are you on Facebook', 'okay, I'll add you'. It's kind of a closing comment in your conversation that you might say to someone.

This kind of moment has become quite common, a kind of social rite aimed at accommodating the influx of voluntary relationships which younger people experience in contemporary times. Importantly, this ritual involves the negotiation of intimacy. 'I added someone that I met at a party', explains Odette, 'who I just thought was interesting, yeah, just a way to stay in touch without getting their mobile number'. Why avoid getting someone's number? This can be interpreted, I argue, as the avoidance of premature intimacy. Participants consider telephone interactions fit for a specific kind of dyadic intimacy between friends. Flash, for example, considers a 'genuine friend' to be someone he would interact with one-on-one or over the phone. Someone who is 'not a friend technically' is, Flash remarks, 'not someone I'd probably ring up'. Telephone intimacy expands to include related rituals, such as asking for someone's number. Facebook, being comparatively public, allows people to make the promise of further friendship without overstepping the bounds of intimacy.

When people travel they form connections which are in certain ways liminal: spontaneous, recreational, transitory. However, these ties are soon distanced as people continue on their journey or return home. Participants value Facebook as a means of staying in contact with these ephemeral personae. Sally expounds:

> Travelling, so – and it's hard to predict, like a lot of people that you meet when travelling, and some of them you keep in contact really well with, and that's what I love about Facebook cause I can keep in contact with my friends overseas really well. Um, whereas a lot of them you end up not interacting with them on Facebook or, um, you might email them or you might talk to them, and you prob – but you're most likely not going to, you just have them there.

This is a common example of how Facebook facilitates the structuration of liminality as a way of resolving the distance generated by a particular kind of mobility. Sally points out that many of these ties become dead wood. They are 'just there': dormant nodes in her egocentric network, and yet, of course, potential audiences.

Some of these contextualised processes lead to the development of stronger ties. However, more often than not they lead to the accumulation of weak ties, 'third-level' friends and 'dead wood'. The promise to 'structure' a liminal connection may serve well as a ritual to negotiate intimacy and lubricate the passing of a social moment. However, future interactions with these ties are minimal.

Overall, this discussion points to the multitude of reasons why people may articulate various social contexts online and expand their Facebook networks. These are often innocent enough at the time, and do not reflect overriding narcissistic compulsions. However, as these ties leave the immediate spatio-temporal fields of one's regular conscious attention and social interactions they come to pose a problem for intimacy, at which time they need to be defined. Participants are burdened with audience definition. They enter a reflexive stage in which they begin to categorise and act toward their connections. The production of terms such as 'second-' and 'third-tier' friends is a symptom of this process which I term the 'bureaucratisation of connection'. Indeed, Facebook anticipates this necessity and affords functions to support it, such as subgrouped 'friends lists'.

In what follows, I consider these problems, first from the perspective of intimate privacy, and then from that of social presence. Both these contingent fields produce a sense of socio-ontological insecurity which drives how my participants behave in regard to Facebook.

Amorphous risk

In Chapters 1 and 2 I argued that privacy and intimacy are importantly related, yet an appropriate framework for this with regard to Facebook has yet to be adequately formulated. Literature suggests that SNS users are reflexive with regard to privacy (Livingstone 2008; Tufekci 2008a; boyd & Hargittai 2010; Madden & Smith 2010; Bateman, Pike, & Butler 2011). Various mediating factors influence this reflexivity, such as trust in the service and in one's connections (Dwyer, Hiltz, & Passerini 2007), confidence and skill at privacy setting (boyd and Hargittai 2010), a desire for the social and self-expressive rewards of publicity (Livingstone 2008; Tufekci 2008a), and a habitual deferment of the perception of risks (Debatin, et al. 2009). Furthermore, it is apparent that whether risks are of an immanently social nature – that is, whether they compromise social contexts – also influences privacy-related behaviour (Raynes-Goldie 2010). Here I add to these ideas, arguing that privacy and intimacy are influenced by social rather than 'amorphous' risks, that intimate privacy is undermined when participants 'lose possession of self', and that this is compounded by the nausea of witnessing the overt public intimacies of others.

In the camp of amorphous risk I place spyware, adware, phishing, government surveillance, cyber-predators, geo-tracking and the like. Flash reflects on these risks:

I'm not one to buy into conspiracy theories by any stretch of the imagination, but, you know, is my, is our information being used for, you know, marketing purposes, you know. How long will it be there? Who's looking at us? Who can see us? So, it's never completely private, anything you put on there.

Flash

This is a common response, evincing concern over hidden watchers, but rather unsure as to who these agents may be. Participants are aware that certain privacy risks exist, yet they find it difficult to define just what these risks are. In this sense they are 'amorphous': without definition. Because they are amorphous they are distanced, removed, fantastical – so much so that, as Flash remarks above, they come to resemble 'conspiracy theories'.

Participants are fuzzily aware of certain amorphous risks. They talk of 'internet scammers' and 'identity theft'. Some participants talk of 'stalkers' and 'stranger danger', and express concern over being located physically by these actors: 'They might not know you [but] they might know you are not home. ... they can go to the pub that you're at' (Sally). Drawing on in-depth interviews, Strater and Lipford (2008), find American undergraduates are also fearful of being located by strangers. Importantly, the online 'stranger' is an amorphous entity. Specific details are lacking, hence media-hyped generalities are used to fill in the blanks (Marwick 2008). Taking cues from the media, strangers come to be defined in terms of their dangerous, criminal, sexual motivations. Facebook worlds are good at complicating oppositions, and much could be said of the role of strangers in this regard. The antagonism between friends and enemies, argues Bauman (1990), constitutes a primary social opposition which produces and organises social knowledge. Strangers exist beyond this opposition; they could be friends, enemies, or neither. Their ambiguity makes them frustratingly hard to interpret and integrate into a social reality. This indeterminate, indefinable character applies to amorphous risks in general. However, staying on the topic of 'stranger danger', the casting of these characters as predators acts to solve and defer this hermeneutic dilemma by bringing the stranger within a familiar opposition, making him or her an *enemy*.

Participants do not take steps to define, understand, and protect themselves against amorphous risks. These risks do not seem likely or proximate enough:

I think people are kind of aware of it and you hear these media reports, um, but people want to be on Facebook so I don't think privacy – it's one of those things you don't really have to think about, and you don't think it's gonna effect you. I think that's what it comes down to.

Sally

This evinces the 'third person effect' thesis proposed by Debatin and colleagues, which argues that 'people expect mass media to have a greater effect on others than on themselves' (2009: 89). Specifically, the authors posit that Facebook users will ascribe the negative effects of using the service to others while ascribing the positive effects to themselves, that is, until they directly experience the former. 'I think it's just psychological' explains Sally. 'You think it's – it might happen to someone else but it wouldn't happen to you. You know, it's, I mean it's really one of those things people kinda know, um, that, yeah, that you just have to be slightly careful but sometimes they're not. ... Out of sight, out of mind, yeah'.

This is not the kind of 'reflexive balance between risk and reward' which Livingstone (2008) speaks of. The fuzzy acknowledgment of risks, the slotting of risks within a binary opposition (friend or enemy), the deferment of risks onto others – this speaks to an un-reflexive attitude.

In the above example, Sally is aware of these amorphous risks because of 'media reports'. Likewise, participants often discuss such risks in relation to 'seeing stories' and 'watching the news'. In a concomitant dual process the news media both produce risks and desensitise the population to them. Risks are spectacularised. They become, as Flash puts it, 'conspiracy theories'. Perhaps this is a prime example of how spectacle encourages passivity while abstracting subjects from their social and material conditions. The spectacle, writes Debord, 'is whatever escapes people's activity, whatever eludes their practical reconsideration and correction. It is the opposite of dialogue' (1994: 11). Witnessing the spectacular representation of risk becomes a false moment of reflexivity. In such instances momentary concern is assuaged with minimal effort and the projection of risks onto others. This undoubtedly serves the interests of institutions like Facebook, whose political economy depends on opening up access and multiplying risk. Hence, amorphous privacy illustrates the limits of a culture of reflexive intimacy as it plays out on Facebook and like SNSs. These limits are set by a familiar form of power – the spectacle – which finds purchase in a new and sophisticated online *despotif*.

Possessing the intimate self

Against amorphous risks, my participants show a great deal of concern with regard to social privacy risk, that is, the need to identify and act toward social contexts. In general, unlike amorphous risks, social risks on Facebook are systemically definable. Put differently: it is much easier to define unwanted audiences composed of intentionally friended social connections than to define those which are composed of, say, clandestine state bureaucrats. Here I wish to move beyond boyd's (2008a) definition of SNS friends as an 'invisible audience', which implies continuous evasion. Instead they embody a form of *virtuality*, a potential becoming. Deleuze and Guattari (1988) conceptualise the 'virtual' as that which is potential. Likewise, the theorist of architectural space, Brian Massumi (1998), views the virtual as 'change', as not a form, but the transition between forms. This seems to contradict the nature of architecture, which produces still-standing forms. However, architecture takes on virtuality, argues Massumi, through the concept of 'topology', the overview of changing still-standing forms. Focus shifts to the 'continuity of variation', and 'still-standing forms appears as residue of a process of change' (1988, 17). Similarly, audiences have two primary forms on Facebook: invisible and visible. However, people do not occupy one or the other, but are constantly transitioning, becoming visible or invisible. The potential becoming of an audience is supremely significant: If it will become, what it will become, and what consequences will result? Hence, audiences on Facebook are both overdetermined – they *will* become – and indeterminate – but where, when, and who?

A liminal connection who becomes dead wood, for instance, begins to transition from visible to invisible the moment he or she is friended. But, perhaps, when looking through one's friend list, that person is identified, becoming visible again, and this causes action. The friend is 'culled' from one's network. Alternatively, perhaps a watcher reveals herself by liking a status update:

> It will be like Harriet 'likes' this and it's like Harriet is my second cousin from New Zealand who I've seen four times in [the] last decade or whatever. The next minute you go 'wow, she's reading that, that's weird' and how much other stuff is she reading, you know, yeah.
>
> Bret

Here, Bret implicitly perceives the Doppler effect of an audience's transition from invisible to visible. He continues to elucidate the type of awareness which results from this:

> It's the strange kind of tip of the iceberg thing I guess or never actually knowing, you know, whenever you do get a response to the stuff

that you're doing, you – you kind of have to assume off the back that there's a whole bunch of other people who are reading or looking at stuff and not responding, um, that's the – yeah, the grey matter, the kind of – and – and that's really interesting.

'Grey matter' is apt. Each potential audience exists by merit of a consciously made connection on behalf of two people. In this sense both parties are aware of each other, even if this awareness has been buried. Hence, their lack of definition is the result of time working on psychology, on 'grey matter'. However, because such ties can become defined, as both parties still have access to each other, they are not completely obscured, not completely 'in the dark'. As a result, moments of indeterminate vision can occur in which people witness unexpected things because of the way weak ties are made visible in public systems such as the News Feed. Hence, many potential audiences on Facebook are neither completely in the light nor drowned in the darkness; they form a 'grey area'.

On the one hand, the grey area can be understood as a field of potential social context conflicts which demand to be defined. As argued in Chapter 2, not all context conflicts involve intimacy. However, when my participants imagine this grey area it worries them in a way which is deeply tied to intimacy.

> I don't feel like, for me it wouldn't feel safe to – to expose myself or to be actually genuinely emotionally vulnerable in that space because, yeah, because I don't feel like it is actually a enclosed or safe world in that way, um, and partly that's a function of me 'friending' people who aren't actually my friends, that they're more like they're acquaintances or they're just people who I know vaguely, um, who I wouldn't be that – or like I think I said my – some girl I went to school with in primary school, um, you know. So in a way I actually don't feel like it's a – a safe space to be actually intimate or vulnerable.
>
> Bret

Here, Bret draws attention to the weak ties which are easily forgotten, 'acquaintances' who are known 'vaguely', a grey area which makes emotionally vulnerable intimacies 'unsafe'. Odette supplies another example:

> Yeah, there's a few photos I've blocked from people, mainly guys that I don't want to see my photos, so I've chosen for them not to have

access to that. ... Mainly because they were romantically interested in me, so I didn't want to have them spying on my photos without my knowledge. It would just be creepy.

Implicit here is the realisation that a grey area exists, after which Odette defines the spying eyes of a problematic audience. This audience is constituted in 'romantic' terms, and in terms of photographs, which carry a particular intimate quality. In this case, Odette seeks to prevent the establishment of a voyeuristic, intimate gaze. In witnessing these photographs I did not see them as intimate. This reveals how intimacy can be a subjective construction based on the expectation of a particular performer–audience relation. More will be said of this shortly.

Why is intimacy so important here? Firstly, because intimate performances, secrets, relationships, photographs, and the like require a certain privacy to remain authentic. Secondly, and more importantly, because the idea of the 'intimate self' – more than, say, the 'professional self' or the 'artistic self' – moving outside of one's control jeopardises one's sense of socio-ontological security. As Bret and Odette imply, the intimate self, when exposed to the grey area, is 'unsafe', 'vulnerable', and the potential effects are 'creepy'. Flash elaborates:

I don't want everyone on there to know everything about me, you know, it's about keeping something for yourself, having a sense of self. Having a sense of privacy ... There's a line in an old Joni Mitchell song, I'm quoting: 'don't let your heart put on a show, don't give yourself away'. And I think that – I mean to each their own, everyone feels differently – but if – I don't want to give too much away. I want to keep something for myself ...

Notice the language of possession here, of not giving the self away, of keeping something for one's self. It seems this loss of personal information amounts to an actual loss of self. The self must not steal away into the ambiguities of the 'grey area'. One must keep 'possession of self', and this is particularly important when it comes to matters of the 'heart'. How does this logic follow? Recall the discussion of performative textuality given in Chapter 2. A performance of self on Facebook is a mediated artefact, a text which can be re-signified, re-*possessed*, in the hands of others. Trivialities become intimacies, jokes become offences, relationships become scandals. Because Facebook mediates the self so effectively, people become aware of the way in which the self as text is circulating beyond their control. The self *acts* beyond itself. With regard to the 'intimate self', my participants experience this as 'sickening' and 'anxious'.

To properly theorise this, I turn to John E. McGrath (2004), who considers the relationship between surveillance and performance. McGrath mobilises Artaud's concept of the 'double' – a representation of the self which we, ourselves, cannot see – to conceptualise what surveillance produces. For example various institutions such as banks and SNSs use 'dataveillance' (Lyon 1994) to collect personal information we cannot view. Institutions access this data to inform judgements on whether we will be denied, say, credit or medical care. If we are denied, then we have encountered our 'data doubles', who have come back to haunt us. McGrath grounds this process in performative theory, drawing on Derrida's and Butler's combined notion of performative iteration. These doubles are performances which can act beyond the intentions of their authors. Importantly, because these doubles can come back to haunt us, we come to fear the invisible spectre of our double.

> [W]e are placed across the border of a representational realm in which we cannot see ourselves, but in which we are nonetheless implicated, conjured. This representational realm-across-the-data-border evokes something in us – our double – which is intimately related to our fears and aporias, perhaps continuing beyond our lives, perhaps bringing about our deaths. (2004: 161)

Facebook causes people to feel insecure about their dispossessed 'intimate doubles'. They fear the intimate double acting beyond their controls, fear it returning in some new and compromising form. Like virtual audiences on Facebook, intimate doubles are virtual, in a state of becoming. The becoming potential of the audience parallels that of the double. For example, participants describe how their friends sometimes post photographs of them which are 'exposing', and which yield less than favourable evaluations. In this situation both an intimate double and an unwanted audience have been actualised. In a sense, when others possess photographs depicting us, they can be said to literally possess a doubled aspect of ourselves. They possess this aspect of the self as a material artefact and control and distribute it as they see fit. Here, to paraphrase Walter Benjamin, we see the work of intimacy in the age of digital reproduction!

Rather than the simple puncturing of a social boundary, it is this process of being doubled and of having one's double leave and return, which constitutes the social-privacy risk to intimacy. This phenomenon can only be partly understood through contextual integrity (Nissenbaum 2004) and situational performance (Goffman 1959), both of which focus on spatial boundaries and a singular, agentic self. These theories do not capture the fear of a 'double' who acts independently.

In response to this problem my participants neither want to completely circumscribe their intimate selves nor to fully publicise them. If they were to shut off every intimate interaction the benefits of publicly performing a connection would be negated. Hence, they develop 'safe' forms of rewarding public intimacy which do not articulate 'intimate selves' that could be dangerously dispossessed. These processes will be addressed in the following chapter.

The desire not to see

Facebook users desire to regulate their personal privacy and that of their social interactions and groups. Broadly, this can be termed the 'desire not to be seen'. Alternatively, when using Facebook my participants also experience the 'desire not to see', moments when they perceive information which they would rather not. Various factors make it particularly hard to regulate this experience. This subverts the agency of vision: the power to look away or not look at all. Altman (1983), argues that privacy is not just about controlling outputs, but inputs as well. Just as a lack of optimisation where informational outputs are concerned can cause psychological problems so, too, can a lack of optimisations of inputs. Hence, someone who achieves no sensory input may become, say, lonely, while someone who achieves too much may feel 'overloaded'. Inputs and outputs are dialectically related. Often a desire to expand one's social group (inputs) may lead to a loss of control over one's personal information (outputs). Inversely, one's personal information may be safe, but one may be subjected to unwelcome disclosures by others. Both problems occur on Facebook, but here I focus on the latter.

Here, the desire not to see is a consequence of having ocular, public access to someone. However, it frequently comes up in relation to indeterminate vision: moments of observation that are completely unexpected and often surprising, jolting, or even shocking. Odette describes how and where indeterminate vision can occur:

> Um, just in the friend's suggestion, um, can also I guess come up in the newsfeed, pictures of yeah, ex boyfriends or girlfriends can appear in the newsfeed if you – not – even if you're not friends with them, if you've got mutual friends it can still appear.

Here, Odette mentions two sites in particular, the 'friends suggestion box', which can appear in the right-hand banner of someone's profile, and the News Feed. The former can present suggestions of friends, whom one may have not wanted to be reminded about. The latter can aggregate and report on activities of people in one's heterogeneous network. Both operate according to protocols which are obscured from view. Odette also recognises how people may encounter the posts of those whom they may not even be Facebook friends with if they share a mutual tie. Odette continues to illustrate how these indeterminate moments can cause the desire not to see:

> I have another friend who's my housemate who has seen pictures of his ex-girlfriend come up, i.e. do you want to add this person as a friend, a friend's suggestion from Facebook and that's also made him upset, um, yeah, mainly just, yeah, people getting quite emotional about Facebook – Facebook doesn't know, you know, who your enemies or friends are, unless you tell them. So if, um, you're not friends with someone and they come up as a suggestion because you have mutual friends they can sort of stir up some emotion, um.... Yeah, well, um, yeah, my housemate who deactivated, this is the same person, said that, um, he felt, yeah, Facebook was in control of his life on Facebook. So, um, yeah, like this girlfriend that he didn't speak to anymore was appearing, um, with her new boyfriend who he also doesn't talk to.

Odette reports that eventually her housemate 'deactivated [his Facebook account] because he didn't like that lack of control'. The desire not to see can often be the manifestation of dredged-up pain. Such moments would not occur if these people had not reclaimed their connection through a public medium such as Facebook. Hence, this bespeaks the contradictions which arise from heterogeneous publics. Facebook networks subsume ties of all sorts: weak, strong, different, similar, reclaimed, sustained, and so forth.

The desire not to see can also exist as a pre-emptive feeling, when the behaviour of certain people is expected to cause negative emotions. After Bret broke up with his girlfriend, Mary, he found a new partner, Jane. This supplies an apt example:

> And I think a day later [Mary] was like 'oh, I just wanted to let you know that I've de-friended you on Facebook, um, this isn't because I hate you or anything but it's just for my own, um, peace of mind'

and I, what I read that to mean was that she just didn't want to see me gushing at some other girl or didn't want to see, you know, whatever. 'Tom and Sarah, blah, blah, blah, love each other so much and really, blah', you know, that kind of stuff. So she – she took us – took me out the picture and I kind of went 'yeah, totally fair enough'.

Bret

In empathising with her position, Bret describes Mary's understanding of how Facebook compromises the desire not to see. Mary would be psychologically harmed by any accidental observation of Bret's and Jane's affections. Hence, Mary pre-empts this subversion of visual agency and 'unfriends' Bret. Again, the contradictions of heterogeneity are at play. Although Mary has recently broken up with Bret, and they probably share very strong bonds, she has moved away from him. They no longer inhabit the same regular spaces.

In these examples, intimacy has an important role. The desire not to see is caused by intense emotions, with their roots in interpersonal relationships. The desire not to see is partly the consequence of the visibility of people who are different and distanced, and who mobilise negative emotions routed in intimate contexts.

People may also experience the desire not to see when they witness certain kinds of performances of connection which fail to negotiate intimacy. This dimension of the desire not to see is different to those explained above, as the observer often may share little personal history with those he or she observes. I call this 'nausea'. John explains:

I find it nauseating to get statements like 'X has just said goodbye to her sister and is already sad'. I don't need to know, you know, I think just keep that inside. The over-emoting in a public space, to people who genuinely don't care and I would be one that genuinely doesn't care.

Nausea is an adverse reaction to the public display of affection. Bret and Penny elaborate:

The other thing that makes me feel awkward is if people are overly gushy and positive and lovey-dovey, like if, you know, couples for example commenting on each other's updates and being all cutesy like that, that makes me feel a little bit ill and gross and that again seems like a – because I was thinking about this, like I'm totally fine with public displays of affection but cyber displays of affection, it feels a bit weird.

Bret

A few friends decided to be horrifically loving toward one another and comment on their previous posts, in the most overly loving manner possible on each others walls. Unfortunately for the 700 or so people connected to these two, the entire thing appeared on our walls!

Penny

Witnessing couples 'over-emoting', 'gushy', being 'lovey dovey', and 'horrifically loving' in a public space causes a feeling of nausea, a 'gross', 'awkward', 'weird' feeling. Participants have at least one or two romantically linked friends who fail to negotiate intimacy in this way. They are not common, nor do they encourage imitation, yet, one cannot help but sometimes stumble across their exchanges. Nausea suggests a disquiet about public intimacy that goes against the idea that such intimacy is the norm, the narcissistic currency of attention. In reality, the relationship between privacy, publicity, performance, observation, and intimacy is far more complex than this idea suggests. As will be argued in the following chapter, people are not only nauseated by such forms of public intimacy, they organise their connections – which can involve culling them, or blocking them – and in this way 'circumscribe vision' such that they will not have to bear it. Likewise, these strategies prevent those occasions when the desire not to see excavates negative interpersonal emotions.

To summarise, participants begin their Facebook careers by adding many ties from different social spheres. As time passes they encounter problems having to do with social privacy. Chief amongst these is the desire not to see, to circumscribe vision and regain one's visual agency. Also, participants experience the feeling that one's intimate self-aspects have flown beyond one's control, have been doubled. This creates a kind of socio-ontological insecurity. I now turn to how heterogeneous publicity and mediated social presence amplify this phenomenon.

Socio-ontological insecurity

Facebook has become an incredibly important tool for communicating with meaningful others and reproducing social life. Facebook has come to facilitate public points of contact with a social world which deeply matters to my participants. These people feel strongly about making an appearance online and being recognised by their Facebook friends. However, Facebook is a mediated public in which modes of appearance are made problematic. This is compounded by the fact that audiences are virtual. They may or may not be watching. Given the heterogeneity and size of people's Facebook publics there is no guarantee that this economy of attention will include oneself. My participants struggle with this divergence between a social world which matters and a mode of social presence which is impoverished and escapes easy understanding. This can lead to 'socio-ontological insecurity'.

Here, I form explicit linkages between social presence and social ontology. I consider social ontology to be an understanding of how human identity is constituted and nourished through experiences with others (Theunissen 1984). When participants feel that their online social identities are removed from a space of interpersonal 'presence', these identities feel insecure. In this state they come to question the 'reality' of Facebook and return to privileging offline life as 'real', while Facebook becomes 'false'. The reader will be sceptical of problematic dichotomies such as 'real/false', especially given the fact that online and offline life are richly entangled. I do not see the offline world as any more real than its online counterpart. Following Goffman (1974), I see these as indicative of 'frames' which my participants take on in order to make sense of certain experiences. Frames are sets of rules which generate the pragmatic reality of specific situations. Frames organise our experience. Chess rules, for example, frame the way we experience chess. Goffman argues that what we consider to be 'real' is based on how an experience is framed and how this relates to other frames.

> When we decide that something is unreal, the reality it isn't need not itself be very real, indeed, can just as well be a dramatisation of events as the events themselves – or a rehearsal of the dramatisation, or a painting of the rehearsal, or a reproduction of the painting. Any of these latter can serve as the original of which something is a mere mock-up, leading one to think that what is sovereign is relationship, not substance. (1974: 560)

The roles we play are copied from one situation to the next, a performative patterning which integrates media experiences. The social situations of offline and online life are equally framed and staged. Their equivalent reality effects are relationally constructed. The fact that participants sometimes consider offline activities more real depends on how they frame these activities in relation to Facebook. These frames – that is, 'the rules' of 'real' experience – are based on *expectations on interpersonal fulfilment through the establishment of dialogical spaces*. When these expectations are not fulfilled in the online realm, then it is framed as 'unreal' in relation to the offline world. This can happen when participants encounter social-presence problems which jeopardise the establishment of dependable dialogical spaces.

In one sense, socio-ontological insecurity is the feeling that, unlike corporeal presence, one's online presence is always diminishing. This provides an unconscious impetus for continually performing the self on Facebook. Odette reflects on this when considering Facebook users:

> Yeah, it's like it's – it's this, um, it's this embodiment of themself that they need to manage and keep returning to – has to remain active because it – because it's part of their identity and even though obviously you've got real people in your real life that you can see face-to-face, yet they still pursue this, um, this sort of yeah, casual communication and interaction with people.

Online identities are an 'embodiment', different from what Odette calls 'face-to-face' and 'real life' embodiment, but still significant. Odette evinces how, unlike the physical body – whose enduring presence is taken for granted – on Facebook presence must be continually worked at and returned to. Notice the compulsion to keep a fresh presence online, to 'remain active'. This compulsion results from experiencing a social embodiment which matters, but which is also fundamentally 'elsewhere'. Contrast this to the physical body, which is experienced as an immanent continuum. The compulsion to regularly update one's online presence is, in part, a desire to 'fill up' the online self with subjectivity, to make it, as Penny remarks, 'worth it all', rather than let it become a separate object.

Unlike the previous Facebook profile interface, the current 'Timeline' interface emphasises the temporality of online social presence. On the one hand, it emphasises the past and asks users to recapitalise on their old posts. On the other hand, it emphasises the present, the need to constantly update. This is only one example of a whole phalanx of applications and device innovations which seek to capitalise on the need for temporal presence, compressing space and time.

> There are so many more applications that are now integrated with Facebook than there was previously. Applications such as Instagram, and Twitter are combined and allow for information to be passed

between them freely [...] So I'm sharing random photos and tweets with my friends that I otherwise wouldn't be sharing on the same platforms. I think it's useful, because it can be hard to track so many accounts across different platforms if you have friends that want to follow your 140 character adventures or to see some amazing picture you took. It's faster, easier and the information is 'liked' by your Facebook friends (keeping them in the loop) and also viewable by the other users of the various platforms from which the information originated.

Penny

Here, Penny links the convergence of wireless Internet, mobile phones, SNSs, and third-party applications. She values how phones can keep open Facebook's real-time chat function. That is, a kind of 'streaming', mediated dialogical space. She values taking photographs with Instagram, which automatically posts images to Facebook, as this can act as a form of nearly instantaneous communication and allows her to receive nearly instantaneous social recognition when her photographs are liked.

Participants are also compelled to update their online personas when they internalise the first-hand judgement of others. Through their own experiences, participants know that first-hand judgment seeks out truth, specifically, performances which appear as 'facts' and can act as 'evidence'. If first-hand judgment falls on an absence of such performances than the 'truth' of someone's identity as it is subjectively perceived is found lacking. To acknowledge the potential surveillance of first-hand judgers is to be disciplined by their gazes to produce the truth of one's self. The punishment for not producing this truth is socio-ontological insecurity.

'I do assume there is an audience', remarks John, 'because nothing that happens on Facebook is private'. But what kind of audience is assumed? Before audiences are defined in any substantive way, I argue, they are defined as first-hand judges. This definition does not come from 'reading' the cues given off by this audience. Audiences are invisible to begin with. Rather, this expectation comes from a projection of one's own experience with first-hand judgment. For example, Sally is concerned with being spied on. Asked why she thinks this is happening, she replies, 'I mean I think a lot of it comes from me doing it myself'. As argued in the previous chapter, people become conscious of first-hand judgment when they engage in information gathering which would be impossible or inappropriate in other mediums. That is, when they 'spy'.

The common expectation that others spy on us amounts to the simple acknowledgment of a first-hand gaze which is ubiquitous and original to the medium in question.

Participants often post content, anticipating the first-hand judgment of their friends. Sally, for instance, posts photographs of her new boyfriend so that her distant friends can be given evidence as to how he looks. Bret, Sally, and Penny post images of their travelling exploits so others can see their exotic adventures first-hand. Recalling the previous chapter, photographs are the cardinal object of first-hand judgement, as it seeks 'evidence' and photographs have an uncanny capacity to depict 'reality'. It is in this way that first-hand judgement demands the production of the truth of people's identities, and why people indeed consider such a 'truth' to exist and be important.

This shifts perspective on the argument that enhanced social presence on SNSs 'limit' the degree to which people can experiment with their identities (Zhao, Grasmuch and Martin 2008), forcing people to be 'honest' (Donath & boyd 2004). Certainly, first-hand judgement conditions 'truth', but 'truth' should not be considered the result of a *limiting* force. Rather, a panoptic regime is at play in which the gaze of others entices the *production* of the self within a truthful paradigm. It is this mode of being which has been constituted by the very nature of Facebook – specifically, the way it transforms observation into a 'truth-act'. The invisible eyes which constitute Facebook ask people to present themselves 'objectively'. Reflecting on the panopticon's disciplining of the subject, Foucault (1977) writes that '"subjects" [are] presented as "objects" to the observation of a power that [is] manifested only by its gaze' (1977: 188). Disciplinary power, Foucault writes, 'produces domains of objects and rituals of truth' (1977: 194). This is exactly what the projection of first-hand judgement does, compelling actors to objectify themselves, to convince others as to the truth of their lives.

The disciplined desire to produce the self in this manner contributes to the insecurity felt when people slip behind in their online updates. However, the compulsion to 'produce the self' in an evidentiary manner can often frustrate participants. The feeling that one has been objectified can make participants yearn for a different kind of sociality, in which identity is conveyed 'dialogically' rather than through an exchange of objects. I return to this shortly.

Alienation through connection

Um, yeah, the meaning is that you have a life really, that you have a social life, um, that you actually see these friends you're friends with on Facebook in reality. Yeah, that's the main – that's the main value.

Odette

Participants want to show – moreover *prove* – to others that they have a 'life'. Better yet, that they have a 'social life'. Hence, a relational existence is at stake, a 'social ontology'. This involves disclosing 'evidence' such as photos, friend connections, invitations to social occasions, and the like. However, participants are not only concerned *that* you were doing something, and *that* it was with others, but '*what* you were doing and *who* you were with' (Odette, my emphasis). Hence, as well as showing the existence of a life, participants want to make sure it is the right kind of life, a life which will identify with others, which will bring esteem, increase social capital, and secure regular performances of connection, thus safeguarding against future insecurities. Hence socio-ontological insecurity has ontological and discursive dimensions.

These are primarily analytic categories. Yet, this analytic duality affords an understanding of how socio-ontological insecurity takes different forms. Hence, someone may appear or feel 'discursively stable' but 'ontologically precarious'. Bret gives an example of such a state of affairs:

I went – went to the Baths for a spa on Friday and overheard this – these two strangers talking about film script, writing their scripts and then developing a novel or something and I was sitting there going 'wow, this is really surreal to be sitting here listening to two strangers talk about the kind of stuff that I spend a lot of my time talking about, but I don't know who they are, so I'm not connected in this'. ... I kind of said to this guy, um, a couple of minutes in or something 'are you talking about film and stuff' and he was like 'yeah, I see you're writer' and it was 'yeah, I do that stuff' and I was like 'yeah', and he was like 'what's your name', and I was like 'Bret Jermaine' and he's like 'I'm Jake Easter', and I was like 'ohh crap, you're my Facebook friend and I should know you' ... I was like 'this is the first time I've ever seen, but I know from Facebook that you're really into posting links to 80s music videos on YouTube like heaps and that's mainly what I know about you'. And oh weird, and it was this – that was the most weird moment going 'oh so you're Jake Easter, I'm already your friend on Facebook', oh I don't – and that means nothing.

Bret realises that he knows Jake discursively, in terms of the persona he has created on Facebook, however he knows nothing of any depth about who Jake 'is'. They lack a socio-ontological connection. It is implied that such a connection comes from the kind of reciprocal sociality that throughout this study has been associated with interpersonal intimacy. Jake is a weak tie, although not entirely 'dead wood', as Bret takes an interest in his posts and, hence, they passively connect through cultural similarities. However, Jake and Bret have not disclosed one personal fact to each other or shared one amiable emotion, as even the most newborn of friends may do. Flash echoes these themes.

When I met Flash for our first interview, and after we had spent some time interacting, he remarked:

> Meeting you in the flesh today is quite different to our email contacts where we were just a few words on the page. I knew you were a person you knew I was a person, but it's a different interaction.

Transcending the formality and sterility of brief textual exchanges, Flash and I formed a friendly bond 'in the flesh'. Before our interview, Flash knew I was a person, but I had no 'being' until we had the chance for an interpersonal interaction. Flash continues this reflection with regard to a weak tie in his Facebook network to whom he was attracted and whom he eventually met in person:

> I mean, you know online when you see someone, whether it's attraction, whether its curiosity, whether you just see someone's photo on the – on the TV, or in the Facebook site it's very different to, you know, meeting them in the flesh in some ways. They become a real person. A *real* person.

I argue that this enhanced sense of 'reality' is not the product of physical co-presence in and of itself, as an *enhanced capability for interpersonal social interaction*. A person, once a 'distant object' of observation, comes to be positioned within a dialogical space. Such a space allows for interpersonal intimacy and, hence, a meaningful connection. While contemplating his experience with Jake at the baths, Bret remarks that this 'almost make[s] me feel slightly more connected and slightly alienated at the same time'. He continues:

> I think I've got, whatever it must be, around 450 friends right now, but if only about 40 of them are actual people who I would want to

hang out with, um, 90 plus percent of those people, to be informed about what they're up to can be a bit alienating

Alienation through connection is a paradoxical feeling of being connected to people without any sense of interpersonal intimacy. This is understandable, given the size of many people's Facebook publics, the heterogeneity of relational contexts therein, and the limited amount of interpersonal interactions a person can realistically engage in. But notice the implicit projection in Bret's words. He is both alienated from these people, and they are alienated from him. In the presence of Jake, Bret feels his own lack of interpersonal being in Jake's eyes, causing awkwardness. 'Oh crap', he reports thinking, 'I should know you'. This is a consciousness of oneself as ontic, but not ontological. As a body with no soul. As a free-floating signifier with no thought act behind it. Hence, even when participants' profiles are rich with self-disclosures they can feel separated.

The accumulation of broad, heterogeneous audiences seemed innocent enough at the time. However, these may become a source of insecurity. This has been discussed in terms of the 'dispossession of self' and 'doubling'. While this phenomenon entails the self moving beyond one's grasp, alienation through connection entails the emptying out of the self – the seeing of oneself, through the eyes of another, as lacking in being. It is no surprise, given these existential problems, that people respond by 'culling' their weak ties. This and other techniques of negotiating intimacy will be discussed in the following chapter.

Where is the real world?

The way in which Facebook mediates people, combined with the way people embody and objectify themselves, sometimes leads to a form of socio-ontological insecurity which favours the offline world as the site of the 'real'. Not all participants reported this feeling, and some participants said they felt this way at some times and not others. This is because Facebook obviously offers meaningful things which the offline world does not, such as the ability to reproduce groups through novel public identification, and the ability to reclaim and sustain distant ties. It seems only when people's online embodiments seem unsatisfactory, or unsuccessful in terms of the performances of connection they seek, that they have their social ontologies challenged and their 'reality frames' transformed. Odette clarifies:

Yeah, I guess Facebook is sort of a false world really. It's a – yeah, it's a non-reality and you don't want to get too consumed in it, you want to be in reality and then share your actual life onto this sort of false world that's there on your computer screen.

One thing which makes the offline world 'reality' and Facebook 'false' is the immediacy people enjoy in their offline social encounters. Recall Odette's earlier comment in which she equates 'real life' to seeing people 'face-to-face'. People can become frustrated by the way in which Facebook is so different from such encounters, as Bret explains:

Um, but you know I constantly kind of feel like maybe I should just, you know, settle my accounts and just send all of my actual friends a message with my phone number saying 'fucking call me, let's go have a coffee, please', you know?

Bret's desire for immediacy stems from a desire for interpersonal interactions. It is the mediation of the interpersonal which can become so frustrating. Sally echoes this when she recounts a conflict between Facebook and face-to-face interaction:

Um, I was at a club the other night and there was a couple of – I could see them, 'cause you know you have it on the phone now, so, I'd spoken to them and then I'd walked off and there was about three of them and they were standing in a group in like a pub, pub-club. And, um, all three of them were on Facebook while there – there – they were together...I thought [that] was really weird, and then I tried to think if I'd ever done something like that, and I have checked Facebook while with other people and I thought that was really kind of weird. Um, but I have done that. Not quite in a club sense, but yeah.

Sally

Here, Facebook, a mediated environment itself, is placed between physical bodies, actually mediating social presence within a physically co-present situation. Sally is unnerved by this subversion of the immediate by the mediated. Suddenly, the value of all those convergent technologies which facilitate immediate online sociality is inverted. In this moment a privileged relation to the offline world is revealed.

In order to further explore the relationship between social ontology and immediacy, I want to turn to the work of Michel Theunissen, in particular his classic text, *The Other: Studies in the Social Ontology of Husserl, Heidegger, Sartre, and Buber* (1984). Theunissen discusses two different socio-ontological paradigms: 'transcendentalism', which he views as chiefly represented by Husserl (but secondarily Heidegger and Sartre), and 'dialogicalism', chiefly represented by Martin Buber. Inspired by Buber (1970), Theunissen sees the former social ontology as that of an 'I–It' relationship, and the latter in terms of an 'I–Thou' relationship.

Transcendentalism, Theunissen argues, holds that the other is always first taken as an object. The other is first and foremost constituted ontically as something in the world. This is because transcendental philosophy sees all exterior phenomenon as derived from the subject–object constituting powers of the transcendental ego. Hence, the Other is not so much a person, but an 'It', moreover, an 'It' derived from the 'I'. In Theunissen's opinion, Husserl's transcendentalism fails in his endeavour to show how the other as object becomes an Other as autonomous agent. Heidegger, Theunissen argues, makes further inroads in this respect, although fundamentally his concept of 'being with' is still only 'got at' through an objectification of the other in terms of the existential analytic of Dasein (the investigation of self-experience). The other remains an 'I–other'. Overall, then, in the transcendental perspective the other is subordinated because of a mediation. Namely, the mediation of beings as 'worldly objects'.

Theunissen constructs linkages between notions of mediation, objectification, and subordination. 'The I–It relationship is', he writes, 'a relationship of mastery and slavery' (1984, 273). That is, in denying the other the power to present his or her being first and foremost, without the need for the mediation of the world, without the need to be objectified, and in simultaneously asserting that the other is ultimately a derivative of the self, Transcendentalism relegates the other to a dominated, disempowered position. On Facebook, as has been argued, people can feel objectified under the invisible gaze of first-hand judges. This feeling makes them feel like objects, rather than beings, subordinate to the power of this gaze. Sometimes this is welcomed and submitted to as a way of producing the 'truth' of the self and gaining the socio-ontological rewards therein. But, as the above examples suggest, sometimes it makes participants feel objectified and alienated. As objects they become other people's prostheses, voyeuristically poached and given nothing in return. In the previous chapter I discussed how prostheses are things which are attached but not integrated; they are at the same time alienated and connected to people. Being an 'it' to someone else's 'I' is akin to being the estranged biography used to facilitate another person's self-realisation.

Against Transcendentalism, Theunissen posits Buber's dialogical ontology. Replacing the 'I–It' relation, Buber investigates the 'I–Thou'. These are distinguished spatially. While the former occupies the space of a single subjectivity, the latter occupies a space of inter-subjective immanence that Buber terms the 'between'. The between neither exists in the 'I' nor in the 'other'. That is, it is not a derivative of any one person's subjectivity. Moreover, it is not an objective 'third thing' which structures an encounter. Rather, it is a metaphysical nothingness. It is best understood as a kind of group ego: 'The Thou-I is, in a certain respect, the "true" subject' (1984: 279). Buber – writing long before the Internet – argues that actors must be spatiotemporally contiguous to form such a space. This affords a relationship of equality rather than subordination. The 'I–Thou' relation entails 'the community of partners of equal rank. Equality of level and of origin can only be reached in this way, that both partners meet each other in action or in passion' (1984: 278). Hence, Buber provides a framework with which to understand how space and social presence affects social ontology. As has been discussed, Facebook does not facilitate an a priori spatial equality. Audiences are virtual. They have, in this sense, the upper hand. This asymmetry causes first-hand judgement and the objectification of identities. Concurrently, people come to privilege offline, co-present spaces.

Can a dialogical space be created on Facebook? As the previous chapters explore, it can indeed. In fact, creating such a space through the performance of connection is one of the chief tasks in which my participants are engaged. However, given that Facebook is heterogeneous, complex, and attention is not only mediated, but can be scarce, these spaces are often stifled, lacking the kind of interpersonal depth which people desire.

Audience capture in an economy of attention

On Facebook at the moment of performance, a person's audience is virtual. That is, it is only potential, expected. The potentiality of an audience is strengthened depending on the regularity of posts a person receives from particular connections. Nevertheless, the possibility of not having an audience is worrying. This is the insecurity of not having one's life acknowledged to exist. What is the point of making oneself visible if there are no eyes to accept this visibility? Furthermore, it is the insecurity of not having this existence socially validated and incorporated into a social group. How can this happen without an audience which can avow, sanction, legitimise, and interact? To clarify, socio-ontological insecurity is not related just to performances which emanate from one's own profile, such as status updates. A person may, say, comment on a friend's content and still feel insecure about whether this comment has been acknowledged and validated until it has been replied to and an audience has become visible.

These issues are further complicated by the fact that one is not only unsure if someone is watching, but that there are potentially more interesting people to watch. In this sense, the requisitioning of gazes on Facebook seems like an 'attention economy'. This concept has been used in various fields, most thoroughly in the advertising industry. However, its basic principle remains relevant here, namely, that many information systems exist as a surplus, while human attention is scarce (Simon 1997). Hence, choices must be made as to what to consume with one's attention. On Facebook, information is publicly broadcast and persists through time. Yet, people are biologically and socially limited in their capacity to consume information (we must sleep and work), as well as personally inclined to choose some forms of content over others.

Asked about how it would feel to have a performance ignored on Facebook, John replied:

> I think that would be terrible – I know this is ridiculous but I think it would make me feel as if I was talking into a void.

Penny echoes this:

> I don't know, if I have something interesting to contribute then I will, if I don't then I don't because it's not interesting and I'm wasting other people's time and then they'll ignore me, which is sad.

These responses are evocative. Failing to capture the attention of an audience would be 'terrible', 'sad', both a feeling of 'talking into a void' – social nothingness and, hence, an insecure socio-ontological state – and of being 'ignored' – a lack of social sanction, of recognition, acceptance, validation. Sally picks up this thought, stating 'You kind of think, well maybe people weren't interested in what you said or don't think it's funny, or something like that'. These themes are further reflected by

Odette, who signals the satisfaction of receiving comments: 'I guess it shows that people are looking at your photos, they're looking at your profile. Your profile is not just there for yourself'.

The need for recognition is epitomised in the various tie functions Facebook offers. These, such as 'likes', signal that an audience has both observed a person's content and 'agrees with' its substance. Sally explains:

> I mean with Facebook changes on your homepage you don't – not necessarily guaranteed people see your posts on their homepage anymore but [receiving likes] shows that either they check your profile or they've read it. It's kind of – at least you know people are actually reading it out there even if they haven't commented. Which I guess is kind of the aim in a way in Facebook. You want people to actually know these things that you're saying. Yeah, so, I like it. If a status update goes past without people liking it it's kind of a weird feeling.

Liking provides reassurance that an audience exists. Notice, though, how Sally has come to depend on liking as socio-ontological assurance. Hence, if she enacts a performance – in this case a status update – and it 'goes past without people liking it' she feels 'weird'. This is a mild feeling of socio-ontological insecurity.

The need to assuage insecurity also aids in understanding people's Facebook rhythms. As discussed last chapter, people's access to their Facebook lives is interstitial. Participants cannot be on Facebook all the time. After intervals offline, they return to Facebook to keep up to date with what their friends are doing. Moreover, they return to check on their own posts, hoping that their endeavours at catching an audience are successful. Key properties of socio-ontological insecurity are 'frequency' and 'compulsion'. This is driven by the desire to keep one's own presence 'fresh', as well as by the need to be assured of the presence of one's audience. Central to this common experience is a kind of delayed gratification. When gratification is delayed, quasi-solipsism looms, and this combination causes people to continue to check back on their performances. Deferral of gratification is not infinite – as I show in the next chapter, people establish reliable patterns of sociality on Facebook – but as long as these mediations are mobilised there is the potential for disappointment and insecurity. This potential, a fundamental problem for the performance of connection, drives much of the novel behaviour Facebook users engage in.

The compulsive need for recognition and validation which socio-ontological insecurity manifests suggests that Facebook encourages the emergence of the 'weak ego' which Lasch, Turkle and others associate with narcissism. Facebook reveals how aspects of selfhood have become insecure. The need for validation, however, should not be overly dramatised as a yawning chasm within the self. It is an important problem, but one that users self-consciously grapple with and invent solutions to. Also, making the self visible, and achieving public recognition is only part of the story. This is but one step in a process by which people seek to establish interpersonal spaces through public visibility.

The possibility of no response and, hence, the haunting potentiality of socio-ontological insecurity, drives forward particular behaviour which mobilises intimacy in performances so as to elicit replies. Hence, an audience must be appealed to through a 'careful' process of choosing content. This is how the problem of socio-ontological insecurity is resolved. The economy of attention on Facebook must be something invested in and, hence, the need to appeal to people's interests which, as discussed in the previous chapter, involves the claiming and crediting of social capital. It is only through the accumulation of specific kinds of capital that this economy of attention can be harnessed and insecurities assuaged. The mobilisation of these capitals shall be discussed in the following chapter.

8
Negotiating Intimacy

Facebook is influencing significant transformations in the nature of social intimacy and public life. Bret is struck by this while reflecting on his time using the service:

> I feel like I had done a lot of talking about Facebook before I joined it because everyone else was excited about it for six months or 12 months earlier, and then for the first few months of joining it I did a hell of a lot of talking about it and it was really exciting and it did feel like it was this paradigm shift, right. And it's – it's really hard to say what it was, but it was – it was amazing to see how different people use it and that some people would become obsessed and update their statuses all the time and that – and that there was this whole, I guess new, social contract being evolved and yeah, levels of appropriate and inappropriate disclosure maybe. And I think some of that stuff is around, for example, how affectionate you are to – to your girlfriend or boyfriend in that sphere in a way that's shared and, you know, I think there is this – this new kind of social contract maybe that Facebook has – has created.

Bret describes a 'new social contract', relating this to issues of public intimacy such as romantic affection. Intimacy is related to 'disclosure'. Bret suggests that what is culturally accepted as an 'appropriate' public disclosure has changed. Yet, Bret is thinking about Facebook's nativity, and he understands that this social contract is 'being evolved'. As people spend more time on Facebook, developing rich online experiences, they come to encounter social problems which influence this evolving contract. That is to say, this contract continues to be 'negotiated'. People shift from an early stage of excitement in which they connect with many people, experiment with a public presence, and invest meaning and value into the social opportunities Facebook creates, to a later stage in which problematic experiences drive a change in intimate behaviour.

In the previous four chapters I have outlined what motivates the participants in my research to use Facebook, their social and self-expressive goals, and the problems which they face in reaching these goals. They want to perform connection in order to enjoy the fruits of sociality in and for itself. This can be especially rewarding where distant ties are involved. They also publicly perform this sociality in order to reflexively constitute and strengthen their social identities. As well as performing connections, people also gather information on their Facebook friends, a process which teaches them about their own level of exposure and the nature of their public identities in the eyes of different others. However, people encounter problems having to do with 'self-possession' and social presence that make the performance of connection and the gathering of information problematic in various ways. In order to solve these problems people engage in the 'negotiation of intimacy'. I use this term to describe a host of techniques which aim to both mobilise intimacies as well as protect and control them.

Organising connection

One way in which my participants resolve problems having to do with social privacy and socio-ontological insecurity involves the organisation of their connections. Users organise their connections such that there is a greater possibility of regular, rewarding performances of connection. In this respect, connections are alerted, mobilised, and positioned such that reciprocal social presence is ensured and socio-ontological insecurity is assuaged. While this process seeks to mobilise intimacy, users are also concerned with preventing intimate privacy problems and, hence, limiting intimacy. For this purpose connections are also organised so that the flow of information is controlled. Overall, an 'I–Thou' space is established and the danger of being doubled and deferred is put out of mind.

Participants gradually become less liberal when it comes to friending others. As Flash relates:

> I suppose I am warier – or at least more careful – about who I send Friend Requests to these days. When I first started using FB in 2007, I would send requests out to almost everyone in my extended social

circle – from close friends to people I'd had a laugh with at parties (but who I might never see again).

Interestingly, Flash touches on the structuration of liminal ties, and implies that he no longer sees merit in this kind of connection. Participants begin to place conditions on friending new connections. They need to have a 'working knowledge of them' (Flash). 'If someone tries to add me that I've never met before, I don't know who they are, then I won't accept that' (Odette). This allows them to establish a sense of interpersonal 'realness': 'I have to actually have seen you in real life there and talked to you, like, you have to exist. Like, some person from India tried to add me. We had no mutual friends, I've never seen them, I will not add you, I don't know who the hell you are, I'm not going to talk to you, goodbye' (Penny). John expounds on this:

> I like – I like to think of whatever I'm doing on Facebook kind of reflects some of my values and one of those values is that, um, when we – we genuinely engage in community we genuinely engage with each other. We don't just – I don't just have 2,000 Facebook friends to have 2,000 friends and I – and I think that's a big difference between me and say my niece, um, oh she has very few as well but her friends tend to have, you know, 1,000, 2,000, 3,000 friends. Now it's just impossible to – to engage with that number of people, um, and you can't have any sort of shared commonality with them other than a number and so I've gone – I've tried to go the other way and said 'well I'd rather have less people and – and know these people'.

Here, John is baffled by enormous networks because it is impossible to 'engage' with most of the people in them. John relates 'engaging' with 'community', a concept which also implies mutual knowledge about one another. Concurrently, John links 'knowing people' with 'shared commonality' such as similar values. As has been argued, similarities are crucial for the performance of connection. Using prior knowledge about someone as a condition for friending them, and as a mode of judging similarities, benefits the performances of connection. Also, John's desire for community bespeaks a desire for some basic level of interpersonal connection such that he does not feel alienated but connected to his Facebook audience.

In a related sense, a connection must have the potential for future sociality. For example, Flash must 'be able to foresee some kind of future relationship with that person offline'. Participants report asking themselves whether they will be friends with a connection in a year's time, and letting this guide whether they will expand their networks. 'Am I going to see you again in person? Am I going to, am I ever going to put something on your wall?' (Sally). Behind these thoughts lies the danger of dead wood ties and the accumulation of a threatening 'grey area'.

Participants also de-friended, or 'culled', Facebook connections in order to resolve problems. Culling was reported to be a kind of ritual process, enacted when people felt that their networks were becoming too large and unwieldy. These moments correspond with socio-ontological insecurity. Culling attempts to make connections more interpersonally accessible, optimising the potential for performances of connection. Culling begins by probing grey areas, defining audiences and questioning their value: 'Basically going through and finding people that I either haven't spoken to in over a year, um, or that I sit there and think: Do I really want them to see my status updates or my photos?' (Sally). In this vein, Flash reflects on a particular connection: 'I just felt it wasn't going anywhere. And he's not – it wasn't a real relationship we were having in any kind of sense. It wasn't meaningful'.

Participants also culled to secure social privacy, both to protect context, and to reduce occasions in which they experience the 'desire not to see'. This desire is sometimes directed at witnessing peoples' banal posts: 'I think it's quite refreshing to have less people on Facebook and – and it does make your homepage a bit more relevant and interesting. Like, sometimes you get these people that, yeah, like, I don't care what game you're playing on Facebook or what you're doing in your life' (Sally). Sometimes it is directed at nauseating posts. When discussing overly emotive status updates, John announces: 'I find – really I mean just want to un-friend them immediately but I can't, um, because I have to explain my issue with them'. This response also evinces the politics of culling. Odette offers a similar example:

Yeah, my other friend who, someone deleted her from Facebook and she got upset about that. So, um, we're friends again now but this is not a person I see in, um, real life, so I've chosen to remain friends with them on Facebook in order to not cause a stir. If I went and deleted them they would get upset because they're an emotional person, so I'd rather just avoid that conflict and stay friends with them on Facebook.

Odette

In the previous Chapter I explored how there is often social pressure to expand one's network. Likewise, there is social pressure to prevent it from being contracted. The social politics of expanding and contracting one's network is at the heart of the culture of intensive intimacy.

As well as organising their networks in general, participants attempt to circumscribe particular audiences for particular performances. In this regard, participants find a privacy setting useful, confirming some of the research I covered in Chapter 2. However, in many cases participants rely on 'likes' and 'tags' to get their friends' attention and engage in a performance of connection. If a person 'likes' a friend's post, this friend is now able to define that person as an audience. Participants were observed to receive many 'likes' from friends when they posted, and to often 'like' the posts of their friends. Over time, participants come to actualise regular interactions and reciprocal 'likes' with a core group of people whom they thus expect as an audience. This amounts to a kind of cognitive organisation of connections.

Importantly, participants do not seek to shut off their social interactions completely, thus Balkanising their Facebook experiences into a collection of virtual private rooms. Sally reflects on those of her friends who give their Facebook friends no access. 'What' she asks 'is the point of Facebook then?' Indeed, a primary motivation for using Facebook involves the performance of connection, which people enjoy because of the way in which it identifies with and draws in others, as well as constitutes and reproduces connections. Hence, if intimacy is to be public, it also involves constructing a specific form of 'safe' public intimacy which does not cause socio-ontological insecurity.

Rules of identification

Shortly after expressing how failing to attract an audience would be like 'talking into a void', John relates: 'I think that the possibility makes me choose my posts, share items quite carefully so as to avoid being "rejected"'. This illustrates how the looming threat of insecurity mobilises certain practices aimed at vouchsafing performances of connection.

Participants learn what not to post when their performances are stifled, as Odette illustrates:

> Just because people don't reply doesn't mean they haven't taken notice. Many people on Facebook are looking but not directly engaging. Sure, it might be a bit disheartening, but it also might

make you think twice about whether people care about that topic or event so much. Maybe you wouldn't post something along those same lines in the future.

Learning what does and does not engage others helps in the gradual process of defining a core audience and encouraging its actualisation over time. Yet, performances of connection are also performances of self, and they must appeal in some way to one's own interests. Hence, similarities are mobilised. Flash expounds on this:

> One way of thinking about your Facebook friends is that they're a kind of audience as much as anything. They're watching you and you're watching them in some respect. You know you'll get their attention when they click on. Particularly when you put up something – not controversial, because I spoke against that earlier – but, something flashy, or something catchy.

And what makes up the substance of this 'catchy' material? Flash continues:

> '[C]atchy', you know, might be some salacious headline about – I don't know – Tony Abbott's sex life or something like that. Or something like: 'Pauline Hanson's going to England', or, or, you know, 'Paris Hilton' something, something, you know. Well you know something catchy, might be amusing, it might be silly, it might be controversial, it might be a piece of writing I admire that I saw, you know, online that I want to draw attention to. It catches my attention. 'Catchy': it catches my attention.

To which I repeat, 'catches *your* attention', and Flash replies:

> Yes, and in some ways maybe I want it to catch other peoples' attention. Either way I – my comment on that, my emphasis on that will tell them something about me.

This idea, that people strategically seek to 'catch' people's attention, is central. Appealing to shared similarities involves walking a fine line between one's own performance of self and the desire for sociality. It entails removing a 'pure self-concern' from the subject matter of one's posts.

If it's of interest to somebody else, even if it's just the one audience I'll still post. But if it's like 'I'm having a lovely cup of coffee', then no. That's not interesting in – in any way.

Penny

This brief but incisive point reveals how central ensuring the performance of connection is. Penny would surely be expressing herself when detailing her cup of coffee. However, in her mind this lacks elements that are capable of inspiring identification from others and, hence, although capable of achieving a performance of self, is incapable of achieving a performance of connection. Pure self-concern fails to negotiate intimacy. Specifically, *it fails to appeal to the interpersonal intimacy of the group.*

Pure self-concern is expressed most commonly through posts which detail everyday trivia. Participants describe these status updates as 'mundane', 'insignificant', 'boring', and 'useless'.

People just put what they're eating or 'I'm having a bagel for breakfast' or – just sort of mundane activities. ... It's about eating and drinking and, yeah, what you're consuming on a day-to-day basis which is something everyone does but they don't feel the need to share that with everyone via a Facebook update.

Odette

Writers have critiqued 'SNS culture' for its supposed preponderance of banal status updates, suggesting these are indicative of normalised narcissism, a need to have even the most minute aspects of one's existence acknowledged (Muther 2009). These assessments resemble Sennett's (1977) critique of 'destructive Gemeinschaft'. Sennett laments the passing of group-oriented play-acting as a mode of public sociality, and its replacement by a narcissistic focus on 'personality', on intimate self-aspects. Sennett writes that, as Enlightenment society moved away from religion to a 'more reflexive condition', belief became 'centred on the immediate life of man himself' (1977: 151).

As the gods are demystified, man mystifies his own condition; his own life is fraught with meaning, yet it remains to be played out. Meaning is immanent in it, yet the person is unlike a stone or fossil which is fixed and so can be studied as a form. (ibid)

Coming to dominance in the eighteenth century, this culture of 'secular immanence' seeks ultimate meaning in the non-transcendent, in emotions, actions, and objects. Anticipating the Freudian revolution to come, secular immanence decrees 'everything counts because every-thing might count' (Sennett 1977: 21). With this in mind, consider this question: 'Why would you subject your friends to your daily minutiae?' (Thompson 2008: n.p.). The critics may reply: Because of a normative self-fascination which has long condoned the fruitless examination of such ephemera as a false means of self-fulfilment.

However, participants report being frustrated and annoyed by these kinds of posts. Sally culls ties 'so their inane or copious links don't come up in my home feed'. Hence, banal status updates, along with the over-emotive updates discussed last chapter, provoke a 'desire not to see'. Participants are wary of these performances because of their own dislike for them, and because they recognise how they alienate audiences. This suggests something counter to Sennett's argument. The fetishisation of material immanence is rejected in favour of group-oriented recognition. Sennett marks the death of interpersonal exchanges based on group conventions. 'For narcissism to be mobilised in a society, for people to focus on intangible tones of feeling and motive, a sense of *group ego* interest must be suspended' (1977: 262, my emphasis). Yet, the careful management of impressions so as to identify with others goes against this position. Interpersonal sociality, recognition through shared inter-ests – these processes suggest that 'group egos' are very much alive.

I now turn to a more thorough analysis of how this process of identifi-cation negotiates intimacy. I again utilise 'social capital' as a framework for understanding how performance and spatialisation negotiates norms, achieves goals, and accumulates intimacy. A 'successful' performance of connection has three analytic parts: the mobilisation of 'resources of identification' within a performance; the social context of a perform-ance; and the sociality which result from a performance. I investigate how intimacy transmits through this signal chain.

Resources of identification

Resources of identification are sign systems which make claims on social capital in order to engage performances of connection. On the one hand, they are families of signs which can be grouped in terms of discursive categories such as 'memory' and 'conviviality'. On the other hand, they are resources which claim on social capital, and, hence, are functions within a social-capital process. They claim on: the personal information or socio-cultural similarities of others; the expectation that others will accept the publication of this information; and the expectation that others will reciprocate socially and join in the performance of connection. As with most resources in a healthy social-capital process, these can cycle to become conditions for the strengthening of connections and the creation of more social capital. For example, a photograph which portrays a group of people sharing a warm, private moment claims on the intimacy of that group. If that group accepts and responds to this publication, socialisation around that photo can generate further intimacy. Intimacy is reinvested. This particular function can, hence, be thought of as 'intimacy capital'. Investment and accumulation of well negotiated intimacy capital will pay off in regular, reciprocal audiences. Investment in badly negotiated intimacy capital can alienate audiences and stifle performances.

I distinguish four key resources of identification, all of which are both signifying strategies and social capital functions. These can be presented in an analytically discrete way. However, as will become clear in the examples given, these 'capitals' enfold and feed off one another. Separating them can be a matter of arbitrary emphasis. To my knowledge, this constitutes a novel form of constructionist discourse analysis.

Intimacy capital

Participants invest intimacy in a performance, either through choosing the media of the performance (which can be helpful as, for example, photographs can transmit intimacy in a seemingly more potent manner), or through choosing and aligning the subject matter and circumscribing an audience through the strategies mentioned earlier in this chapter. Investment in intimacy can either attract an audience or stifle a performance. This depends on the 'intensity' of the intimacy involved. However, this intensity is not based on a transcendental scale; rather, it is the product of situational context. Hence, the way a participant organises connections to facilitate this context, or fails to do this, will condition the intensity of intimacy and, hence, its effectiveness in mobilising a performance of connection. Intimacy capital can be thought of a as a 'meta-capital', as often the other three capital resources are composed of signs which have an intimate nature.

Relational capital

When someone signifies direct relation to another person, he or she is claiming on relational capital. In a broad sense, a publicly displayed 'friends list' signifies relational capital. Also, all public interactions, such as posting a comment on a person's wall, claim on relational capital. Photographs make claims on relational capital by relating oneself to the embodied identities of one's friends. As has been argued, this form of relational capital is a chief example of how people collaborate in authoring their social identities. However, if these depictions are too intimate or unattractive, or if they compromise social contexts, then they can be thought of as bad investments of relational capital. In this case the resource claimed can in fact be thought of as stolen, and the person depicted has lost possession of his or her identity, has been 'doubled'. Congruent with other studies, (Besmer and Lipford 2009; Madden and Smith 2010), my participants find un-tagging to be a common, but ineffectual, resolution to this problem.

Importantly, relational capital should not be confused with the social capital *process* as a whole. This would confuse social capital with connections in and of themselves. It would simplify a process which also involves history, norms, and resources with one element, namely, relationality. It would stifle the analytic ability to understand how connections are self-consciously performed in the social capital process as signs which act as resources.

Memory capital

Participants are fond of posting photographs and status updates which recall bygone social occasions. If others can identify with these performances, then they can be said to mobilise memory. If people respond to these performances with social interactions which continue to share memories, then memory capital has been reinvested. This, in turn, strengthens the mnemonic character of social capital. It strengthens 'remembering' as a norm which influences social capital. Put differently, it becomes normative to claim on memory capital. The preponderance of Facebook threads which 'remember' attests to this. Memories are often quite intimate, hence memory capital can also be considered a form of intimacy capital.

Photographs have an important relationship to memory, given that they freeze moments in time. For participants in this study, one of the most common kinds of photographs depict social events in which either a few people are attending, say, with the backdrop of a restaurant, café or dining room, or in which a smaller group is singled out from a larger house party, dance floor, wedding, or the like. These convivial moments project the affection and warmth of social connections. For example, Bret is pictured on the perimeter of around 20 friends huddled in a precarious attempt at a 'group shot'. In the comic melee people are smiling and laughing, barely able to hold their poses, while trying to fix their eyes on the camera. It is Bret's birthday party, and the moment is filled with posterity. It includes many people and, likewise, tags many people. Memory capital and relational capital are deployed, while intimacy capital is implied in the show of friendship, through the closeness of bodies, stolen glances, and the group-privacy of the shot, which is especially meaningful to this group and their friends.

Cultural capital

Of course, participants identify with others through shared cultural biographies and interests. Facebook allows the ethnographer a fantastic opportunity to clearly see these cultural affiliations when participants affiliate themselves with Facebook pages and groups and post links to content such as YouTube videos. Allow me to draw selectively on my participants' Facebook pages so as to convey their cultural position: 'I grew up in Australia in the 90s'; 'Movies you watched on VHS as a kiddy in the 90's'; 'One Million Gen Y's with respect for the RSL and ANZACS'; 'Fresh Prince'; and 'I miss the Spice Girls Impulse deodorant'. These suggest a distinct generational membership. 'I Love cheesy eighties songs', and, 'When I was younger I would record my favourite songs off the radio onto tape' evinces a related nostalgic pride. 'Let's Get Melbourne on the World Monopoly Board'; 'Melbourne is better than Sydney'; 'Bitch Please... I'm from the Northern Suburbs' evoke both pride and a loyalty to place. Interestingly common are pages and groups which comically refer to widespread experiences: 'Yelling "STAY!" at a non-living object that keeps falling over'; 'I hate it when you're trying to be serious, but then you accidentally smile :)'; '63 Notifications Later and I regret Liking Your Status'. It is the fact that people share these experiences which makes these pages funny. This self-consciousness of affinity further points toward similarity and group experiences as dominant aspects of life on Facebook. Overall, such tokens constitute cultural capital when they identify with others and facilitate a performance of connection.

Performance context

All performances have contexts which influence how resources are mobilised. The context of a performance is set partly by the way users have organised connections to create an online public space. It is also set by its subject form and matter, the media used, and the social relationality of the people it depicts, discusses, tags, and so forth.

Subject form and matter

Performances can take on general, non-discrete 'forms' such as: assertions of tastes, values, and opinions; reflections; jokes; and memories/experiences. Within these forms a vast panoply of sub-forms and subject matters can unfold. Although in-depth cataloguing of these may be an interesting endeavour, it is enough for the purposes of this task to recognise that every performance is about something, and this frames the deployment of resources of identification.

Media used

Different media have different effects on the constitution of intimacy. This is due to their different performative affordances and constraints. Photographs, for example, allow for the performance of the corporeal body and embodied social relations. They also afford the *imaging* of private social scenes. Moreover, photographs have a special relationship to memory, fixing moments in time. Photographs, therefore, enable the mobilisation of intimacy and memory capital in specific ways. Finally, photographs are the cardinal object of first-hand judgement. They have the ability to give 'evidence' to people about the nature of one's offline social life and, hence, resolve that element of socio-ontological insecurity which requires the recognition of such a life.

The norms which influence photographic performances have evolved for participants over the course of their Facebook experiences. Cheap digital cameras and camera-phones as well as photo sharing on Facebook has engendered the normalisation of abundance. This 'abundance' has, in turn, allowed for novel modes of self-expression, and has influenced how participants negotiate intimacy through photographs. Sally explains:

> Well when I first joined I only put up – I wouldn't put up too many. I know there was a limit back then, but it seemed a bit over the top. Like – it's like, you know, back when your parents would say it's rude to talk about yourself all the time. So it's kind of like well if you put a hundred photos of you up isn't that a bit vain? Um, it's less so now for some reason 'cause people just put on more random ones and I now feel it's a bit more acceptable.

Sally began using Facebook in 2007 when photo sharing between her group of friends was only beginning. Why, at this time, would an abundance of photographs be considered vain? As argued above, pure self-concern entails a failure to mobilise interpersonal intimacy. Hence, an abundance of photographs was 'read' as self-concerned rather than group-concerned. However, according to Sally it has become 'acceptable to put up a hundred photos of what you've been up to', because 'they've built up over time'. Photographs are archived on Facebook, yet social life continues to produce photographed moments. This normalises the inevitable existence of abundance. A critical mass is reached, at which point it can no longer be 'vain' to possess a surplus of photographs.

Sally associates this quantitative shift with a qualitative one: it becomes appropriate to post 'random photos':

> Well I think there's two camps with the random photos, like, the less 'posey' and everything where you've got holiday snaps where they don't just put up the main ones, you know, picking the best or anything, they just put up everything. 'Cause now Facebook, as well, there's no limit on album numbers, so you can put hundreds of photos in there. So that's kind of random in that sense, like, um. Whereas there's also the random, like, say, a few of my friends have really odd things in their mobile uploads particularly. So you've got things like signs, or they've got a picture of, you know, things on the back of the toilet wall, which I think before digital photography you'd never take a photo of that, like, what a waste of film, so. Um, yeah, funny, ah, often funny things.

In this respect, Sally appreciates Facebook's integration with mobile camera phones, which allow one to be 'just connected in, and you could, um, put those photos up'. Penny explores the effect of Instagram[1] on this phenomenon:

> I've noticed, though, that the photos that go up from instagram are always slightly different to the one you find uploaded from a traditional camera. Because of people using their mobile phones (which go everywhere, instead of cameras which you would just take for special occasions), the photos tend to be much more naturalised and spur of the moment. My friends Facebook Instagram photos show very little posing, of either individuals or groups.

Contrary to Frohne's ideas, put forward in Chapter 1, the mobility and ease of photography seems to have lessened the way in which the camera solicits poses. For most of the twentieth century photography was – in the spheres of photojournalism, art and family life – constrained by the cost of analogue prints. Furthermore, both artistic photography and personal photography sort out significant moments to capture. This was due to a romantic aesthetic lineage (Scharf 1974), and because it served to reproduce bonds by focusing on positive familial events (Chalfen 1998). Hence, as Bazin and Gray (1960) argue, adopting a term made famous by Cartier-Bresson (1952), photography sought to capture 'decisive moments'. Digital photography transcends the spatio-temporal and economic constraints of its analogue predecessor. Images can be produced, reviewed, uploaded, and shared with little time and effort. Digital replicability significantly reduces costs. The convergence of phones, cameras, and broadband connections allows for mobile photo sharing, a near-instantaneous form of visual communication. Furthermore, as Van Dijck argues, digital photography is part of a 'larger transformation in which the self becomes the centre of a virtual universe made up of informational and spatial flows' (2008: 62–63). That is, digital personal photography accompanies mobility, individualisation, and the emergence of networked, personal communities.

Hence, '[u]nlike the traditional camera', write Daisuke and Ito, 'the camera phone is an intimate and ubiquitous presence that invites a new kind of personal awareness, a persistent alertness to the visually newsworthy that makes amateur photojournalists out of its users' (2003: n.p.). In this way photography's 'decisive moment' is devalued. The authors also imply that camera phones have democratised the experience of photography and empowered the everyday layperson's aesthetic gaze. 'Camera phones capture the more fleeting and unexpected moments of surprise, beauty and adoration in the everyday' (2004: n.p.). For instance, when I asked Penny why she posted some close-up photographs of a tiny snail, she replied that they 'fit on a thumb nail' and are 'adorable'. Importantly, Penny states: 'I don't actively search for snails. I was gardening'. These pictures are the product of a spontaneous aesthetic moment. In this way new forms of cultural capital are developing which can be mobilised so as to perform connection.

Sally explains how 'random' photos such as these, photographs which evince one's aesthetic, spontaneous, and funny side, are no longer 'vain' because they have accumulated online. In not being vain they are interpersonal, able to transmit resources of identification. This is not only due to the resources themselves, but to the nascent norms associated with the socio-technical development of photo-convergent media.

Social relationality

The social makeup and internal relationality of a performance is critical to the way it negotiates intimacy. These factors are part of the context of a performance, but they have such an influence on the negotiation of intimacy that they require special attention. I find performances can be solo, dyadic, group, or 'ego-propping'.

Solo performances

A 'solo performance' articulates a single person's identity. For example, a status update which gives mention to no one else, or a photo depicting a single body. Solo photographic performances have a social structure which can evoke a sense of intimacy and even exposure.

> Well it's weird on Facebook because a lot of the photos feel a bit too intimate for me so I didn't want to look at them or I'd flick through them quickly. And then – more the group shots that they'd posed for I was more happy to look at, 'cause I felt like when – you know, they were expecting someone to look at that.
>
> Sally

Photographs which depict individuals seem 'too intimate' to Sally, and this repels her, making her 'flick through them quickly'. The source of this aversion is revealed when she compares these photographs to those which depict groups. Sally is 'happy to look' at these. There is no feeling of repulsion. Rather, these photographs seem to expect and condone a public audience:

> Well I guess 'cause the group ones are often – you're posing for it. It's much more – even though you're posing for it as an individual as well it feels like you kinda know that other people are gonna look at them. I don't know why, I guess 'cause you know other people in the photo are probably gonna show it around, that sort of thing.
>
> Sally

Sally implies that a different kind of 'posing' happens when someone is in a group. She suggests a performative stance which anticipates and, hence, condones publicity. Group contexts engender the expectation of the social remediation and distribution of images. Sally, as an audience, projects an understanding of this expectation onto these photographs and is thus able to traverse through these optical spaces without feeling she is a trespasser. On the other hand, solo photographs lack this sociality, this performative stance and, hence, this expectation. When the eye crosses into such spaces a sense of trespass is imbued and thus a sense of voyeuristic intimacy (discussed in Chapter 6).

Having said this, certain solo photographs do receive social responses and seem to negotiate away their repulsive qualities. They achieve this by mobilising resources of identification. For instance, a photograph depicts Odette on her own in her living room, appearing drunk. She is posing in a comedic manner, her eyes wide and manic, knees bent, arms outstretched, her hands clasping some invisible object in an absurd manner. There is humility and mock self-deprecation here. Odette claims on the sense of humour and affection which she shares with her friends. These friends are able to *sense* this humour and expand on it:

> **Dave**
> Oh fantastic choice

> **Bradley**
> I have no idea what is going on here but I can only assume it involved the ingestion of alcohol.

> **Susanne**
> LOVELY ;)

> **Dave**
> You know, you really are the classiest person I know!

> **Conner**
> Watch where you're pointing that butt, gurl... You don't want nothin' flammable nearby! Not with what's coming out that end...

> **Letty**
> Actually I think she's cleaning...

> **James**
> Hahahaha that is awesome!

> **Paul**
> INVISIBLE TRYCICLE!

> **Sandy**
> I firmly believe this should still be your profile pic!!! Lol
> 'how's the lemonade girls???'

> **Craig**
> lol

What results constitutes a great example of an 'in-joke', an ideal performance of connection. If the combination of a kind of media and a form of internal relationality – photography and a solo performance – has a socio-technical effect on intimacy, this intimacy can be negotiated through identification and playfulness.

Dyadic performances

These can involve a photograph of two people, a status update which gives mention to another person; any performance which tags another person, and posts on a specific person's wall which are thus directly addressed to someone. As Simmel (1950) argues, dyads have an innate intimacy, born out of the structure of the dyadic bond in which two people are bound by a mutual fatefulness which would be destroyed if one party left. Furthermore, dyads, in excluding all others, can seem to take on the appearance of a secretive union. They appear to share mutual knowledge a third party could not possess. They have an exclusivity which makes the private spaces they create sharper, and the public gazes which penetrate these spaces more prone to 'exposing' intimacies. Dyadic performances thus have a specific relation to the 'capitals'. They claim on the relational capital of a single connection; they claim on the more 'intense' intimacy capital of this connection; and it is similar with shared memories and cultural interests. Hence, dyadic performances usually attract dyadic sociality, as others do not find much to identify with and, hence, cannot credit the claims being made.

Group-based performances

These give mention to, include, or depict a group. Status updates which mention more than one other person or link to a 'group page' are examples of group performances. So are photographs which depict more than two people socialising, and performances which tag multiple people. Group-based performances were commonly found to attract group-based sociality as well as long, reciprocal threads. As I argue in more depth shortly, a kind of gregarious group-ego forms, a prime example of well-negotiated intimacy.

Ego-propping

This is a common practice on Facebook which can be understood through looking at a performance's internal relationality. Ego-propping describes the use of resources of identification – collective signifiers of sameness – to identify with a group, while simultaneously using other elements of a performance to elevate the self within this group. Hence, resources of identification are used both to attract the attention and sociality of others, focused on the self, while simultaneously mediating this self-focus such that one does not come across as self-obsessed.

Ego-propping often occurs through an experience-based subject form which I term an 'occasion of pride'. A trip overseas, for example, is an occasion of pride which attracts people's cultural interest while simultaneously focusing their attention on a courageous vagabond. Asking participants to complete a diary of their most memorable experiences on Facebook, Sas and colleagues (2009) notice a similar phenomenon. The authors identify a form of performance they term 'genuine self expression', posts which describe 'significant positive events in one's own life' such as a 'new job, new partner or holidays in exotic places'. These are 'quickly shared through group messages, status updates and uploaded photos, so that they can be publicly celebrated' (2009: 122).

Ego-propping is conditioned by a reciprocal social capital process. Consider the following update:

Flash
a hot day to be doing the graduation thing…

In this concise expression a graduation serves as an ego-prop. This resource claims on Flash's friends who have done and are doing degrees, to offer their recognition and support. The reference to it being a 'hot day' serves as a rhetorical device, a textual frame which makes this announcement more blasé, a marker of cool nonchalance which downplays the esteem-based intentions of the post. In response, Raymond writes:

Raymond
enjoy the champagne/daiquiri/gin/pimms/etc at the end of it. id say its EXTREMELY well deserved.

Flash
you're too kind, Raymond – was great to run into you the other day, and be assured, there IS a light at the end of the PhD tunnel!! :)

The esteem which Raymond bestows on Flash is reciprocated by Flash's support of Raymond's own studies. This incisive exchange reveals how ego-props take place within a greater framework – the reproduction of connections through interpersonal intimacy. But note that this exchange could only have taken place if a point of identification existed between the two.

A photo depicting Bret illustrates the ego-propping process more dramatically. Bret is in the centre of the shot, striking a dramatic pose while wearing a garish costume which leaves much of his naked body exposed. However, he is positioned among various others at a party who, although not focused on, are also wearing costumes. These personae are involved in a shared cultural interest: 'dressing up'. Bret confirms that many of his Facebook friends are 'arty' and 'exhibitionists'.

> I consider myself to be an exhibitionist and I guess Facebook, some of the things that it does, I think mainly the shared photo albums and the status updates instantly become a way to just extend that, that sort of extroversion or that exhibitionism and while in theory you could post boring photos on, I suppose, or sedate photos, it seems like mainly people post photos of trashy parties and fancy dress parties and stuff, ah, and that's mainly what I would do as well.

For Bret and his friends, 'exhibitionism' indicates a shared cultural practice and aesthetic. Hence, as well as focusing on Bret, this photo identifies with others through relational and cultural capital. Manifesting as costumed personae in a theatrical setting, these resources are, in this context, ego-props. Concurrently, Bret receives esteem: 'Oh Mr Bret, you are a god. A god made out of...pet accessories and...the Swing machine...but a god no less.' In this humorous response one can see the aesthetic lexicon which meaningfully connects Bret with his friends. This esteem negotiates the intimate body in a productive fashion. A potentially exposing picture of Bret has been socially acknowledged and validated.

Bret supplies another relevant example:

> Like I went for this trip...and posting that photo album up online was really a thing of, like, that was such a wonderful show-off thing, and it was wanting to share it but it was also like going, you know 'this is the kind of crazy New Zealand life that is here', and yeah, I think I even talked about this last time as well and you just go 'oh my God, that's incredible' and you go 'yeah, I'm incredible, that's a fact', you know, like the fact that it enables that can be – can be really validating and...it feels like the level it operates on is a – a level of ego.

These photographs serve to 'show off' and ingratiate Bret's ego. What struck me about them was the way they mediate this focus on ego with collectively appealing signifiers, such as the awesome spectacle of a white water rapid. Bret is successful in his ego-propping, as these resulting posts confirm:

> Amazing!
> Hardcore water rat!
> This is truly the stuff of legend. They'll write fables about you Bret! Hell, maybe I will!
> That is total insanity. NZ is HARDCORE

Occasions of pride are themselves ego-props, as they both appeal to a socio-cultural domain of similar interests and elevate the self within this domain. The final comment above nicely illustrates this. The poster makes reference to the main element in the prop, the New Zealand bush, without making direct reference to Bret. Thus, Bret has managed to assert the scene as much as he has himself, and did not 'exhaust' the image with his ego. When photographs are used as ego-props another important factor comes into play, namely, first-hand judgement. Photographs give indubitable evidence to first-hand judgment. So, in the example above, Bret 'warrants' his esteem by actually showing 'first-hand' his trek in an exotic locale. However, ego-propping is a delicate balancing act. If people do not mobilise resources of identification properly they may come across as egotistical, and the performance of connection will be stifled.

To summarise, an important part of the context of a performance is the way in which it implies others, either directly or indirectly, mobilising relational capital. Performances which seem to expose intimate scenes without the social buffer of relational capital can seem like they have badly negotiated intimacy, and thus repulse people. This exposure is particularly potent with regard to photographs. Yet, people can utilise resources of identification to negotiate away this repulsive intimacy and attract a connection. For performances which desire personal esteem and recognition, resources are mobilised to appeal to the intimacy of the group.

Resultant sociality

A 'successful' performance garners a social response. Overall, in both dyadic and group interactions I observed three dominant modes of sociality: 'remembering', 'esteem', and 'playfulness'. These play out differently depending on whether a group or dyad is involved inasmuch as these factors generally seem more exclusive and, hence, intimate when dyads socialise.

Remembering

When memory capital is successful in attracting social interaction it usually sparks sociality which 'remembers'. Research has found that when people talk about memories, a process termed 'rehearsing', it increases the intimacy related to those memories and reflexively strengthens relationships (Nicole & Bluck 2007). Regular interaction of this kind can cause the 'habituation of the memory's emotional effect' (ibid: 1094). Fostering intimacy in this manner, I argue, is a prime activity on Facebook. The habituation of memory as a form of social intimacy serves to reproduce social connections through the performance of connection.

Here, I focus specifically on remembering which occurs around photographs, because photography has a special relationship to memory, and because scholarship has yet to thoroughly explore how photography on Facebook takes place within the logic of social capital and identification. Memory capital is found abundantly in travel photographs. Sally and five friends are perched atop a mound of dirt and rock, balancing on an arterial network of tree roots, with a sun-spattered forest rising behind them. Sally is not the centre of this photograph; the group is in focus. Neither is she given centrality as the photograph's owner, as she did not post it. Hence, this is a group performance, rather than an ego-prop. This photograph is found in an album entitled 'Borneo08 – Phase 2b (trek)', so the viewer is assured of its context: rugged travelling in exotic locales. Relational capital is present, and confirmed in the tagging of those depicted. Cultural capital comes through the travelling context: if not an experience people have shared, then one they most probably desire. But the photo itself lacks the cliché which the album title evokes. This is not a photo of famous monuments or people garbed in tourist keepsakes. The bush is too 'plain', and the authentic enjoyment of those pictured too much the centre of the photograph. This private group and the affection they share mobilise intimacy capital. Memory frames the entire affair, and the successful investment of memory capital is confirmed in the resultant sociality, which 'remembers':

Sally
aw good photo. its our lion king pride rock...the one i managed to hit my head on, because you can easily miss it, it just comes outta nowhere!

Bianca
omg i remember that.
It looked so painful...but yes of course it just comes out of nowhere! NOT.

> **Sally**
> yes, just further proof I am uncoordinated, as if falling down hills into trees about 5x a time a day wasn't enough. It was the jerrycan's fault!!! haha

In this sample, Sally and Bianca continue to remember an experience which the photograph provokes, expanding it, telling stories. This is also an example of 'playfulness', evinced in Sally's self-deprecation, which Bianca picks up on and joins in with mock sarcasm. Importantly, this playfulness is the emotional accretion of the process of remembering and, hence, is always associated with fragments of an experience – a 'jerrycan', 'falling down hills into trees', a 'lion king pride rock'. There is also a sense, however that this playfulness transcends the memory-orientated subject matter, signifying the enjoyment of sociality in and for itself.

Earlier, I argued that dyadic performances often circumscribe dyadic audiences so, therefore, resultant threads are usually between two people and perpetuate an intimacy which excludes all but this coupling. This can be seen in relation to remembering. A photograph depicts Sally and her friend Lupé leaning against a bale of hay, smiling broadly at the camera, rugged up in duffle coats and hoodies, paper-wrapped fortified wine bottle in one hand, and a crowd of revellers in the background. In the caption below the photo the viewer learns part of the context of this performance: 'Fancy seating at the Livestock Music Festival!!' The album title to the right of the photograph reveals more: 'Ireland – 2006'. Overall, the performance context of this photograph is a dyadic travel photo, depicting conviviality, fun-loving, and the liminality of foreign lands and eclectic events. Although some of this cultural capital may be appealing to a broader group, the memory, relational, and intimacy capital at play emanate from an experience which only two people can truly identify with. Hence, this photograph provokes a dyadic thread:

> **Lupé**
> sally I could shoot ya for not burning this photo. nice bottle of buckfast between the legs!!!

> **Sally**
> this photo is brilliant!
> ah the buckfast ... that stuff was deadly. and not in the way irish use the word, but actually death-inducing

> **Lupé**
> you know the song 'buck fast – will get ya f!!c'd fast!!' happy days xx
>
> This exchange makes reference to mutual memories, centring around unpleasant experiences with a local form of liquor. It emanates an aura of sentimentality corollary to a performance of connection in which Lupé and Sally reaffirm their shared history and relationship.

Facebook's profile upgrade, the Timeline interface, seems to encourage the mobilisation of memory capital and remembering. A person's entire Facebook history can now be accessed through a reverse chronological date system, and the person can add key life-moments all the way back to birth.

> I haven't filled in my timeline completely, such as adding significant life moments, and therefore I don't really see it as a timeline of my life. Would I add life moments? At first I would have said no, but I think I would consider it now. Some friends have shared some older photos recently and that was cool and some funny conversations came out of it. It was a bit of an insight into what people considered life moments – a 4 day holiday in 2002 is not a life moment!
>
> Sally

This response has two enlightening aspects. First, Sally does not find Timeline appealing until she recognises that some friends are using it to post old photographs, claim on memory capital, and establish performances of connection. These are 'funny conversations', hence playful interactions. Second, Sally puzzles at how people interpret 'life moments'. Yes, it is common for people to post information regarding their travelling escapades. These are occasions of pride. However, it is important to consider these occasion in terms of what they are not – *love and tragedy*. The great moments in life can swing from great love to tragic death. It is interesting that these kinds of intimacies do not appear in timelines; instead, people negotiate intimacy so as to encourage playfulness, rather than nauseatingly public affection or remorse.

Esteem

Esteem giving is very close to the kind of 'partner responsiveness' that is central to the development of interpersonal intimacy (Reis & Shaver 1988). According to Honneth (2007), esteem is a form of recognition that strengthens social relationships by establishing moral, affective bonds between people. I read esteem on Facebook in this light. Esteem,

I argue, has two primary dimensions, 'supportive' and 'supplementing'. Supportive esteem is designed to help someone who is going through an emotional problem or crisis. For this reason this form of esteem can range from mild to more intense, although it usually remains in the former end of the spectrum given the way intense emotionality can 'nauseate' people and stifle performances of connection. Take, for example, this simple exchange:

Penny
There are too many people that are smarter than me at [redacted], its very upsetting.

Chris
ah well. you'll always be a smart cookie up here in hicksville :)

Penny
naww. thanks. =)

On the other hand, supplemental esteem aims to enhance a person's already positive state of mind, and is much more widespread. Supplementary esteem can take the form of congratulations, praise, admiration, honour, and so forth. For instance, a common example of supplementary esteem on Facebook involves people getting birthday well wishes. Supplementary esteem is usually the result of a successful ego-prop.

Penny is pictured in multiple photographs in an album that documents a college party which involves being covered in paint. Each image is set amongst the ambience of dance floors and clotting crowds of college students. Written on their clothes, poses, alcoholic beverages, and in the florescent primary colours of dappled paint is an easily read code which celebrates autonomous, uninhibited fun, as well as a certain membership, a cultural belonging that implies social fields that expand outward from the specific – a university cohort – to the general – an age group, a mythology of youthfulness and promiscuity. These photographs are invested with cultural capital which both positions Penny within a group and elevates her status. She is given an aura of 'cool'. The ego-prop is successful:

---

hey! loving the photos haha such a messy night!

---

so looks like you had fun being covered in paint!
did you get to throw it at each other??

> im starting to think i should let you convince me next time...
> xoxo

> OMG unfair!
> If i had known this i would have come.
> ok next time i will listen to your wise opinions!

Esteem, in being related to ego-propping, is often the result of the performance of an 'occasion of pride'. Thus, esteem is associated with trips, achievements, birthdays, successes, and so forth. Odette has posted an image in which she stands next to a large banner which reads, 'congrats Odette'. This photograph is within an album entitled 'thesis banquet', and in other images the viewer finds out that Odette's friends have thrown a congratulatory party for her thesis completion. A comment below this image reads 'awww!! that's so sweet of them!!' Hence, Odette has her relational identity – and the fact that she has friends who care for her – confirmed and validated with this response.

For my participants, playfulness is the social spirit of Facebook. Sociality, in and for itself, constitutes one side of the performance of connection. Playfulness is the highest form of that sociality. Participants begin to play when they discuss fun things which interest them. They post funny clips from YouTube, favourite comedy moments, embarrassing dating videos, and candid political gaffs, to name just a few. They share memes, which establish a kind of play-frame through the re-signification of the same hilarious image with different text. They recall funny events. They share funny stories. Most of all, they make 'witty', 'pithy' status updates, which are often sarcastic, ironic, and lightly self-deprecating. These mobilise resources of identification so as to establish fun and conviviality interactions. Importantly, playful interactions usually involve three or more people, are imbued with a gregarious kind of intimacy, and signify a 'group ego'.

Playfulness

Playfulness has two dimensions. Firstly, it entails social interactions in which each party expresses knowledge and responds to others in a good-hearted, lively, and humorous manner. This can extend to becoming mischievous and melodramatic, can detour into satirical jibing, or darken into black humour and shock-horror. That is, partners 'play' with the subject at hand. These characteristics resemble what Boxer and Cortés-Conde (1997) call 'conversational joking', a kind of 'situational humour' that emerges through interactions. Based on group-specific social conventions, actors cue others to a playful mood. A 'play frame [is] created by participants, with a backdrop of in-group knowledge' (1997: 277). These playful cues can also be thought of as 'resources of identification'. Cultural capital is one such resource which commonly anticipates playfulness, as it claims that others come and engage in the aesthetic, creative sides of their identities.

Secondly, playfulness entails an emotional aura which accretes from these kinds of social interactions. This aura signifies the enjoyment of sociality in and for itself. Additionally, it signifies the shared interpersonal histories of those socialising. According to Boxer and Cortés-Conde, playfulness can strengthen the relational identities which make up a group:

> We believe that it is in situational humour that one can observe with most clarity the RID [relational identity development], because in joking and teasing we can display the intimacy of our identities as friends, family members, and members of an in-group. (1997: 282)

Note how this resembles the way in which participants use performances of connection to reproduce connections. That is, the way they publicly perform intimacy so as to strengthen aspects of their social relationships and identities. I argue that, when public intimacy is well negotiated, the intimacy which becomes instrumental in reproducing connections is exactly that emotional aura which accretes from playfulness, *not deeply personal disclosures*.

Witness how this aura emerges out of the following thread:

Flash
is high-fiving the bloke who hosted 'Rage' last night – best line-up of videos in a long time!!

Greg
I think you manipulated the list, Flash. What's this about Malcolm McLaren, Neneh Cherry AND Fleetwood Mac?

Flash
And I still have 'Steppin' Out' in my head – genius!!

Osuka
wow, makes me wish i'd been watching...

Flash
and buffalo stance!!

Osuka oooh yeah! so who was programming?

Flash i actually can't remember... i was so enthralled with what was on the screen... and poor David had to sit back and endure my musical tastes (not all of which we share :)

Flash alas, one ommission – James Reyne 'Hammerhead'! :)

Osuka hahahaha poor Greg ;-)

Osuka I picked up an Australian Crawl album yesterday... haven't played it yet! it will have to be an occasion when you are there :-)

Flash oh, i WILL be there if Mr. Reyne is on stereo!

Flash OMG!! – 'Slave to the Rhythm' was playing loud n clear on Parliament Station tonight!!

Greg With the addition of 'Hammerhead' and 'Slave To The Rhythm', that's your musical fantasy lived out. The next time I watch late night Rage, I hope to get a decent deal.

Here, three posters trade cultural capital. They construct a cultural field consisting of locations and musical tastes. They creatively *play* with these tokens, and in the process reveal that they *know* things about one another, that they share an affectionate history. An emotional aura emerges. There is the sense that this playfulness transcends the subject matter of this sociality and signals the enjoyment of sociality in and for itself. Flash's original reference to 'high fiving' cues this 'play frame', and this is greatly expanded on in the resulting thread. The magnitude of playfulness increases in accordance with the expanding dimensions of a private social space.

As the following thread nicely illustrates, playfulness is a self-conscious, creative practice:

Bret cacked myself at Dave Hughes' show 'HUGHSING AROUND'. can't wait for Wil Anderson's new show 'WILARIOUS'.

> **Jerry**
> If he hasn't done 'Wilarious' yet, you could probably make big bux selling him that title. GO TOM!

> **Bret**
> i'm gonna PAT THAT!

> **Bret**
> And in 2011, it's 'Born To Be Wil-d'.

> **Selene**
> draining my Wil to live.

> **Jerry**
> I'm looking forward to his DVD, 'The Wils Are (a)Live!!!'

Here Bret and his friends express a creative form of group sociality by engaging in word*play*. Flash instigates a similar process:

> **Flash**
> doing the needful on a Sunday morning

> **Hunter**
> what is it with everyone using the word 'needful' these days? :P

> **Flash**
> Hunter, if you ain't doing the needful now, perhaps you never will! :)

> **Craig**
> I prefer doing 'mindful'.

> **Flash**
> you have to be mindful that you're doing the needful

What kind of intimacy is being negotiated here? These are not extreme emotions, but they nevertheless signal the warmth of an interpersonal bond. Convivial warmth and affection – these are the signifiers of well-negotiated public intimacy. Beyond the cynicism that both users and academics share about Facebook, there is a central aspect of fun to the experience, deeply routed in the interpersonal, which is too often overlooked, underestimated, or misconstrued.

I define this as 'gregarious intimacy'. A gregarious person is often though to be light-hearted and playful. 'Gregarious' refers to someone who enjoys merging with crowds, who revels in herd mentality and disindividuation. Now, people do not 'disindividuate' on Facebook. However the emotional aura which emerges from playful sociality does signify a kind of 'group ego'. In Chapter 4 I discussed how performances of connection create intimate social spaces which expand when others identify with those within them and join in the interaction. Also, throughout this book I have discussed the enjoyment people can feel when they experience an unpredictable moment caused by the heterogeneous nature of Facebook publicity. Such moments are enjoyable when the eye recognises similarity rather than difference, conviviality rather than conflict, warmth rather than overt emotion. Part of the enjoyment of group, gregarious sociality on Facebook is that it is open to these broad publics and, hence, allows unexpected people to identify with those socialising and join in. It is this ability to form fun, creative, playful interactions with an unpredictably expansive set of friends which is valued about Facebook. Again, I find Deleuze and Guattari's definition of 'virtuality' as that which is 'becoming' useful. The social membership which constitutes gregarious space is not exclusive and set, as with dyadic space. Rather, it is unfixed and open-ended, always becoming. In this sense, gregarious intimacy is a kind of virtuality. However, in my time spent with my participants on Facebook I noticed that regular group sociality involved four or five regular friends. However, now and again threads burgeoned into large social space with many participants, and these were more often than not playful.

In aiming to create these kinds of spaces, not only routinely, but strategically, through the right kind of investment in intimacy and other forms of capital, people positively negotiate intimacy. This is in contrast to the negative negotiation of intimacy which occurs when people organise networks and audiences so as to shut off spaces. Recalling the questions regarding authenticity and regionality posed in Chapter 2, gregarious intimacy can be seen as an authentic 'middle region'. It is authentic in the sense that it desires true interpersonal connection and abstracts the kind of self-concerned malaise characteristic of overt public intimacy. It is a middle region in the sense that deep back-region intimacy is abstracted, as is the kind of rigid formality, politeness, and decorum constitutive of front regionality (Meyrowitz 1985). Recalling Bret, who is careful to exclude vulnerable emotionality from Facebook because it is 'unsafe', gregarious intimacy is a 'safe' form of public intimacy. The intimate self which is constructed lacks the emotional and biographical information necessary to make it vulnerable when circulating beyond the performance of connection.

In this Chapter I have looked at how my participants negotiate intimacy in order to actualise regular performances of connection and, hence, a regular sense of interpersonal fulfilment on Facebook. On the one hand this involves circumscribing social spaces by organising connections. On the other, it involves mobilising specific forms of intimacy to generate specific kinds of interactions. In regard to the latter, I have, much like Goffman, constructed the performance of self as a strategic, dialogical process. However, I have conceptualised this element of strategy in terms of social capital resources. Participants want to capture the attention and sociality of others. It is this process of capturing an audience and encouraging it to reciprocate which makes a social capital framework valuable, especially when considering public sociality itself to be a social resource which is claimed on by the performer and credited by the responding audience when intimacy capital is well invested.

Turkle writes: 'Social media ask us to represent ourselves in simplified ways' (2011: 185). I think this has become somewhat of a naïve clique. It neglects the various processes which occur around the camera, outside of the shot. It neglects how people mobilise resources of identification. It misses the complexity of performance context, the influence of convergent media, first-hand judgement, internal relationality, ego-propping, and the like. Most importantly, it does not take into account how performances extend into social interactions, becoming complex performances of connection. The self-presentations on Facebook are not simplistic, but are rich, layered processes.

Overall, the ways in which my participants negotiate intimacy to achieve interpersonal goals and overcome problems involves the cultivation of various new social skills and sensitivities. The organisation of connections so as to afford meaningful performances of connection involves audience definition, network contraction, privacy setting, and tagging savvy, extending interpersonal aptitudes into novel technical domains. The negotiation of intimacy through resources of identification is a skill which results from learning about the nature of Facebook's heterogeneous publicity, about first-hand judgement, nauseating posts, and the delayed gratification caused by an attention economy. Hence, this is likewise a subtle form of social skill. Hence, on Facebook, public intimacy is neither simplistic, nor deskilled. Being highly skilled and complex it can be called intensive. The solutions to the problems put forward in the previous chapter are constitutive, like the problems themselves, of intensive intimacy.

Not every performance leads to group sociality, a playful aura, a group ego and, hence, gregarious intimacy. Dyadic sociality and ego-propping reveal complex relationships between self, other, and group. The commonality of dyadic interactions suggests a desire for different degrees of private intimacy in public. Also, the commonality of ego-propping suggests a continuing desire for individual attention and esteem. However, these gradations do not overtake what I consider to be the central, and most common, kind of public intimacy on Facebook. They exist alongside gregarious intimacy. Hence, Facebook is a realm in which forms of individual, dyadic, and group realisation are occurring.

Facebook did not create gregarious intimacy. Indeed, gregarious intimacy is a kind of basic social process which is common to the many kinds of convivial social spaces one can imagine. Facebook *affords* the creation of gregarious spaces composed of people are who spatiotemporally discontinuous. Moreover, it allows these spaces to occur in a trans-mobile, online, persistent representation space which is low in cost and easy to access. Hence, it allows gregarious spaces to occur with distant and proximate friends in an easy, ritualistic fashion.

Conclusion

In a mobile world in which people face nebulous contingencies in their efforts to sustain important relationships, a service such as Facebook capitalises on a growing need for intimacy. People make use of Facebook's bounded publics to perform their connections and reproduce the intimacy therein. However, Facebook also puts intimacy at risk. The pressure to capitalise on social connections from various situations in life and with various 'degrees' of intimacy can cause the accumulation of heterogeneous personal networks. The public spaces which result endanger the capacity for Facebook to positively service interpersonal intimacy. On the one hand, this doubles and dispossesses the intimate self and demands that intimacy be carefully controlled. On the other hand, it mediates people and potentially alienates and objectifies them. This threatens the interpersonal recognition which they desire, producing a looming state of socio-ontological insecurity. In order to assuage this insecurity, people mobilise intimacy, carefully targeting the interpersonal fabric which binds them to those who matter.

The way in which my participants organise connections and mobilise resources of identification illustrates how intimacy, as that core aspect of the interpersonal, has come to involve socio-technical strategies which go far beyond what is generally considered intimate. So much more must be made explicit, evaluated, decided, and acted on. For instance, as discussed in Chapter 7, what I have called liminal ties are no longer ephemeral. They must be structured into one's personal network as a way of negotiating the intimacy of liminal moments. Yet, it is likely these ties will become dead wood and subsequently culled. Gone is a time when such people were not a problem; now they make up a 'grey area' – a problematic zone which lacks definition and thus must be defined.

Estranged ties also pose challenges. They afford the construction of self through the comparison of intimacies. Yet, this can fail to morally validate the self. Moreover, it may lead to guilt over 'spying'. The value of these ties and their existence in one's network must thus be decided and acted upon.

Choices aimed at negotiating intimacy abound: Is a connection close enough such that I can address him or her? Or do I have to wait for some kind of 'trigger' to negotiate intimacy and establish a meaningful interaction? Who may be embarrassed if I post or tag this image? Have I posted too much? Does this post appeal to the interests of others? Who should be included in this social space? How vulnerable am I and my friends to this network of people?

People do not seek to close off spaces, to transform Facebook into a tightly Balkanised patchwork of interactions. They seek the pleasure of belonging that comes from annexing private space from public space. They seek the potential, unpredictable expansion of private space which often occurs when identifying with friends from a broader public space. However, they must carefully negotiate intimacy so that the public intimacy which results from these private spaces does not nauseate and alienate audiences. This requires a judicious investment of well-negotiated intimacy capital. Playfulness is the ultimate result of these processes. That is, sociality which accretes an emotional aura that, in turn, signifies a group ego.

I have argued that many of these processes can be thought of in terms of intensive intimacy, which can be conceptualised as a terrain of struggle between the 'I–Thou' and the 'I–it'. It is important to recognise that my participants were spurred on from a state of intensive intimacy into a state of *reflexive intimacy*, in which they developed techniques to address the problems associated with the 'I–it' state-of-mind. This reflexive stage follows an earlier stage in which the initial 'buzz' of Facebook causes people to expand their networks and indiscriminately publicise their personal details. Importantly, this is not a teleological process. Facebook continues to innovate, and new contingencies can engender new habits and risks. Hence, I have emphasised that intensive intimacy exists prior to reflexive intimacy. Extrinsic contingencies need not ultimately cause enduring awareness, concern, and agency. Concurrently, intensive intimacy need not always be experienced as frustration, or as a sense of insecurity. Indeed, the laboriousness of interpersonal sociality – for, example, the careful tagging and editing of self-disclosures – can be experienced as fun.

Future research can expand in various ways on the ideas presented in this book. I would like to briefly cover three: the relationship between intensive intimacy and political economy; the need for research into further service innovations; and the emergence of locative social media.

I have argued that intimacy possesses a laborious quality. The concept of 'social labour' is also associated with political economy. Facebook creates revenue by mining user data and using it to construct personally tailored advertisements. Facebook transforms social relations and self-expression, *transforms intimacy*, into immaterial commodities. 'Social labour' indicates the laborious quality of interpersonal life as well as the way in which sociality creates value for capitalists. Various writers have explored the nature of immaterial capitalism, social labour, subjectivity, and surveillance on Facebook, and I do not wish here to take up an in-depth discussion of these interesting issues. I merely wish to indicate the potential of integrating some of the ideas I have discussed in this book with a political economy approach. The commodification of social life, subjectivity, and intimacy entails an inversion of what Foucault (1977) calls 'disciplinary power'. It entails something closer to how Hardt and Negri (2009) re-theorise Foucault's notion of 'bio-power', which now emanates as much from cognition, affect, and language as it does from the body's sinews. Relying on the production of subjectivity, this mode of power encourages and seduces rather than disciplines. However, 'consumed consumers', as Bauman (2007) would say, cannot be given complete freedom. They are managed rather than coerced, directed rather than disciplined. We see this subtle interference happening on Facebook, where constant innovation seeks to steer the way in which users publicise and share their intimacies. Corporate surveillance which determines modes of publicity can be understood as a key *structure* which acts on intimacy. Hence, we can understand intensive intimacy through looking at these broader structures. We can likewise frame intensive intimacy in these structural terms. In which case theories of intensive intimacy can be integrated into the phalanx of already existing powerful critical theories.

Facebook continues to innovate as a convergence of different media, content platforms, applications, and industries. It is interesting to examine how these new affordances may serve to dampen or heighten intensive interpersonal labour. For example, Instagram posts camera phone photographs automatically to Facebook, hence bypassing the labour of selecting, editing, collocating, and tagging. Does this provide a new kind of convenience, or does it subvert the kind of control over resources of identification needed to negotiate intimacy?

In 2011, Facebook integrated new 'frictionless sharing' protocols into its third-party application architecture. 'Frictionless sharing' describes the way in which Facebook will take note of what a user reads, watches, and listens to on integrated applications such as Spotify,[1] and post these links to his or her timeline. The intentional human act of sharing is bypassed. Selecting certain content over others is integral to how users perform their identity. Frictionless sharing undermines this act. Agency seems to have migrated from our neural architecture to Facebook's sharing architecture (arguably both involve a dynamic execution of super-complex hidden software protocols). This is a further development in what Monovich (2000) calls 'automation', the way in which digital algorithms take up human work. However, while previously this was prevalent in serving us *personalised content*, such as through search filters, it now services our social networks with the *contents of our personas*. The Facebook Company seems to think that their users will welcome this displacement of agency. Users want to share, no matter what. However, to me this seems to engender another form of 'doubling', another data self which acts beyond the self. Perhaps people desire friction. Friction implies close presence, it implies rubbing up against people. The insecurity which the intimate double engenders stems from not knowing who one's doppelganger is rubbing up against.

Research into continuing innovations will be necessary so that we can keep up with this socio-technical juggernaut. Because these innovations involve policy, planning, protocols, and people, frameworks such as Actor Network Theory – which traces the translation of agency through social and technical stages (Latour 2005) – are highly useful.

Given the growing convergence between social media and related devices, it is also valuable to examine how intensive intimacy plays out in different, but related, media ecologies. How does it play out on different SNSs with specific cultures of use? How does it relate to other dominant cyber-phenomena such as gaming? What forms of intimacy exist in gameplay or roleplay? Most importantly, how does the negotiation of intimacy deal with emergent forms of mobile and locative media?

Locative social media (LSM) are fast becoming a crucial aspect of the emerging social technoscape. As social media have increasingly come to dominate the Internet so, too, has the Internet come to pervade physical places through mobile media. LSM applications, used predominantly on smartphones, are reconfiguring the relationship between places and social networks (Gordon & De Souza e Silva 2011). Here lies the opportunity for fruitful research into how LSM influence intimacy as it relates to identity, relationships, and place.

In general, LSM combine online social networks with GPS technology, allowing users to locate one another in physical space. For example, this can be achieved by geo-tagging a Facebook post, or 'checking in' to a FourSquare location.[2] Most applications also allow users to augment places with user-generated content. For example, Gypsii allows users to 'create' places, which involves taking photos of specific locations and tagging them with relevant comments. These place-impressions become publicly available on the Gypsii network. Such LSM ask users publicly and subjectively map, visualise, and annotate place. Although there are numerous different kinds of locative social applications, they usually offer profiles, privacy settings, and the equivalent of News Feeds.

As Sutko and de Souza e Silva (2011: 808) note, while much has been written about locative media games and artworks, little has been said about the role in everyday life of LSM such as FourSquare or Facebook Places. That is, little has been said of applications which are primarily used to sustain interpersonal bonds and reproduce social life. Such applications mobilise categories which have been central to this book, such as space/place, performance, playfulness, memory, and surveillance.

LSM trace part of their lineage to mobile phones. Research suggests that mobile phone use can strengthen interpersonal bonds by allowing social ties to coordinate and communicate when they are not physically present (Ling 2008). However, phones and other mobile media also act as shields or escape routes (Campbell 2004). They allow people to block out their proximate surroundings, negating chance public encounters and spontaneous sociability (Habuchi 2005). Hence, while these media may positively increase existing social capital, they may prevent the formation of new social capital. Moreover, phones introduce private interpersonal spaces into public places. The rupture of public space by personal, private space suggests that norms of public intimacy are being destabilised and negotiated. Similar to Facebook, the public strengthening of mediated interpersonal bonds may play out in such a way as to disturb onlookers and disrupt public equilibrium (Caporael & Xie 2003). Alternatively, onlookers may be quietly intrigued by the conversations they are forced to overhear (Fortunati 2011). Again, this possibility is reminiscent of Facebook, where public disclosures can both fascinate and nauseate. The way in which digital media introduce forms of publicity which mobilise both the desire to see and not to see (or hear and not to hear, as the case may be) suggests ongoing, contradictory forces of inclusion and exclusion in modern media culture, significantly governed by intimacy thresholds.

To reiterate, a problem associated with mobile phones is that they allow for private spaces to impede on public spaces. In one sense, LSM resolve this problem by facilitating co-present sociality. Users signal their presence in a specific location and attract their friends to come and hang out. It would be interesting to map changes in how social ties negotiate intimacy as they transition from the online network into the networked locality. For example, an interesting aspect of how people negotiate intimacy relates to the feeling of insecure anticipation which accompanies waiting for a reply to a public status update. Here the Deleuzian virtuality of the audience is critical: the 'who', 'what', and 'when' of the becoming response. When thinking about LSM we can add a new category: 'where'. Who will I meet? What will we do? When will they come? *Where will we be?* Certainly, physical public locations are heavily encoded with specific behavioural norms. The introduction of 'whereness' will significantly affect how intimacy is negotiated in relation to social norms. Will this further intensify the negotiation of intimacy? How will people negotiate intimacy in response?

Yet, while LSM may continue to enhance already existing social bonds, it is a matter of debate as to whether they will facilitate sociality with the urban public. For example, Humphreys (2008) examines the now defunct LSM application, 'Dodgeball'. She finds that using 'Dodgeball' can lead to 'social molecularisation'. That is, a 'collective movement through an urban environment' in which users are aware of the movements of other 'Dodgeball' users, but engage less with the urban public (2008: 354).

> Dodgeball becomes another means of maintaining and reinforcing social bonds. Even when my informants did meet new people through Dodgeball, these people were fairly demographically similar. While urban areas are diverse environments, Dodgeball may contribute to an illusion of 'looser' sociality despite reinforcing homophilous tendencies. (Humphreys 2008: 356)

In this book I have suggested that SNSs such as Facebook mobilise and emphasise intimacy and similarity. What I find interesting here is how this mobilisation may be at odds with a heterogeneous, yet integrated and interactive, public realm. This is certainly a concern when considering urban ideals such as cosmopolitanism and cultural citizenship (Bridge 2006).

As it stands, scholars are attempting to understand what kinds of mobile and locative media will produce heterophilic, engaged public spaces (Hampton, Livio, Goulet 2010; Gordon & De Silva e Souza). For example, de Souza e Silva and Hjorth (2009) suggest that the 'gamification' of interpersonal LSM may lead to the strengthening of interpersonal bonds as well as to engagement with public spaces and strangers. Locative games have a playful, explorative element which often requires that players engage in conversations with the strangers who happen to occupy the game-space. Recalling the previous chapter, it is interesting that playfulness again appears at the threshold of private and public sociality. An understanding of play, publicity, and place as they relateto the contradictions between intimacy and community may be well informed by ludological approaches. It may be that game contexts allow for an intimacy of playful movement and exploration: exploration, the unknown, and discovery all play a role in intimacy. When learning about intimate life, children explore bodies, secrets, taboos, and meanings. Adults explore each other's personalities. Can this be mapped on the city?

The relationship between intimacy and place will also be determined by the kinds of places within which LSM are used, as well as the relationship between these places. For example, liminal zones such as night clubs and pubs will have different social logics to city squares and parks. Here, intimacy will be negotiated in a different manner, as will the relationships between strangers and strong friends.

LSM afford the performance of place. For example, my participants sometimes attached geo-tags to their posts, letting their friends know where they were when they updated. These tags have a cultural content which constructs the self. But this is just one way in which place can be performed. Another way involves camera phone photographs which image-map specific locals. Ito and Okabe (2003) discuss how camera phones empower amateur photographers with a new aesthetic relationship to their surroundings. Similarly, Van House (2009) describes the act of collocating photographs online as a kind of narrative performance. Locative social media which offer geo-tagged photographs expand on this phenomenon. Hjorth and Gu (2012) argue that taking locative images amounts to a kind of self-construction through 'emplaced visualities'. The photographer simultaneously gives a place a subject meaning, while using that place to construct his or her subjectivity. Elsewhere, Hjorth (2007) argues that because these acts involve reflection and feeling they render a certain intimacy to spaces. Places come to reflect one's inner self.

This can be expanded to include various kinds of locative perform-ances, such as annotations and check-ins, which potentially render places with the kind of information which accretes from interpersonal intimacy. I have theorised the performance of intimacy through the concept of 'intimacy capital', arguing that elements of a performance can come to represent a claim on intimacy capital which specifically desires an interpersonal response. It would be interesting to examine how check-ins, annotations, and so forth enter into this process.

Overall, these media afford the simultaneous performance of place, self, and connection. However, due to the nature of these applications, the performance of connection takes on new properties. Certain LSM applications, such as Whrrl, establish groups or 'societies' based around shared tastes, rather than around interpersonal histories. Hence, users will connect with people who enjoy similar things in order to seek out particular 'taste-places'. Because connecting with these people is an act which is publicly performed on the social network, this can be read as a particular kind of performance of connection: the performance of affinity. How does this mobilise cultural capital to negotiate intimacy?

As well as coordinating connections and performing places, LSM also allow for the movement through, and occupation of, place to be recorded and, hence, to become an objected of mediated memory. Here, we see an interesting form of memory capital which potentially mobi-lises intimacy and engenders performances of connection.

LSM open up new kinds of information to the mediated and invisible gaze of one's online peers. It is interesting to ponder how we watch each other through location-based services. Does witnessing someone 'check in' to a physical location amount to the kind of 'first-hand' knowledge I discussed in Chapter 6? What do we desire to see, and what do we desire not to see? For instance, I can image a situation in which a person would rather not have seen his or her ex-partner check in to a restaurant with a romantic rival. Hence, place, networks, intimacy, and the agency of vision are all potentially made problematic by LSM.

LSM also provide new challenges for privacy and for the control of social contexts. LSM can betray one's physical location and poten-tiate physical invasions and even danger. They can be used to perform place – however some performances may contradict a persona fostered in a different social context. Today, a certain amount of digital literacy is required to control one's privacy. However, privacy is a key struc-ture within what Ulrich Beck (1992) calls 'risk society', and David Lyon (1994) calls 'surveillance society'. That is, privacy/surveillance risks are often multiplying beyond our awareness of them. They are what I have called 'amorphous'. With new social technologies such as LSM these amorphous risks may elude even the digitally literate until the damage has been done.

For example, tech-gurus and academics alike are eagerly expecting the 'web of things' paradigm to come to full fruition. That is, the pervasive embedding of computer intelligence in physical spaces and objects such that users (and, of course, businesses) can extract digital value from their surroundings. Will the 'web of things' further compli-cate the object relations of cyber-intimacy? Will intimate physical spaces become geo-tagged, live-rendered, and frictionless – shared as people move through, and interact with, them? It is now already quite possible for Facebook to share the combined locations of two secret lovers without their intention such that their friends will perceive that they regularly meet on a certain park bench or in a certain hotel room. Will this create a 4D shadow, an intimate double so complete that the resulting intensification of intimacy will permeate and disrupt our deepest sense of interpersonal existence? Academic research into surveillance and mobilities is already voluminous, but this only multi-ples potential conceptual meeting points on these issues.

Despite these possibilities, Facebook is not an inherently negative or positive phenomenon – whatever these terms may mean. Rather, it is part of a broader shift in contemporary society toward mediated systems which intensify interpersonal intimacy. It is increasingly difficult to refuse to participate in these systems, which can itself be a worrying thought. However, whether this leads to 'good' or 'bad' outcomes depends on what one looks at, and how it is framed. For example, Facebook's increasingly pervasive surveillance of its users causes obvious moral disquiet. On the other hand, an analyses of how Facebook facilitates distant intimacy must recognise new forms of positive interpersonal bonding. Overall, Facebook is too broad and heterogeneous an assemblage for simplistic conclusions. Moreover, it and the socio-technical paradigm it represents is still relatively young and evolving. This grand social experiment is open-ended. It is hard to say what things will be like when a time before Facebook is diffi-cult to recall. We must be sensitive to the many cultures and processes which make up this emergent unknown. That is, to the many intima-cies which are intensifying, struggling, dimming, and igniting – that are, in the end, transforming through flows in digital space.

Notes

1 Discovering Intimacy on Facebook

1. While Sennett described the privatisation of intimacy, he also describes its simultaneous incursion into the public spaces of the nineteenth-century city. Various factors caused this, such as the cultural adoption of 'secular immanence', and the destruction of non-intimate social conventions originally fostered to lubricate urban transactions with strangers. Consequently, according to Sennett, urban sociality came to focus on the immanent aspects of intimate selfhood, rather than on shared conventions free of personal malaise.

2 Frameworks: Privacy, Performance, Social Capital

1. For an informative running list of Facebook's privacy issues, visit the website 'Consumer Watchdog': http://www.consumerwatchdog.org

4 The Performance of Connection

1. It should be noted that Twitter and Facebook are quite different services. The former is open to the public at large, the latter to personally constructed publics. The former is based on micro-blogs, while the latter converges various forms of interactive content shared between friends.
2. A 'UDL' is a form of 'alco-pop' alcoholic beverage associated with youth binge drinking in Australia.

5 Distant Intimacy

1. See the conclusion for a more detailed discussion of the relationship between intimacy and locative social media.

6 Prosthetic Intimacy

1. Sally is using the Australian vernacular 'bogan' in a popular pejoratives sense, to indicate a person of lower economic status and cultural tastes.

8 Negotiating Intimacy

1. Instagram is a smartphone application which allows users to take a photograph, have it filtered in such a way as to appear like a Polaroid camera shot, and have it easily posted on his or her Facebook Timeline.

Conclusion

1. Spotify, like many Facebook applications, is a third-party entertainment service. It allows users to choose and listen to streaming music.
2. FourSquare 'check ins' are tags attached to social maps which indicate to a user's friends that he or she is occupying a particular place. Here, social networks are visualised in terms of cartographic proximity.

Bibliography

Aboujaoude, E. (2011) *Virtually You: The Dangerous Powers of the E-Personality*. New York: Norton.

Acquisti, A. & Gross, R. (2006) 'Imagined Communities: Awareness, Information Sharing, and Privacy on the Facebook'. Paper presented at the Proceedings of 6th Workshop on Privacy Enhancing Technologies, Cambridge, UK.

Albrechtslund, A. (2008) 'Online Social Networking as Participatory Surveillance'. *First Monday, 13*(3).

Allan, G. (1998) 'Friendship, Sociology and Social Structure'. *Journal of Social and Personal Relationships, 15*(5) 685–702.

—— (2001) 'Personal Relationships in Late Modernity'. *Personal Relationships, 8* 325–339.

—— (2008) 'Flexibility, Friendship, and Family'. *Personal Relationships, 15* 1–16.

Allan, G. & Crow, G. (1991) 'Privatisation, Home-Centredness and Leisure'. *Leisure Studies, 10* 19–32.

Altman, I. (1983) *Behaviour and the Natural Environment*. New York: Plenum Press.

Aristotle (1998) *The Nichomachean Ethics* (D. Ross, Trans.). New York: Oxford University Press.

Bankston, C. & Zhou, M. (2002) 'Social Capital as Process: The Meanings and Problems of a Theoretical Metaphor'. *Sociological Inquiry, 72*(2) 285–317.

Barker, V. (2009) 'Older Adolescents' Motivations for Social Network Site Use: The Influence of Gender, Group Identity, and Collective Self-Esteem'. *Cyber Psychology and Behaviour, 12*(2) 209–213.

Barthes, R. (1981) *Camera Lucida: Reflections on Photography* (R. Howard, Trans.). New York: Hill and Wang.

—— (1985) 'Rhetoric of the Image'. (R. Howard, Trans.) *The Responsibility of Forms*. Berkeley: University of California Press.

Bateman, P. J., Pike, J. C. & Butler, B. S. (2011) 'To Disclose or Not: Publicness in Social Networking Sites'. *Information Technology and People, 21*(1) 78–100.

Bauman, Z. (1990) 'Modernity and Ambivalence'. *Theory, Culture and Society, 7*(2) 143–169.

—— (2000) *Liquid Modernity*. Cambridge, UK: Polity Press.

—— (2007) *Consuming Life*. Cambridge, UK: Polity Press.

Beck, U. (1992) *Risk Society: Towards a New Modernity* (M. Ritter, Trans.). London: Sage.

Beck, U. & Beck-Gernsheim, E. (2002) *Individualization: Institutionalized, Individualism and its Social and Political Consequences*. London: Sage.

Becker, J. A. H., Johnson, A. J., Craig, E. A., Gilchrist, E. S., Haigh, M. M., & Lan, L. T. (2009) 'Friendships are Flexible, Not Fragile: Turning Points in Geographically Close and Long-Distance Friendships'. *Journal of Social and Personal Relationships, 26*(4) 347–369.

Bellah, R. N., Madsen, R., Sullivan, W. M., Swidler, A. & Tipton, S. M. (1985) *Habits of the Heart: Individualism and Commitment in American Life*. Berkley: University of California Press.

Bennett, C. J. (2011) 'In Defence of Privacy: The Concept and the Regime'. *Surveillance & Society, 8*(4) 485–496.

Berger, J. (1982) 'Appearances'. In J. Berger & J. Mohr (Eds.), *Another Way of Telling.* 81–130. New York: Vintage Books.

Besmer, A. & Lipford, H. (2009) *Tagged Photos: Concerns, Perceptions, and Protections.* Paper presented at the 27th International Conference Extended Abstracts on Human Factors in Computing Systems, Boston.

Bilandzic, M. & Foth, M. (2012) 'A Review of Locative Media, Mobile and Embodied Spatial Interaction'. *International Journal of Human-Computer Studies, 70*(1) 66–71.

Binder, J. F., Howes, A. & Smart, D. (2012) 'Harmony and Tension on Social Network Sites'. *Information, Communication and Society, iFirst Article,* http://dx.doi.org/10.1080/1369118X.2011.648949.

Blatterer, H. (2010) 'Social Networking, Privacy, and the Pursuit of Visibility'. In H. Blatterer, P. Johnson & M. R. Markus (Eds.), *Modern Privacy: Shifting Boundaries, New Forms.* 73–87. New York: Palgrave Macmillan.

Blumer, H. (1969) *Symbolic Interactionism.* Edgewood Cliffs, NJ: Prentice-Hall.

Blunt, A. (2007) 'Cultural Geographies of Migration: Mobility, Transnationality and Diaspora'. *Progress in Human Geography, 31*(5) 684–694.

Bourdieu, P. (1984) *Distinction: A Social Critique of the Judgement of Taste* (N. Richards, Trans.). Cambridge, MA: Harvard University Press.

—— (1986) 'The Forms of Capital'. In J. G. Richardson (Ed.), *Handbook for Theory and Research for the Sociology of Education.* 241–258. New York: Greenwood.

Boxer, D. & Cortés-Conde, F. (1997) 'From Bonding to Biting: Conversational Joking and Identity Display'. *Journal of Pragmatics, 27* 275–294.

boyd, d. (2006) 'Friends, Friendsters, and MySpace Top 8: Writing Community Into Being on Social Network Sites'. *First Monday, 11*(12).

—— (2008a) 'Why Youth Love Social Network Sites: The Role of Networked Publics in Teenage Social Life'. In D. Buckingham (Ed.), *Youth, Identity and Digital Media.* 119–142. Cambridge, MA: MIT Press.

—— (2008b) 'Facebook's Privacy Trainwreck'. *Convergence: The International Journal of Research into New Media Technologies, 14*(1) 13–20.

—— (2011) 'Dear Voyeur, meet Flâneur… Sincerely, Social Media'. *Surveillance & Society, 8*(4) 505–507.

boyd, d. & Ellison, N. (2008) 'Social Network Sites: Definition, History, and Scholarship'. *Journal of Computer-Mediated Communication, 13* 210–230.

boyd, d. & Hargittai, E. (2010) 'Facebook Privacy Settings: Who Cares?'. *First Monday, 15*(8).

Bridge, G. (2006) 'The Paradox of Cosmopolitan Urbanism: Rationality, Difference and the Circuits of Cultural Capital'. In J. Binnie, J. Holloway, S. Millington, & C. Young (Eds.) *Cosmopolitan Urbanism.* New York: Routledge.

Buber, M. (1970) *I and Thou* (W. Kaufmann, Trans.). New York: Charles Scribner's Sons.

Buffardi, L. & Campbell, K. (2008) 'Narcissus and Social Networking Web Sites'. *Personality and Social Psychology Bulletin, 34* 1303–1314.

Burgoon, J. K., Parrott, R., Le Poire, B. A., Kelley, D. L., Walther, J. B. & Perry, D. (1989) 'Maintaining and Restoring Privacy through Communication in

Different Types of Relationships'. *Journal of Social and Personal Relationships, 6* 131–158.

Burkart, G. (2010) 'When Privacy Goes Public: New Media and the Transformation of the Culture of Confession'. In H. Blatterer, P. Johnson & M. Markus (Eds.), *Modern Privacy: Shifting Boundaries, New Forms.* 23–38. New York: Palgrave Macmillan.

Burke, M., Marlow, C. & Lento, T. (2010) 'Social Network Activity and Social Well-Being'. Paper presented at the 28th Conference on Computer-Human Interaction, Atlanta.

Butler, J. (1990) *Gender Trouble: Feminism and the Subversion of Identity.* New York: Routledge.

—— (1993) *Bodies that Matter: On the Discursive Limits of 'Sex'.* New York: Routledge.

Campbell, S. W. (2004) 'Normative Mobile Phone Use in Public Settings'. Paper presented at the annual meeting of the National Communication Association, Chicago.

Campbell, S. W. & Park, Y. J. (2008) 'Social Implications of Mobile Telephony: The Rise of Personal Communication Society'. *Sociology Compass, 2*(2) 371–387.

Cartier-Bresson, H. (1952) *The Decisive Moment.* New York: Simon and Schuster.

Castells, M. (1996) *The Information Age: The Rise of the Network Society.* Malden: Blackwell.

Chalfen, R. (1998) 'Interpreting Family Photography as Pictorial Communication'. In J. Prosser (Ed.), *Image-Based Research: A Sourcebook for Qualitative Researchers.* 214–34. London: Falmer Press.

Christofides, E., Muise, A. & Desmarais, S. (2009) 'Information Disclosure and Control on Facebook: Are They Two Sides of the Same Coin of Two Different Processes?'. *Cyber Psychology and Behaviour, 12*(3) 341–345.

—— (2012) 'Hey Mom, What's on Your Facebook? Comparing Facebook Disclosure and Privacy in Adolescents and Aduls'. *Social Psychology and Personality Science, 3*(1) 48–54.

Coleman, J. (1988) 'Social Capital in the Creation of Human Capital'. *The American Journal of Sociology, 94*(95–120).

Caporael, L. R. & Xie, B. (2003) 'Breaking Time and Place: Mobile Technologies and Reconstituted Identities'. In J. Katz (Ed.) *Machines that Become Us: the Social Context of Communication Technology.* New Brunswick, NJ: Transaction Publishers.

De Vos, J. (2010) 'Christopher Lasch's *The Culture of Narcissism*: The Failure of a Critique of Psychological Politics'. *Theory Psychology, 20*(4) 528–548.

Debatin, B., Lovejoy, J. P., Horn, A. & Hughes, B. N. (2009) 'Facebook and Online Privacy: Attitudes, Behaviors, and Unintended Consequences'. *Journal of Computer-Mediated Communication, 15* 83–108.

Debord, G. (1994) *Society of the Spectacle* (D. Nicholson-Smith, Trans.). New York: Zone Books.

Deleuze, G. & Guattari, F. (1988) *A Thousand Plateaus: Capitalism and Schizophrenia* (B. Massumi, Trans.). London: Athlone Press.

Derrida, J. (1976) *Of Grammatology* (G. C. Spivak, Trans.). Baltimore: Johns Hopkins Press.

De Souza e Silva, A. & Hjorth, L. (2009) 'Urban Spaces as Playful Spaces: A Historical Approach to Mobile Urban Games'. *Simulation and Gaming, 40*(5) 602–625.

DiMicco, J. M. & Millen, D. R. (2007) 'Identity Management: Multiple Presentations of Self in Facebook'. Paper presented at the International ACM Conference on Supporting Group Work, Sanibel Island, FL.

Donath, J. & boyd, d. (2004) 'Public Displays of Connection'. *BT Technology Journal, 22*(4) 71–82.

Duck, S. (2007) *Human Relationships* (4th ed.). London: Sage.

Dwyer, C., Hiltz, S. R. & Passerini, K. (2007) 'Trust and Privacy Concern Within Social Networking Sites: A Comparison of Facebook and MySpace'. Paper presented at the Americas Conference on Information Systems, Keystone, CO.

Ellison, N., Steinfield, C. & Lampe, C. (2007) 'The Benefits of Facebook 'Friends': Social Capital and College Students' Use of Online Social Network Sites'. *Journal of Computer-Mediated Communication, 12*(4) 1143–1168.

—— (2011) 'Connection Strategies: Social Capital Implications of Facebook-enabled Communication Practices'. *New Media & Society, 13*(6) 873–892.

Enli, G. S. & Thumim, N. (2012) 'Socialising and Self-Representation Online: Exploring Facebook'. *Observatorio (OBS*) Journal, 6*(1) 87–105.

Eynon, R., Fry, J. & Schroeder, R. (2008) 'The Ethics of Internet Research'. In N. Fielding, R. M. Lee & G. Blank (Eds.), *The Sage Handbook of Online Research Methods.* 23–41.

Fogel, J. & Nehmad, E. (2009) 'Internet Social Network Communities: Risk Taking, Trust, and Privacy Concerns'. *Computers in Human Behaviour, 25* 153–160.

Forest, A. L. & Wood, J. V. (2012) 'When Social Networking is Not Working: Individuals With Low Self-Esteem Recognize but Do Not Reap the Benefits of Self-Disclosure on Facebook'. *Psychological Science, 23*(3) 295–302.

Fortunati, L. (2005) 'The Mobile Phone and Self-Presentation'. Paper presented at the Front Stage/Back Stage: Mobile Communication and the Renegotiation of the Social Sphere Conference, Grimstad, Norway.

Foucault, M. (1977) *Discipline and Punish: The Birth of the Prison.* London: Allen Lane.

Freud, S. (1962) *Three Essays on the Theory of Sexuality* (J. Stratchey, Trans.). London: Hogarth Press.

Frohne, U. (2002) 'Screen Tests: Media Narcissism, Theatricality and the Internalized Observer'. In T. Levin, U. Frohne & P. Weibel (Eds.), *CTRL_Space.* 253–277. Cambridge, MA: MIT Press.

Gaensbauer, D. (1987) 'Trespassing and Voyeurism in the Novels of Virginia Woolf and Marguerite Duras'. *Comparative Literature Studies, 24*(2) 192–201.

Giddens, A. (1991) *Modernity and Self-Identity: Self and Society in the Late Modern Age.* Cambridge, UK: Polity.

—— (1992) *The Transformation of Intimacy: Sexuality, Love and Eroticism in Modern Societies.* Cambridge, UK: Polity Press.

Glaser, B. (1998) *Doing Grounded Theory: Issues and Discussions.* Mill Valley, CA: Sociology Press.

Goffman, E. (1959) *The Presentation of Self in Everyday Life.* Garden City: Doubleday.

—— (1971) *Relations in Public: Microstudies of the Public Order*. New York: Basic Books.

—— (1974) *Frame Analysis: An Essay on the Organisation of Experience*. Cambridge, MA: Harvard University Press.

Goggin, G. (2010) 'Moveable Types: Youth and the Emergence of Mobile Social Media in Australia'. *Media Asia, 37*(4) 224–231.

—— (2011) 'Mobile Internet: New Social Technologies' *Global Mobile Media*. 116–137. New York: Routledge.

Gordon, E. & de Souza e Silva, A. (2011) *Net Locality: Why Location Matters in a Networked World*. Malden, MA: Wiley-Blackwell

Granovetter, M. (1973) 'The Strength of Weak Ties'. *American Journal of Sociology, 78*(6) 1360–1380.

Gunning, T. (2008) 'What's the Point of an Index? or, Faking Photographs'. In K. Beckman & J. Ma (Eds.), *Still Moving: Between Cinema and Photography*. 23–40. Durham and London: Duke University Press.

Habuchi, I. (2005) 'Accelerated Reflexivity'. In M. Ito, D. Okabe & M. Matsuda (Eds.) *Personal, Portable, Pedestrian: Mobile Phones in Japanese Life*. Cambridge, MA: MIT Press

Hall, C. M. & Williams, A. M. (2002) 'Tourism, Migration, Circulation and Mobility: The Contingencies of Time and Place'. In C. M. Hall & A. M. Williams (Eds.), *Tourism and Migration: New Relations Between Production and Consumption*. 1–52. Dordrecht: Kluwer.

Hampton, K. N., Livio, O. & Goulet, L. S. (2010) 'The Social Life of Wireless Urban Spaces: Internet Use, Social Networks, and the Public Realm'. *Journal of Communication*, 60(4) 701–722.

Hampton, K. N. & Gupta, N. (2008) 'Community and Social Interaction in the Wireless City: Wi-Fi Use in Public and Semi-Public Spaces'. *Society, 10*(6) 831–850.

Hardt, M. & Negri, A. (2009) *Commonwealth*. Cambridge, MA: Belknap Press.

Harvey, D. (1990) *The Condition of Postmodernity: An Enquiry into the Origins of Cultural Change*. Oxford: Blackwell.

Hearn, A. (2008) "Meat, Mask, Burden': Probing the Contours of the Branded 'Self''. *Journal of Consumer Culture, 8*(2) 197–217.

Hine, C. (2000) *Virtual Ethnography*. Thousand Oaks, CA: Sage.

Hjorth, L. (2007) 'Snapshots of Almost Contact: A Case Study on South Korea'. *Continuum, 21*(2) 227–238.

—— (2008) 'Being Real in the Mobile Reel: A Case Study on Convergent Mobile Media as New Media and a Sense of Place'. *Convergence: The International Journal of Research into New Media Technologies, 14*(1) 91–204.

Hjorth, L. & Gu, K (2012) 'The Place of Emplaced Visualities: A Case Study of Smartphone Visuality and Location-Based Social Media in Shanghai, China'. *Continuum, 26*(5) 699–713.

Holstein, J. A. & Gubrium, J. F. (2008) 'Constructionist Impulses in Ethnographic Fieldwork'. In J. A. Holstein & J. F. Gubrium (Eds.), *Handbook of Constructionist Research*. 373–395. New York: The Guilford Press.

Honneth, A. (2007) 'Recognition as Ideology'. In B. van den Brink & D. Owen (Eds.), *Recognition and Power: Axel Honneth and the Tradition of Critical Social Theory*. 323–347. New York: Cambridge University Press.

Hull, G., Lipford, H. R. & Latulipe, C. (2010) 'Contextual Gaps: Privacy Issues on Facebook'. *Ethics and Information Technology* 1–14.

Humphreys, L. (2007) 'Mobile Social Networks and Social Practice: A Case Study of Dodgeball'. *Journal of Computer-Mediated Communication 13*(1). Available at: http://jcmcindianaedu/ vol13/issue1/humphreyshtml

Ibrahim, Y. (2008) 'The New Risk Communities: Social Networking Sites and Risk'. *Journal of Media and Cultural Politics, 4*(2) 245–253.

—— (2010) 'Social Networking Sites (SNS) and the 'Narcissistic Turn': The Politics of Self-Exposure'. In S. Rummler & K. B. Ng (Eds.), *Collaborative Technologies and Applications for Interactive Information Design: Emerging Trends in User Experience*. 82–95. Hershey, PA: IGI Global.

Illouz, E. (2007) *Cold Intimacies: The Making of Emotional Capitalism*. Cambridge, UK: Polity Press.

Inness, J. C. (1992) *Privacy, Intimacy, and Isolation*. New York: Oxford University Press.

Ito, M. & Okabe, D. (2003) *Camera Phones Changing the Definition of Picture-Worthy*. Japan Media Review report. http://www.ojr.org/japan/wireless/1062208524.php

Jamieson, L. (1998) *Intimacy: Personal Relationships in Modern Societies*. Oxford: Blackwell.

Jenkins, R. (2004) *Social Identity* (2nd ed.). London: Routledge.

Joinson, A. (2008) 'Looking at', 'Looking up' or 'Keeping up with' People? Motives and Uses of Facebook'. Paper presented at the Computer Human Interaction, Florence.

Katsh, E. (1989) *The Electronic Media and the Transformation of Law*. Oxford: Oxford University Press.

Kilminster, R. (2008) 'Narcissism or Informationalization? Christopher Lasch, Norbert Elias and Social Diagnosis'. *Theory, Culture and Society, 25* 131–151.

Kirkpatrick, D. (2010) *The Facebook Effect: The Inside Story of the Company that is Connecting the World*. New York: Simon and Schuster.

Kolek, E. & Saunders, D. (2008) 'Online Disclosures: An Empirical Examination of Undergraduate Facebook Profiles'. *National Association of Student Personnel Administrators, 45*(1).

Kramer, A. D. I. (2012) 'The Spread of Emotion Via Facebook'. Paper presented at the 12th Annual Conference on Computer–Human Interaction, Austin, TX.

Lampe, C., Ellison, N. & Steinfield, C. (2006) 'A Face(book) in the Crowd: Social Searching vs. Social Browsing'. Paper presented at the 20th Anniversary Conference on Computer Supported Cooperative Work, Banff, AB.

Larsen, J., Axhausen, K. & Urry, J. (2006) 'Geographies of Social Networks: Meetings, Travel and Communications'. *Mobilities, 1*(2) 261–283.

Lasch, C. (1979) *The Culture of Narcissism: American Life in an Age of Diminishing Expectations*. New York: Norton.

Latour, B. (2005) *Reassembling the Social: an Introduction to Actor-Network Theory*. Oxford: Oxford University Press

Laurenceau, J., Pietromonaco, P. R. & Barret, L. F. (1998) 'Intimacy as an Interpersonal Process: The Importance of Self-Disclosure, Partner Disclosure, and Perceived Partner Responsiveness in Interpersonal Exchanges'. *Journal of Personality and Social Psychology, 74*(5) 1238–1251.

Lenhart, A. & Madden, M. (2007a) *Social Networking Websites and Teens: An Overview*. Pew Internet and American Life Project report. Retrieved 5–5–2011 from http://www.pewinternet.org/Reports/2007/Social-Networking-Websites-and-Teens.aspx

—— (2007b) *Teens, Privacy, and Online Social Networks*. Pew Internet and American Life Project report. Retrieved 21–9–2009 from http://www.pewinternet.org/Reports/2007/Teens-Privacy-and-Online-Social-Networks.aspx

Ling, R. (2008) *New Tech, New Ties: How Mobile Communication is Reshaping Social Cohesion*. Cambridge, MA: MIT Press.

Lipford, H. R., Hull, G., Latulipe, C., Besmer, A. & Watson, J. (2009) 'Visible Flows: Contextual Integrity and the Design of Privacy Mechanisms on Social Network Sites'. Paper presented at the International Conference on Computational Science and Engineering, Vancouver.

Liu, H. (2008) 'Social Network Profiles as Taste Performances'. *Journal of Computer-Mediated Communication, 13*(1) 252–275.

Livingstone, S. (2008) 'Taking Risky Opportunities in Youthful Content Creation: Teenagers' Use of Social Networking Sites for Intimacy, Privacy and Self-Expression'. *New Media & Society, 10*(3) 393–411.

Lury, C. (1998) *Prosthetic Culture: Photography, Memory and Identity*. London: Routledge.

Lyon, D. (1994) *The Electronic Eye: The Rise of Surveillance Society*. Minneapolis: University of Minnesota Press.

Madden, M. & Smith, A. (2010) *Reputation Management and Social Media*. Pew Internet and American Life Project report. Retrieved 5–4–2011 from http://pewinternet.org/Reports/2010/Reputation-Management.aspx

Maffesoli, M. (1996) *The Time of the Tribes: The Decline of Individualism in Mass Society*. Thousand Oaks, CA: Sage.

Mallan, K. (2009) 'Look at Me! Look at Me! Self Representation and Self-Exposure Through Online Networks'. *Digital Culture and Education, 1*(1) 51–66.

Manago, A. M., Taylor, T. & Greenfield, P. M. (2012) 'Me and My 400 Friends: The Anatomy of College Students' Facebook Networks, their Communication Patterns, and Well-Being'. *Developmental Psychology, 48*(2) 369–380.

Manovich, L. (2000) 'The Language of New Media'. MIT Press report.

Marden, B., Joinson, A. & Shanker, A. (2012) 'Every Post You Make, Every Pic You Take, I'll be Watching You: Behind Social Spheres on Facebook'. Paper presented at the Hawaii International Conference on System Sciences.

Markham, A. N. (2004) 'Representation in Online Ethnographies: A Matter of Conext Sensitivity'. In M. D. Johns, S. L. S. Chen & J. Hall (Eds.), *Online Social Research: Methods, Issues and Ethics*. 141–157. New York: Peter Lang.

Marlow, C. (2009) *Maintained Social Relationships on Facebook*. Facebook Data Team report. Retrieved 6th November 2009 from http://www.facebook.com/note.php?note_id=55257228858&ref=mf

Marshall, T. C., Bejanyan, K., Castro, G. D. & Lee, R. A. (2012) 'Attachment Styles as Predictors of Facebook-Related Jelousy and Surveillance in Romantic Relationships'. *Personal Relationships* pre-publication release.

Marwick, A. (2008) 'To Catch a Predator? The MySpace Moral Panic'. *First Monday, 13*(6).

Massumi, B. (1998) 'Sensing the Virtual, Building the Insensible'. *Architectural Design, 68*(5/6) 16–24.

Mauss, M. (1969) *The Gift: Forms and Functions of Exchange in Archaic Societies* (I. Cunnison, Trans.). London: Cohen and West.

McGrath, J. (2004) *Loving Big Brother: Performance, Privacy and Surveillance Space*. London: Routledge.

Mehdizadeh, S. (2010) 'Self-Presentation 2.0: Narcissism and Self-Esteem on Facebook'. *Cyberpsychology, Behavior, and Social Networking, 13*(4) 357–364.

Mendelson, A. & Papacharissi, Z. (2011) 'Look at Us: Collective Narcissism in College Student Facebook Photo Galleries' *A Networked Self: Identity, Community, and Culture on Social Network Sites*. 251–273. New York: Routledge.

Meyrowitz, J. (1985) *No Sense of Place: The Impact of Electronic Media on Social Behavior*. New York: Oxford University Press.

Muise, A., Christofides, E. & Desmarais, S. (2009) 'More Information Than You Ever Wanted: Does Facebook Bring out the Green-Eyed Monster of Jealousy?'. *Cyberpsychology and Behaviour, 12*(4) 441–444.

Muther, C. (2009) Antisocial Status. Online news article published by *The Boston Globe*. Retrieved 30th October 2011, from http://www.boston.com/lifestyle/articles/2009/05/07/antisocial_status

Nicole, A. & Bluck, S. (2007) 'I'll Keep You in Mind: The intimacy Function of Autobiographical Memory'. *Applied Cognitive Psychology, 21* 1091–1111.

Nissenbaum, H. (1997) 'Toward an Approach to Privacy in Public: Challenges of Information Technology'. *Ethics and Behaviour, 7*(3) 207–219.

—— (2004) 'Privacy as Contextual Integrity'. *Washington Law Review, 79* 102–39.

Ong, E. Y. L., Ang, R. P., Ho, J. C. M., Lim, J. C. Y., Goh, D. H., Lee, C. S., et al. (2011) 'Narcissism, Extraversion and Adolescents' Self-Presentation on Facebook'. *Personality and Individual Differences, 50* 180–185.

Pahl, R. (2005) 'Are all Communities, Communities in the Mind?'. *Sociological Review Monograph, 53*(4) 621–640.

Pahl, R. & Wallace, C. D. (1988) 'Neither Angels in Marble nor Rebels in Red: Privatisation and Working-Class Consciousness'. In D. Rose (Ed.), *Social Stratification and Economic Change*. London: Hutchinson.

Papp, L. M., Danielewicz, J. & Cayemberg, C. (2011) '"Are We Facebook Official?" Implications of Dating Partners' Facebook Use and Profiles for Intimate Relationship Satisfaction'. *12*(2) 85–90.

Park, N., Jin, B. & Jin, S. A. (2011) 'Effects of Self-Disclosure on Relational Intimacy in Facebook'. *Computers in Human Behaviour, 27*(5) 1974–1983.

Parks, M. & Floyd, K. (1996) 'Meanings for Closeness and Intimacy in Friendship'. *Journal of Social and Personal Relationships, 13*(1) 85–107.

Pempek, T., Yermolayeva, Y. & Calvert, S. (2009) 'College Students' Social Networking Experiences on Facebook'. *Journal of Applied Developmental Psychology, 30* 227–238.

Portes, A. (1998) 'Social Capital: Its Origins and Applications in Modern Sociology'. *Annual Review of Sociology, 24* 1–24.

Prager, K. J. (1995) *The Psychology of Intimacy*. New York: Guilford Press.

Putnam, R. (2000) *Bowling Alone: The Collapse and Revival of American Community*. New York: Simon and Schuster.

Raynes-Goldie, K. (2010) 'Aliases, Creeping, and Wall Cleaning: Understanding Privacy in the Age of Facebook'. *First Monday, 15*(1).

Reis, H. T. & Shaver, P. (1988) 'Intimacy as an Interpersonal Process'. In S. Duck (Ed.), *Handbook of Personal Relationships*. 367–389. Chichester: Wiley.

Richardson, I. (2007) 'Pocket Technospaces: The Bodily Incorporation of Mobile Media'. *Continuum: Journal of Media and Cultural Studies, 21*(2) 205–215.

Rill, B. (2006) 'Rave, Communitas, and Embodied Idealism'. *Music Therapy Today, 12*(3) 648–661.

Robards, B. (2012) 'Leaving MySpace, Joining Facebook: 'Growing Up' on Social Networks'. *Continuum: Journal of Media and Cultural Studies, 26*(3) 385–398.

Roderick, C. (2010) 'Commodifying Self: A Grounded Theory Study'. *The Grounded Theory Review, 9*(1) 41–63.

Rose, G. (2001) *Visual Methodologies: an Introduction to the Interpretation of Visual Materials.* London: Sage.

Rosen, C. (2007) 'Virtual Friendship and the New Narcissism'. *The New Atlantis, 17* 15–31.

Ross, C., Orr, E. S., Sisic, M., Arseneault, J., Simmering, M. & Orr, R. R. (2009) 'Personality and Motivations Associated with Facebook Use'. *Computers in Human Behaviour, 25*(2) 578–586.

Sas, C., Dix, A., Hart, J. & Su, R. (2009) 'Dramaturgical Capitalization of Positive Emotions: The Answer for Facebook Success?' Paper presented at the 23rd British HCI Group Annual Conference on People and Computers: Celebrating People and Technology.

Sassen, S. (1998) *Globalisation and its Discontents.* New York: New Press.

Scharf, A. (1974) *Art and Photography.* Baltimore: Penguin.

Schofield, C. P. & Joinson, A. (2008) 'Privacy, Trust, and Disclosure Online'. In B. Azy (Ed.), *Psychological Aspects of Cyberspace: Theory, Research, Applications.* 13–31. New York: Cambridge University Press.

Schonfeld, E. (2009) 'Facebook Photos Pulls Away From The Pack'. Retrieved 9th October 2010, from http://techcrunch.com/2009/02/22/facebook-photos-pulls-away-from-the-pack/

Sedekides, C., Wildschut, T. & Baden, D. (2004) 'Nostalgia: Conceptual Issues and Existential Functions'. In J. Greenber, S. Koole & T. Pyszczynski (Eds.), *Handbook of Experimental Existential Psychology.* 200–214. New York: Guilford Press.

Sennett, R. (1977) *The Fall of Public Man.* New York: Knopf.

Sheller, M. & Urry, J. (2006a) 'The New Mobilities Paradigm'. *Environment and Planning, 38* 207–226.

—— (2006b) 'Introduction: Mobile Cities, Urban Mobilities'. In M. Sheller & J. Urry (Eds.), *Mobile Technologies of the City.* 1–18. New York: Routledge.

Shin, D. (2010) 'The Effects of Trust, Security and Privacy in Social Networking: A Security-Based Approach to Understand the Pattern of Adoption'. *Interacting with Computers, 22* 428–438.

Simmel, G. (1950) *The Sociology of George Simmel.* Clencoe: Free Press.

Simmons, O. E., Hadden, S. C. & Glaser, B. G. (1994) 'The Study of Basic Social Processes'. In B. Glaser (Ed.), *More Grounded Theory Methodology.* Mill Valley: Sociology Press.

Simon, H. A. (1997) 'Designing Organizations for an Information-Rich World'. In D. M. Lamberton (Ed.), *The Economics of Communication and Information.* 187–203. Cheltenham: Edward Elgar.

Skeels, M. M. & Grudin, J. (2009) 'When Social Networks Cross Boundaries: A Case Study of Workplace Use of Facebook and LinkedIn'. Paper presented at the Supporting Group Work, Sanibel Island, FL.

Sontag, S. (1973) *On Photography.* New York: Picador.

St John, G. (2006) 'Electronic Dance Music Culture and Religion: An Overview'. *Culture and Religion, 7*(1) 1–25.

Steinfield, C., Ellison, N. & Lampe, C. (2008) 'Social Capital, Self-Esteem, and Use of Online Social Network Sites: A Longitudinal Analysis'. *Journal of Applied Developmental Psychology, 29* 434–445.

Strater, K. & Lipford, H. R. (2008) 'Strategies and Struggles with Privacy in an Online Social Networking Community'. Paper presented at the 22nd British HCI Group Annual Conference on HCI: People and Computers XXII: Culture, Creativity, Interaction, Liverpool.

Stutzman, F. (2006) 'An Evaluation of Identity Sharing Behaviour in Social Network Communities'. Paper presented at the International Digital Media and Arts Association and IMS Code Conference, Oxford.

Stutzman, F. & Kramer-Duffield, J. (2010) 'Friends Only: Examining a Privacy-Enhancing Behaviour in Facebook'. Paper presented at the Computer-Human Interaction, Georgia.

Sundén, J. (2003) *Material Virtualities*. New York: Peter Lang.

Sutko, D. M. & de Souza e Silva, A. (2010) 'Location-aware Mobile Media and Urban Sociability'. *New Media and Society, 13*(5) 807–823.

Theunissen, M. (1984) *The Other: Studies in the Social Ontology of Husserl, Heidegger, Sartre, and Buber* (C. Macann, Trans.). Cambridge, MA: MIT Press.

Thompson, C. (2008) Brave New World of Digital Intimacy. Online news article published by *The New York Times*. Retrieved 5th August 2011, from http://www.nytimes.com/2008/09/07/magazine/07awareness-t.html?pagewanted=all

Tokunaga, R. S. (2011) 'Friend Me or You'll Strain Us: Understanding Negative Events That Occur over Social Networking Sites'. *Cyberpsychology, Behavior, and Social Networking, 14*(7) 425–432.

Tong, S. T., Van Der Heide, B., Langwell, L. & Walther, J. B. (2008) 'Too Much of a Good Thing? The Relationship Between Number of Friends and Interpersonal Impressions on Facebook'. *Journal of Computer-Mediated Communication, 13*(3) 531–549.

Tönnies, F. (1963) *Gemeinschaft und Gesellschaft* (C. P. Loomis, Trans.). New York: Harper and Row.

Tufekci, Z. (2008a) 'Can You See Me Now? Audience and Disclosure Regulation in Online Social Network Sites'. *Bulletin of Science Technology Society, 28*(1) 20–36.

—— (2008b) 'Grooming, Gossip, Facebook, and MySpace'. *Information, Communication and Society, 11*(4) 544–564.

Turkle, S. (1994) 'Constructions and Reconstructions of Self in Virtual Reality: Playing in the MUDs'. *Mind, Culture and Activity, 1*(3) 143–155.

—— (1995) *Life on the Screen: Identity in the Age of the Internet*. New York: Simon and Schuster.

—— (2011) *Alone Together: Why We Expect More from Technology and Less from Each Other*. New York: Basic Books.

Turner, V. (1969) 'Liminality and Communitas' *The Ritual Process: Structure and Anti-Structure*. 94–130. London: Routledge.

Tyler, I. (2007) 'From "the me Decade" to "the me Millenium": The Cultural History of Narcissism'. *International Journal of Cultural Studies, 10* 343–363.

Urry, J. (2003) 'Social Networks, Travel and Talk'. *British Journal of Sociology, 54*(2) 155–175.

Utz, S. & Beukeboom, C. (2011) 'The Role of Social Network Sites in Romantic Relationships: Effects on Jealousy and Relationship Happiness'. *Journal of Computer-Mediated Communication, 16*(4) 511–527.

Valadez, J. & Clignet, R. (2005) 'On the Ambiguities of a Sociological Analysis of the Culture of Narcissism'. *The Sociological Quarterly, 28*(4) 455–472.

Valenzuela, S., Park, N. & Kee, K. K. (2009) 'Is There Social Capital in a Social Network Site?: Facebook Use and College Students' Life Satisfaction, Trust, and Participation'. *Journal of Computer-Mediated Communication, 14* 875–901.

Valesco-Martin, J. (2011) 'Self-disclosure in Social Media'. Paper presented at the Annual Conference on Human Factors in Computing Systems, Vancouver.

Van Der Heide, B., Angelo, J. D. D. & Schumaker, E. M. (2012) 'The Effects of Verbal Versus Photographic Self-Presentation on Impression Formation in Facebook'. *Journal of Communication, 62*(1) 98–116.

Van Dijck, J. (2008) 'Digital Photography: Communication, Identity, Memory'. *Visual Communication, 7*(1) 57–76.

Van House, N. (2009) 'Collocated Photosharing, Story-Telling, and the Performance of Self'. *International Journal of Human-Computer Interaction, 67* 1073–1086.

Vitak, J., Lampe, C., Gray, R. & Ellison, N. B. (2012) '"Why Won't You Be My Facebook Friend?" Strategies for Managing Context Collapse in the Workplace'. Paper presented at the 2012 iConference, Toronto.

Walther, J. B. & Parks, M. R. (2002) 'Cues Filtered Out, Cues Filtered In: Computer Mediated Communication and Relationships'. In M. L. Knapp & J. A. Daly (Eds.), *Handbook of Interpersonal Communication*. Thousand Oaks, CA: Sage.

Walther, J. B., Van Der Heide, B., Sang-Yeon, K., Westerman, D. & Tong, S. T. (2008) 'The Role of Friends' Appearance and Behavior on Evaluations of Individuals on Facebook: Are We Known by the Company We Keep?'. *Human Communication Research, 34* 28–49.

Warren, S. & Brandeis, L. D. (1890) 'The Right to Privacy'. *Harvard Law Review, 4* 193–220.

Wellman, B. (2002) 'Little Boxes, Globalization, and Networked Individualism'. In M. Tanabe, P. Besselaar & T. Ishida (Eds.), *Digital Cities 2: Computational and Sociological Approaches*. 10–25. Berlin: Springer.

West, A., Lewis, J. & Currie, P. (2009) 'Students' Facebook "Friend": Public and Private Spheres'. *Journal of Youth Studies, 12*(6) 615–627.

Westin, A. (1970) *Privacy and Freedom*. New York: Atheneum.

Westlake, E. J. (2008) 'Friend Me if You Facebook: Generation Y and Performative Surveillance'. *The Drama Review, 52*(4) 21–40.

Wilkinson, J. (2010) 'Personal Communities: Responsible Individualism or Another Fall for Public [Man]?'. *Sociology, 44*(3) 453–470.

Williams, D. (2006) 'On and Off the "Net: Scales for Social Capital in an Online Era"'. *Journal of Computer-Mediated Communication, 11* 593–628.

Zhao, S., Grasmuch, S. & Martin, J. (2008) 'Identity Construction on Facebook: Digital Empowerment in Anchored Relationships'. *Computers in Human Behaviour, 24* 1816–1836.

Zywica, J. & Danowski, J. (2008) 'The Faces of Facebookers: Investigating Social Enhancement and Social Compensation Hypotheses; Predicting Facebook and Offline Popularity from Sociability and Self-Esteem, and Mapping the Meanings of Popularity with Semantic Networks'. *Journal of Computer-Mediated Communication, 14* 1–34.

Index

Authors

Aristotle
  Nicomachean Ethics, 27
Barthes, R., 16, 17, 55
Bauman, Z., 20, 21, 122, 178
Berger, J., 16, 53, 72, 73, 85, 86
  see also photographs and
    photography, private
    photographs
Bourdieu, P., 67
  see also social capital
Buber, M.
  'I-thou' and 'I-it', 2, 4, 21, 140, 141,
    146, 177
Butler, J., 45
boyd, d., 8, 10, 11, 12, 32, 33, 34, 35,
  39, 41, 115, 118, 124
  networked public, 39, 67
Castells, M., 78, 79
Debord, G., 123
Deleuze, G., 124, 173, 181
Derrida, J., 44, 45
Foucault, M., 17, 135, 178
  see also panopticon
Frohne, U., 24, 157
Giddens, A., 9, 11, 19, 20, 28, 33
  pure relationship, 19, 27
Goffman, E., 36, 37–41, 128, 174
  impression management, 38
  regionality, 39, 173
  dialogical performance, 38, 39, 44
  tie signs, 63, 73, 74
  frames, 132
Guattari, F., 124, 173
Honneth, A., 167
Illouz, E., 9, 20, 21, 110
Lasch, C., 21, 22, 144
Livingstone, S., 10, 33, 43, 60, 123
Lury, C., 107–8
Meyrowitz, J., 41, 42, 173
Nissenbaum, H., 30, 35, 128
Putnam, R., 28, 46, 47, 78, 79

  see also social capital
Sennett, R., 13, 26, 109, 151,
  152, 185
Simmel, G., 64, 161
Theunissen, M., 140, 141
Turkle, S., 13, 22, 23, 108, 109, 144,
  174
Wolf, V., 102
Zuckerberg, M., 2, 35
alienation through connection, 135–8
attention economy, 141

belonging, 61, 62, 67
body/embodiment, 21, 58, 133, 138,
  156, 159, 163

community
  intimacy/community dichotomy,
    27, 28, 182
  personal communities, 12, 79
  sense of, 82, 147
cosmopolitanism, 181, 182
'culling' social ties, 148
cultural capital, 155

desire not to see, 129–31
discourse analysis, 52, 53
distant ties, 11, 12, 77–94
  as estranged ties, 77, 103
Doctor Phil, 20
doubling of the self, 2

ego-propping, 161–4, 169
esteem giving, 164, 167
ethnography, 51–3, 55
existentialism, 80, 81

first-hand judgement, 110–14, 134,
  135, 156, 183
Freudianism
  scopophilia, 101
  therapy, 20
frictionless sharing, 179